Capitalist Development in the Twentieth Century
An Evolutionary-Keynesian Analysis

Capitalism in the twentieth century has been marked by periods of persistent bad performance alternating with episodes of good performance. Much current economic research ignores this phenomenon; other work concentrates almost exclusively on developing technology as its cause. Cornwall and Cornwall draw upon Schumpeterian, institutional and Keynesian economics to investigate how far these swings in performance can be explained as integral to capitalist development. The authors consider the macroeconomic record of the developed capitalist economies over the past hundred years (including rates of growth, inflation and unemployment) as well as the interaction of economic variables with the changing structural features of the economy in the course of industrialization and transformation. This approach allows for changes both in the economic structure and in the economic variables to be generated within the system.

This innovative and original approach will be essential reading for macroeconomists and economic historians.

JOHN CORNWALL, FRSC, is Professor Emeritus in the Economics Department, Dalhousie University. His many publications include *Growth and Stability in a Mature Economy* (1972), *Modern Capitalism: its Growth and Transformation* (1977), and *Economic Breakdown and Recovery: Theory and Policy* (1994).

WENDY CORNWALL is Professor of Economics in the Economics Department at Mount Saint Vincent University. Her publications include *Economic Recovery for Canada: a Policy Framework* (with J. Cornwall, 1984) and *A Model of the Canadian Financial Flow Matrix* (with J. A. Brox, 1989).

Capitalist Development
in the Twentieth Century
An Evolutionary-Keynesian Analysis

JOHN CORNWALL AND
WENDY CORNWALL

CAMBRIDGE
UNIVERSITY PRESS

PUBLISHED BY THE PRESS SYNDICATE OF THE UNIVERSITY OF CAMBRIDGE
The Pitt Building, Trumpington Street, Cambridge, United Kingdom

CAMBRIDGE UNIVERSITY PRESS
The Edinburgh Building, Cambridge CB2 2RU, UK
40 West 20th Street, New York, NY 10011–4211, USA
10 Stamford Road, Oakleigh, VIC 3166, Australia
Ruiz de Alarcón 13, 28014 Madrid, Spain
Dock House, The Waterfront, Cape Town 8001, South Africa

http://www.cambridge.org

© Cambridge University Press 2001

First published 2001

Printed in the United Kingdom at the University Press, Cambridge

Typeface Monotype Times New Roman 10/12pt   *System* QuarkXPress™   [SE]

A catalogue record for this book is available from the British Library

Library of Congress Cataloguing-in-Publication data
Cornwall, John.
Capitalist development in the twentieth century / John Cornwall and Wendy Cornwall.
    p. cm.
Includes bibliographical references and index.
ISBN 0 521 34149 3
1. Economic history – 20th century. 2. Economic development. 3. Capitalism.
I. Cornwall, Wendy A. II. Title.
HC54.C73   2001
330.12′2 – dc21   00-069752

ISBN 0 521 34149 3 hardback

HC
54
.C73
2001

Contents

Figures

Tables

Foreword

David Colander

True macroeconomists are hard to find these days. They seem to have dug themselves into the woodwork in response to the new classical, and their new Keynesian clone, population explosion. When you find a true Keynesian, you have found a treasure, and the Cornwalls are true, unrepentant Keynesians.

I call their analysis 'true New Keynesian'. (I can't simply call it New Keynesian, because that term has been hijacked by a set of writing that often has little to do with either Keynes or macro, but is actually a combination of partial equilibrium analysis and new monetarism going under a Keynesian label.) It is Keynesian because it retains a framework within which aggregate demand can play a role in affecting the long-run performance of the economy. It is new because it incorporates new ideas that are relevant for the exposition. The Cornwalls have carefully followed the modern developments in macroeconomics, adapted those aspects of it they consider advances, and eliminated those aspects of it that they find fads.

In this well-structured book they present, in a wonderfully clear style, a framework that 'explains' the stylized facts of macroeconomic development of the industrial nations during the past hundred years. They consider these stylized facts in historical sequence, arguing that the facts trace out a pattern of alternating episodes of poor and superior macroeconomic performance. The framework they use is evolutionary; it is neither completely self-regulating nor knife-edge. The system adapts, but adapts slowly, to events and disturbances. Using their updated, evolutionary model, they explain the past and give us insight into the future.

The Cornwalls' work is an example of the direction the macro profession would likely have gone had it not become lost in overly formal rational expectations models. It blends elements of three traditions: Schumpeterian, Svennilsonian, and Keynesian. The big change from the early Keynesian work is a switch from a focus only on the short run to a focus on the intermediate run. In this intermediate run there are many possible directions the economy might take. Which it takes is not a priori determined.

This intermediate-run approach replaces the sterile concept of a unique long-run equilibrium with multiple equilibria. Agents are forward looking, but not so forward looking as to push our credulity over the limit. This intermediate-run approach directs us to think of the economy as a path-dependent process, where hysteresis rules. There's no predetermined future. Which way the economy goes depends on how institutions and government policy deal with our problems.

The Cornwalls' Keynesian macroeconomics admits to its deductive limitations. It recognizes the macroeconomy as a complex system from which one cannot build up from first principles to a complete understanding. Instead, one must build down, developing a contextual macroeconomic analysis through an understanding and appreciation of the economy's institutions. It is an analysis in time. A name for it would be Charles Peirce's term, abduction. Abduction is not deduction, not induction, but a sensible blend of the two. In abduction the role of theory is to create a reasonable story that 'explains' the facts. Using abduction one is careful not to claim a model is more than what it is – a reasonable story.

The Cornwalls' overriding policy interest is in keeping unemployment as low as possible. That interest guides their analysis. They argue that a defining feature of the golden age was full employment. They contrast that golden age with the latest episode of neoliberalism where there has been much more unemployment. Drawing on their historical analysis they argue that, to achieve high employment, government, capital, and labour must create and sustain an institutional environment that makes social bargains possible and relieves the economy of constraints on aggregate demand. The golden age achieved this through an activist government. It worked because of a willingness by labour to abandon unrestricted collective bargaining and accept moderate wage demands in exchange for full employment, an expanded welfare state, and 'fair' treatment in the workplace.

The political forces that led society to create such golden age institutions have changed in the past thirty years, leading to a breakdown of those institutions and the establishment of a neoliberal regime. The defining characteristics of this modern neoliberal regime are a focus on price stability and an elimination of the institutions necessary for full employment. The Cornwalls argue that the neoliberal institutions place too strong a constraint on aggregate demand and are therefore inconsistent with the full employment goal. Whether institutions can change to become consistent with full employment is an open question. Based on history, the Cornwalls argue that some kind of big push – a precipitating event – is necessary for the right kind of institutional change, and that this is unlikely in the near future.

I don't agree with everything in this book but I agree with much of it, and I can highly recommend it to all. It is a sensible blend of institutional knowledge and analytic understanding. It is insightful and instructive, and it will give the reader an excellent sense of what the real issues in macro are.

To Dan, Ian and Isabel

W.C.

To the memory of my parents

J.C.

Preface

This book deals with economic development, and with macroeconomic performance in the context of capitalist development. In addition to explaining the macroeconomic record, for example rates of growth, inflation and unemployment, we explain the interaction of economic variables with the changing structural features of the economy in the course of capitalist industrialization and transformation. This requires a framework suited to analysing a more complex economic reality than mainstream economic theory can encompass. This complexity arises from two sources. First, we include institutions among the structural variables, and the impact of the distribution of economic and political power on these institutions. Second, we examine the interaction of economic performance with the structure of the economy to show how each causes changes in the other. This reaches beyond the 'intellectual autarky' of equilibrium analysis, in which structural variables influence the endogenous economic variables but are themselves subject only to unexplained change. Instead, our framework allows for changes both in the economic structure and in the performance variables to be generated within the system. In contrast to this evolutionary approach, mainstream theory focuses on equilibrium states and restricts itself to the less demanding task of establishing conditions for the existence and stability of the equilibrium.

To use our approach is to make what Nelson (1995, p. 85) refers to as 'an intellectual bet that the price of added complexity is worth paying to buy the better ability to devise and work with a theory that rings right'. The bet is that an evolutionary approach will lead to an understanding of capitalist performance that is denied to those whose work is confined within the mainstream equilibrium framework. In the course of supporting our approach, we shall argue that mainstream macroeconomic theory has not been able to develop an adequate explanation of periods of malfunction, such as the past quarter-century of high unemployment, or even of episodes of superior performance such as capitalism's 'golden age'.

The 'Evolutionary-Keynesian' description of our approach that appears in the sub-title requires comment. The Keynesian component is chosen to suggest the critical role aggregate demand plays in our framework, echoing the message of the *General Theory*. We maintain there is no automatic tendency for the private sector of an affluent capitalist system to generate full employment levels of aggregate demand. Further, in our view Keynes underestimated the central role of aggregate demand in driving the economy, hence we will speak of an extension of the Keynesian model. The 'evolutionary' component of the subtitle is chosen to emphasize endogenous processes involving structural change in our explanation of macroeconomic development. For example, we will model development as a process in which performance generates change in technologies and institutions, which in turn alters performance. This changed performance subsequently induces further structural changes in an endogenous evolutionary process.

Institutions are an essential ingredient in our analysis. They are the laws, customs and norms that guide interactions among individuals in a society. We argue that it is impossible to explain the way an economy works, whether in the short or the long run, without including institutions as part of the economic structure. The mainstream view is that a mark of progress in any field of economics is the rigorous development of its micro foundations, whereas we emphasize institutions to make explicit the 'macroeconomic foundations of microeconomics', that is, the way the institutional framework places constraints on individual decision-making (Colander, 1996, 1999).

This study builds on and extends earlier work by the authors in three ways. First, rather than limit the analysis to the post-World War II period, we have set for ourselves the more ambitious goal of including a period covering approximately the twentieth century. Second, our earlier work was more informal and restrictive in its integration of structural features of the economy with the usual economic variables; it focused on the influence of institutions on macroeconomic performance ('institutions matter') and how performance affects institutions. In this study, we have attempted to construct a full-fledged framework for modelling the interaction of economic performance with economic structures, especially institutions and technology, in an evolutionary process that incorporates the causal linkages between historical episodes. Third, shifts in the distribution of economic and political power are given a key role in accounting for institutional change.

Because of the complexity of the subject matter, and because some of the topics covered will be unfamiliar to many economists, we have tried to keep the presentation of our ideas as non-technical as possible. In addition, and in the hope that it will make the work accessible to economists whatever their special fields might be, we have provided background material for the less familiar topics.

We are indebted to the following for providing financial support during the course of writing this book: the Social Science and Humanities Research Council of Canada; the Office of the Dean of the School of Science and Dean Warwick Kimmins, and the Department of Economics, both at Dalhousie University; and the Internal Research Fund at Mount Saint Vincent University. We would like to thank Philip Arestis, Peter Burton, Sean Hargreaves Heap, Geoff Harcourt, Kurt Rothschild, Gouranga Rao, Peter Riach, Peter Skott and Tony Thirlwall for their comments and helpful criticisms. Most of all, we would like to express our gratitude to Mark Setterfield for his extremely thorough reading of the complete manuscript, his numerous helpful suggestions for improving the book, and his encouragement throughout its writing.

Parts of chapters 4, 6 and 10 were originally published in the *Journal of Post Keynesian Economics*, Summer 1997, the *International Papers in Political Economy*, No. 3, 1999, and *Economica*, May 1994, respectively, and are reprinted here by permission of M.E. Sharpe, Inc., the University of East London and the London School of Economics and Political Science. Material in chapters 5 and 8 is included by permission of Macmillan Press and chapter 11 includes work reprinted by permission of Edward Elgar Publishing. Table 2.5 is taken from Western and Beckett, *American Journal of Sociology* (January 1999), and is reprinted with the permission of the University of Chicago.

Part I
Framework

Introduction

This book examines macroeconomic development of the industrial nations during the past 100 years. Among the more notable features of capitalism's progress over this period have been alternating episodes of superior and poor economic performance. The main task of the book is to develop and apply a framework that explains these episodes and the causal linkages between them. The episodes to be analysed include the Great Depression, the golden age that followed World War II, and the current episode of high unemployment that began in the 1970s.

Underlying our explanation of these historical developments is an assumption about how developed capitalist economies function that contrasts sharply with the mainstream perception. Mainstream neoclassical thought sees a capitalist system as inherently self-regulating: given some exogenous disturbance, mechanisms operate to steer the economy back to its full employment growth path. In our view, capitalism is not self-regulating, nor is it doomed to self-destruct as some crude Marxian versions of capitalism's development claim. Instead, we see alternating episodes of superior and poor performance as a normal part of capitalist development, and trace them to structural changes. Those who would argue that capitalism is self-regulating (given the usual provisos) not only must believe that an invisible hand is rapidly and continuously clearing markets and providing the signals needed for efficient resource allocation; they must also believe that this same invisible hand is selecting the technologies and institutions from the evolving structural framework that guarantee markets work in this fashion. We shall argue that this is asking too much of any invisible hand.

There are other differences in the two approaches, but of greatest importance are the ways in which each treats structural change, history and aggregate demand (AD). The term 'evolutionary' used in the sub-title of this study indicates an emphasis on endogenously generated change in both the economic and structural variables of the system. 'Keynesian' is included to emphasize the independent role for AD in generating these changes. An initial set of structural variables, including institutions, determines the performance of the economy, especially the level and rate of growth of AD, and it is performance that eventually induces changes in the economic structure. Because of the interaction between structures and macroeconomic performance, the current performance of the economy depends upon its past, including previous changes in structures, and its future performance depends upon what happens today. Therefore, explaining how an economy develops over time, including an explanation of alternating periods of malfunction and superior macroeconomic performance, requires an evolutionary approach in which 'history matters'; the future will only be understood and explained in terms of what happens today, just as events of today find their causes in the past.

Change cannot be analysed within the mainstream neoclassical framework. For example, rooted in mechanics, the neoclassical growth model can describe only the response of the system to changes that occur outside the model, that is, in the structural variables. When a structural variable changes, the system's sole response is to restore equilibrium, the original one if the change is temporary, a new one if it is permanent. Any temporary shock, no matter how large or small or when it occurs or which structural variable is involved, has no long-run effect; the economy returns to the previous equilibrium. If the change is permanent, the economy moves to a new equilibrium; the previous equilibrium or behaviour of the economy has no impact on the new one. It is as though history did not exist.

Another important difference in the two approaches is the way each treats AD. Again using neoclassical growth theory, there is no independent role for aggregate demand; it merely adjusts passively to a growing aggregate supply. Our reasons for rejecting supply-determined equilibrium processes are taken up in chapters 3 and 4. Here we simply point out that the occurrence of lengthy periods of high unemployment is evidence of the inadequacy of an approach that assumes AD is always sufficient to match aggregate supply. Long periods of high unemployment reveal a failure of any mechanism automatically to raise AD to output levels dictated by aggregate supply conditions.

We propose a new framework of analysis, an alternative to two familiar approaches to modelling long-run macroeconomic dynamics. It differs from the usual long-run theories of capitalist development, for example, long cycle and stages of development theories, by relying heavily upon traditional analytical techniques. It also contrasts markedly with the more formal steady-state growth theories, both the old and new forms of full employment models as well as the older Keynesian versions, by incorporating structural change, especially the evolving institutional framework, and the influence of power on institutions as integral parts of the analysis. Our framework can be described as blending elements from three traditions: that associated with Schumpeter (1934) and Svennilson (1954), with its emphasis on structural change and transformation as an integral feature of economic development; that of institutional economics, with its stress on rules, laws, customs and beliefs as structural forces influencing economic and political behaviour; and that of Keynesian economics, with its emphasis on aggregate demand as a key determinant of economic performance and outcomes. These are the roots that have led us to call our approach evolutionary-Keynesian.

Why stress unemployment?

Our study also differs from other theories of capitalist development and from formal growth theories by emphasizing the long-run unemployment record of the developed economies, as well as their growth performance as they evolve and transform over the long run. There are several reasons for this; two in particular deserve comment here. One is the glaring neglect of the unemployment problem by the economics profession, both inside and outside the universities. High unemployment has been a problem for some time, and seems likely to continue to be so. The record needs to be set straight. Another reason is that to neglect the unemployment dimension of economic performance and development is to overlook one of the most important indicators of economic and social welfare loss over the course of capitalism's development.

Consider the unemployment record of the golden age compared with unemployment in the 1990s. For the period 1955–73, the unemployment rate for the 16 OECD economies listed in table I.1 averaged 2.4 per cent, providing ample evidence that developed capitalist economies can solve the unemployment problem. A repeat of the 1930s, widely anticipated to follow World War II, could be and was avoided. Unfortunately the golden age was to be followed by a considerable deterioration in the unemployment picture that continues today. Comparing the 1955–73 record with the latest figures for the 1990s, average unemployment rates have tripled (from 2.4 to 7.5 per cent). If we consider only the last five years for which data are available (1994–8), the rate has risen almost 230 per cent. Improvement in unemployment during the 1990s was confined primarily to the English-speaking economies. In terms of the numbers of unemployed workers, figure I.1 adds Ireland and New Zealand to the sample and shows an increase from 8 million workers in 1961 to 25.3 million in 1998, yet there appeared to be

Table I.1 *Unemployment rates for 16 OECD countries: 1955–1998 (%)*

Country	1955–73	1990–93	1994–98	1990–98
Australia	2.0	9.6	8.6	9.0
Austria	2.1	4.0[b]	4.2	4.2[c]
Belgium	2.4	7.4	9.7	8.7
Canada	5.1	10.3	9.4	9.8
Denmark	2.1	8.9	6.6	7.6
Finland	2.0	9.5	14.1	12.1
France	1.9	10.2	12.1	11.2
Germany[a]	1.4	5.4	9.0	7.4
Italy	5.2	9.3	11.9	10.8
Japan	1.5	2.2	3.4	2.9
Netherlands	1.8	6.1	5.9	6.0
Norway	2.0	5.8	4.6	5.1
Sweden	1.8	4.9	9.2	7.3
Switzerland	0.0	3.0[d]	3.9[e]	3.5[f]
United Kingdom	2.8	9.1	8.0	8.5
United States	4.8	6.7	5.3	5.9
Unweighted average	2.4	7.0	7.9	7.5

Notes:
[a] West Germany prior to 1991.
[b] 1993 only.
[c] 1993–98.
[d] 1991–93.
[e] 1994–97.
[f] 1991–97.
Sources: Maddison (1991), Table C.6; OECD, *Economic Outlook*, 66, December 1999, Annex Table 22.

growing disregard for the problem. This was particularly true of economies that had shown improvement in the 1990s. As high unemployment entered its third decade, the authorities and the economics profession seemed to see the growth of aggregate output, the rising stock market and the achievement of low inflation and balanced budgets as more worthy of attention. Our view is that much of the justification for this lack of concern with high unemployment and its attendant welfare costs is based on factually incorrect diagnoses of the nature of unemployment, or of the effect of stimulative policy, or both. Stimulative aggregate demand policies are a necessary condition for regaining full employment because most of the unemployment is involuntary and not to be blamed on labour. But such policies are not sufficient for recovery because sustained full employment has unaccept-

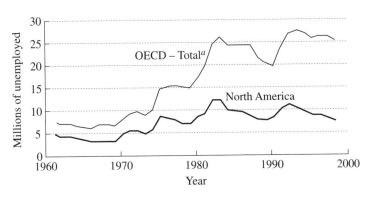

Figure I.1 Unemployed workers: 18 OECD countries and North America, 1961–1998
Note:
[a] Australia, Austria, Belgium, Canada, Denmark, Finland, France, Germany (West Germany prior to 1991), Ireland, Italy, Japan, the Netherlands, New Zealand, Norway, Sweden, Switzerland, the United Kingdom and the United States.
Sources: OECD, *Labour Force Statistics*, various issues; OECD, *Economic Outlook*, 65, June 1999.

able impacts on other goals of society, for example low inflation. From our perspective, the past growth of unemployment and its current slow recovery justifies our emphasis on unemployment in this study.

Modelling capitalist development

In developing our framework we have been guided by a belief that the value of macroeconomic dynamics lies in its ability to explain historical processes. Given that our objective is to explain a rather complex reality, we have felt it essential to employ a variety of techniques. Historical and descriptive narratives are used, as well as analytical techniques. For example, non-linear dynamics and the cyclical models based on this kind of mathematics are used in chapter 8 to explain the sources of the Great Depression in the United States. The theory is not set out in equations but is developed in the narrative. Other chapters employ a formal theoretical approach, using equations to set out the ideas, and some employ econometric techniques and utilize econometric results from our own and other studies to support a point. Yet others turn to case studies. Whenever possible we use the term 'framework' rather than 'model' (although the term 'modelling' cannot be avoided) to avoid disappointing readers who prefer to have everything set out in a system of equations. However, when discussing components of our framework, the term 'model' is used.

The book is divided into three parts. Part I outlines the framework for analysing economic development over the past century, part II utilizes this framework to explain capitalist development in the twentieth century and part III focuses on the role of power and its likely contribution to the course of development in the near future.

1 Economic development and economic performance

1 Introduction

Looking back over the twentieth century at what are now the advanced capitalist economies, one of the more outstanding characteristics of macroeconomic development has been the radical transformation of their economic structures, i.e. the tastes, technologies and institutions that shape economic activity. The fourfold increase in real per capita income since the early years of the twentieth century is not the result of balanced growth, with output expanding at the same rate in every sector. Instead, growth has been accompanied by large shifts in the composition of output and in the sectoral distribution of capital and labour, transformations that have led economic historians and economists to distinguish among epochs of capitalism, such as the 'industrial' and 'post-industrial' phases. But this observation barely scratches the surface. These transformations are themselves made possible by technological change, as within each sector industries grow and decay, product and process innovation are commonplace and resources continuously reallocated. And with technological change there have been changes in the lifestyle of individuals that go far beyond those implied by mere increases in income, however large, and, beyond even this, changes in society itself. A well-known example is the advent of the 'age of steam', which introduced the factory system and urbanization. In the case of such sweeping change to the type of work and its organization, and to how and where people lived, it is relatively easy to recognize that new rules and norms would become established to govern behaviour under these new conditions. The point to be made here is that capitalism transforms itself continuously, and that change is both pervasive and radical. There are no 'givens' in the long run, or even in the intermediate run. Technologies, tastes and institutions change, and a change in one can trigger events or trends that lead to changes in the others.

7

2 Development or performance?

Our main concern is to explain macroeconomic performance in the advanced capitalist economies over a period covering roughly the twentieth century. Nevertheless, we have chosen to use 'development' in the title, rather than 'performance', because of the structural changes that have taken place over this period. These are incorporated into our analytical framework, which is designed to explain not only key indicators of macroeconomic performance, for example GDP and unemployment, but also the interaction of performance with the evolving economic structure that accompanies industrialization and transformation.

This cannot be done within the mainstream framework. The neoclassical model simply responds to exogenous forces; given a change in economic structure, the model's sole response is to restore equilibrium. The cause of all long-run economic change is to be found outside the economy. Observation of the historical course of capitalism demonstrates the falsity of this view. History shows that performance and structural change are inseparable in real economies. And, although some structural change may be traced to exogenous causes, much of it is endogenous. For example, products and processes are the result of innovation, the search for different and improved goods and methods of production. Even when the underlying scientific knowledge is properly classified as exogenous, its adaptation to commercial use is a central activity of the capitalist economy, the task of entrepreneurs. The alternative framework we use is therefore evolutionary, that is, it gives a central place to endogenous structural change as the process by which capitalist economies transform themselves.

This approach demonstrates some sharp differences from neoclassical theory. First, we treat institutions – the rules, laws and customs that define acceptable social behaviour – as well as tastes and technology as part of the structure of the economy. Moreover, as part of the structure they undergo change. Therefore we also investigate the process by which economic variables and outcomes induce institutional change, as well as change in the other structural variables. Second, power is introduced into the analysis both as an important influence on economic performance through the power of organized interest groups to affect institutions, for example the impact of unionization on welfare legislation, and as a force affected by the economy, for example the effect of full employment on union density. This focus on organized interest groups affects the way in which we treat tastes. Our concern is with collective preferences, so that where consumer theory considers income as the means of optimizing individual preferences, we consider power (whether economic or political) as the means of achieving group preferences. Before an interest group can affect institutions, it must acquire and exercise sufficient power.

3 Institutions and institutional change

The decision to incorporate institutions in our analysis stems in part from the belief that capitalist development cannot be modelled adequately if they are omitted. They are an integral part of the structural framework. Institutions act as cognitive devices (Hodgson, 1993); by encapsulating information about the probable actions of others, they reduce uncertainty, giving stability to social and economic relations. However, in doing so they simultaneously regulate behaviour, which must conform to the established norms, which reduces conflict. More generally, because they guide behaviour, institutions such as tastes and technology affect the manner in which the economy performs, for example whether growth proceeds rapidly or slowly, whether it is accompanied by serious inflation, whether the rising affluence is denied to large segments of the population through unemployment. As a result, any explanation of economic performance, and of why it differs among countries or from one period of time to another, requires study of the way in which institutions affect economic processes.

The impact of institutions on performance is only part of the story. Change is central to capitalism, both economic and institutional change. For many early economists, change was capitalism's overwhelming characteristic, making its development incomprehensible except as a historical process. As Heilbroner (1986, p. 143) notes, all the great political economists describe 'dramas of social as well as material evolution' brought about by capitalism. Following this tradition, we maintain that long-run macroeconomic performance is one of the most powerful causes of institutional change. And because institutional change alters behaviour, future economic performance is also affected. A similar view is appropriate with respect to the more familiar structural features treated as exogenous in neoclassical analysis. To emphasize this last point further, our approach to modelling macroeconomic performance differs from the neoclassical approach not simply by including institutions as additional structural features affecting performance, but more fundamentally because it considers the impact of performance on tastes, technologies and, especially, institutions. Long-run performance is modelled as the outcome of an interaction between economic performance and the structure of the economy. Economic performance in the short run is always constrained by some initial set of structures, but in the long run economic performance induces changes in the structural framework, creating a causal sequence of events. In more familiar terms, economic performance and structural change over time can be envisaged as an interaction between the demand side of the economy and the 'supply side', where the latter is to be viewed in terms of an expanded list of structural characteristics.

4 Some benefits

Clearly this cannot be the whole picture as disturbances and trends independent of the performance of the economy can have a significant impact on economic performance and structures. But we maintain that highlighting the interaction between performance and economic structure is the key to understanding the basic processes of macroeconomic development. It also has other benefits. First, by incorporating the induced effects of economic performance on the economic structure and the effect of changed structure on economic performance in subsequent periods, an endogenous evolutionary chain of causation is established. Economic performance in a more recent period is explained in terms of economic events at an earlier period, and the future is similarly related to the present. This is to be contrasted with the lack of explanatory power of neoclassical growth dynamics in which long-run movements in the economic variables are merely traced to elements of an unexplained exogenous structure.

Second, this inclusion not only permits a more satisfactory explanation of events, but provides more information on which to base remedial policies in the event of economic malfunction. Thus, if poor economic performance can be attributed to structural change, which is in turn related to economic performance at an earlier point in time, both poor and superior performance can be explained endogenously within a common framework, a possibility ruled out in neoclassical analysis. Further, our approach gives policy makers some indication of what might be done to improve performance by identifying 'ports of entry' for policy intervention, clues and opportunities overlooked when the source of difficulty can be assigned only to some exogenous force. We intend to support these views in part II of the book in our explanation of some of the more important macroeconomic developments in the advanced capitalist economies during the twentieth century.

5 What drives the system?

In a study of macroeconomic performance and evolving economic structure, a decision must be made about which performance variables and economic structures to study. In this section we argue that the choice of performance variables is dictated by which forces drive the economy. For example, if economic development is a process in which aggregate demand

(AD) adjusts passively to supply forces, as in neoclassical growth theory, supply-side variables such as rates of growth of the labour force and technological progress are of chief interest. On the other hand, if growth is a process in which AD induces adjustments on the supply side, the focus is on Keynesian variables, for example rates of growth of investment, fiscal and monetary policies and unemployment. As suggested in the introduction to part I and to be treated in detail in chapter 4, our emphasis is on AD and its rate of growth, both because of its direct impact on output and unemployment, the stuff of traditional Keynesian economics, and because of its indirect impact on the structure of the economy.

Consider the following observations. In a world devoid of invisible hands, full employment even in some long run is not guaranteed; the output and unemployment record will depend upon AD and its growth. As well as the usual Keynesian variables, the level and growth of AD directly influence the behaviour of other economic variables such as the growth of productivity and per capita incomes. This is especially likely when AD growth causes or is caused by investment growth. The negative intertemporal correlation shown in table 2.1 between unemployment rates and per capita income growth rates illustrates this connection, as do the econometric results of chapter 10. Less obvious, but no less important, is the effect of rising levels of per capita incomes and affluence that growing AD and output generate. They alter the distribution of sectoral output and employment, the result of differences in sectoral income elasticities of demand and sectoral levels and rates of growth of productivity. These distributional effects induce structural changes on the supply side. For example, AD and its growth influence the choice of production techniques, the growth of investment and the growth of the labour force through induced effects on participation rates and immigration. Finally, growing incomes and rising affluence induce institutional changes, for example by shifting the distribution of power from capital to labour and by raising the aspirations of ordinary workers. Directly and indirectly, AD has a crucial role to play in economic development. In contrast, slow-growing or stagnant AD leads to high unemployment and low output growth, bringing these and related aspects of transformation to a halt.

An emphasis on AD as a prime driving force behind economic growth and development might appear unusual, as there exists a large literature emphasizing entrepreneurial innovation, in particular the adoption of new product and process embodied investment, as the engine of growth. The works of Schumpeter immediately come to mind. But Schumpeter's assumption of full employment whatever the position of the economy should also remind us of the general neglect of the demand side in the development literature. At the very least our approach can be seen as filling this gap in development theory. Further, there is no conflict between our emphasizing the importance of AD and others choosing to stress entrepreneurial innovation and technology in the study of economic development. Rather they are complementary and partially overlapping approaches. It is enough to note that the degree to which entrepreneurs are willing to undertake innovation activities and bear the risks of implementing new ideas will greatly depend upon the rewards to such activities; this is heavily dependent upon the state of AD. The level and growth of AD provide the key to explaining both the lower turning points of a growth cycle (something which is missing in Schumpeter's work) and differences in the supply of entrepreneurial skills along alternative long-run growth paths (Baumol, 1968). To quote Goodwin (1991, p. 32),

> But because the level and growth rate of demand plays so great a role in productive decisions, especially in the case of new and risky projects, various innovations are launched and/or rapidly expanded in a rising market: then the requisite investment required further accelerates the already buoyant market. . . . Thus the Kahn–Keynes multiplication of expansive and contractive demand furnishes a crucial missing link for Schumpeter's innovative theory of technological evolution.

Treating AD as the driving force in economic growth and development in this study dictates the choice of performance variables to study. We have singled out the unemployment rate for special attention, judging it to be the best measure of the state of AD. There are three additional reasons for choosing the unemployment record. First, the ability of an economic system to provide employment for anyone wanting to work is a widely accepted indicator of national economic well-being.[1] Second, other dimensions of macroeconomic performance are related to the overall state of the labour market and these also have welfare implications, some of which we wish to study; for example, the growth of productivity and incomes, the incidence of poverty and crime, the degree of inequality in the distribution of incomes. Third, other important aspects of macroeconomic performance are negatively related to unemployment performance, and this raises the issue of trade-offs between macro goals. Thus periods of high involuntary unemployment are attributed in the first instance to a deficiency of AD. When these deficiencies occur they are traced to the adverse effects of higher levels of AD and lower unemployment on other economic and political goals, for example price stability, external balance, capital's control of the workplace. Conversely, when periods of full employment levels of AD occur, this reflects an absence of adverse side-effects of full employment on potentially competing macroeconomic goals. Thus, in explaining

---

[1] Keynes saw full employment as essential for reconciling capitalism and democracy.

unemployment, the analysis is automatically extended to include and explain additional dimensions of macroeconomic performance.

6 Selecting components of the economic structure

The criterion we adopt in choosing which components of the economic structure to study is largely dictated by our emphasis on explaining unemployment trends. As we will argue, periods of high and low unemployment, and of poor or superior performance in general, depend ultimately upon prevailing institutions because of their impact on AD. An obvious example is a law forbidding government deficits; even when private demand is weak it will prevent the use of stimulative fiscal policies, making higher unemployment inevitable. The Maastricht criteria are relevant examples of such constraints on AD. Of equal interest are those cases in which trade-offs between macroeconomic goals are involved. As will be discussed at some length in chapter 5, institutions affecting the labour market can lead to a poorly placed Phillips curve and a politically unacceptable rate of inflation under full employment conditions. The post-war record shows that in such cases restrictive AD policies are used to combat potential inflationary tendencies. To relieve the economy of restrictions on AD and to improve unemployment *and* inflation performance, policy-induced changes in institutions must precede the use of stimulative AD policies. On the other hand, at a different time or in another economy, the menu of unemployment–inflation choices open to the authorities may contain a number of politically acceptable options. In this case, it is shown that elements of the institutional framework allow low unemployment and low inflation to be achieved simultaneously. One of our aims is to determine which institutions permit low rates of unemployment because their presence allows the economy to avoid the adverse side-effects of high levels of AD.

7 Evidence

Given the central role of structural change in economic development, it becomes clear that recurrent crises resemble each other only with respect to their most prominent manifestation, such as lengthy periods of high unemployment. In every other dimension they can be expected to differ, because the economic structure differs. Thus history does not repeat itself, but rather traces out a sequence of episodes, each with its distinct structural characteristics. For example, a given exogenous shock may have no effect, or it may trigger a sequence of events that culminate in a crisis, depending on the economic structure. Let us suppose that the second result obtains; again, depending on the economic structure, the process of transmitting the shock will differ, as will the set of performance variables affected and the extent to which each changes. Therefore, not only is the same exogenous shock applied to the same economy at different phases of its development expected to yield different results, but these results are expected to take effect via different processes.

This clearly presents a problem for the analyst, for, no matter how accurate the data, the structure of the economy is changing in the long run. For an individual economy, the available statistical evidence is inadequate to test an explanation of economic performance; any results would be highly speculative. This, however, is only part of the broader picture presented here. We stress the importance of endogenous change, in particular the way in which economic performance induces structural change that in turn alters the economic processes. In view of this, poor performance and even crisis may be the product of the cumulative effects of endogenous change. This presents an even greater dilemma: given the evolutionary nature of economic development, how is it possible to determine whether a poor performance in some country is to be attributed, for example, to a set of unfortunate institutions rather than to exogenous disturbances?

While the data do not permit us to test our proposals for an individual economy, we make use of multi-country analysis. Although the development of an economy involves a continuous evolution of its economic structure, we believe that the advanced capitalist economies have experienced broadly similar evolutionary paths over the past century, particularly since World War II, and that they will continue to do so. Much of the explanation of the similarities is implicit in section 5, which discussed the direct and indirect impacts of AD on the economy. Not only have all these economies responded to AD pressures in the manner described in that section, but historically there has been substantial similarity in average AD pressures across countries. Stagnant AD conditions were a common feature during the 1930s, as were strong and growing AD during the 'golden age' of capitalism and the reversion to stagnant conditions since the mid-1970s.

There were also supranational changes, largely external to any individual economy but affecting all of them, that led to similarities in development patterns. These include the increasing international linkages brought about by the rapid expansion of trade, and the changed international monetary regime following the breakdown of the Bretton Woods Agreement. The impact of deregulated international capital flows, especially since the 1980s, on AD policies within each economy is a case in point. To these can be added long-run forces. These, while not entirely exogenous, must because of our ignorance be treated as such. They affect the structural framework and performance of all economies in a similar way (for example, the spread of free education and the extension of the franchise).

8 Similar development patterns, different performances

In the previous sections we have noted that there are parallels in the development patterns of the advanced capitalist economies. However, we do not take the position, made popular by social scientists in the early part of the post-World War II period, that there is an inherent tendency for industrialized economies to undergo convergence of their economic structures (Kerr, 1960). In fact, case studies of the industrial relations systems and other institutions of the developed capitalist economies show examples of both divergence and convergence in the course of their development. Institutional divergence has resulted in different economic performance because of the effect of institutions on economic processes. Underlying these events, however, is the long-run development pattern shared among them as they move through the stages of industrialization and modernization and on toward post-industrialism; it is against this background of broadly similar experience that these differences in economic performance and structure stand out so clearly. And it is these differences that provide the evidence essential to an investigation of the impact of economic structure on economic performance.

In summary, the approach to be used in this study is to explain similarities in the development patterns of a group of economies in terms of similar interactions of economic performance variables and economic structures, and then to account for differences in economic performance between these economies in terms of differences in the evolving structural framework, especially their institutions. This task can be divided into three parts, with institutional differences used as an example. First, it is necessary to determine the process that enables institutional differences to generate performance differences among economies. For example, cross-country analysis of the golden age in chapter 5 shows a wide variation in unemployment rates and almost no variation in rates of inflation. Although other influences were at work, this can be largely attributed to differences in institutions of the labour market, in particular to how effectively they can contain rates of inflation at low rates of unemployment. Similar cross-country analysis can be used to examine other periods. The second task is to determine when certain institutions have changed sufficiently that new constraints on AD are in operation or old constraints have been removed, and to identify how and how strongly they affect economic performance. Radical alterations in macroeconomic performance are clues to such changes. Once it is established that significant institutional change has occurred, the investigation proceeds to determine whether it is endogenous (that is, can be attributed to the cumulative impact of past macroeconomic performance) or whether and to what extent exogenous forces were involved. The final task is to combine these results in the form of a causal chain illustrating the interaction of performance and structures.

9 Historical laws and predictions

Our analysis of macroeconomic performance employs a framework in which key aspects of an evolving structure are explained. This may appear to some as a quest for historical laws of macroeconomic development with all the ambitious predictive connotations this usually carries. It is not our intention to engage in what we believe would be so fruitless a task. Instead, the task we have set ourselves reduces to answering two quite straightforward questions. First, what part do economic structures, especially institutions, play in the determination of differences in economic performance? And, second, how does economic performance itself influence these structures?

Our efforts to answer these questions necessarily depend on the past experience of a limited number of economies. Can our findings be applied to economies beyond this sample, and can they be used for prediction? In assessing their general applicability, we are faced with the complications arising from the centrality of institutions to the analysis, and the fact that institutions tend to be country specific. We maintain that there have been and will continue to be important similarities between the development patterns of the advanced capitalist economies. For this reason, an understanding of the role of institutions and the causes and results of institutional change in these economies will provide valuable information for policy makers. Furthermore, in the absence of catastrophes, there is every reason to believe that the newly industrialized countries (NICs) will experience similar patterns of development. It also seems reasonable to expect that the rate at which the NICs will transform themselves will be as rapid as, perhaps more rapid than, the rate experienced by the present industrial leaders when they were at a comparable level of development. Given these similarities, the experience of the advanced capitalist economies is relevant, and with some modification our analysis would be applicable.

Because the NICs appear to be following the paths of the advanced capitalist economies, there is the possibility that our results might be used for medium- or longer-term forecasting. However, such forecasts would be very speculative, subject to error stemming from unforeseen shocks, from structural changes unrelated to their past economic performance, and from the unique features of a country's historical development. Predictions become even more perilous when considering the likely evolving performance of the already industrialized economies. For example, the 1950s and 1960s were a period of rapid and sustained growth and low unemployment in the advanced capitalist economies. Viewing the future from the vantage point of, say, the late 1960s to early 1970s, a forecast of continued superior macroeconomic performance would have appeared reasonable and was the view held by the overwhelming majority of macroeconomists at the time. In retrospect, the late 1960s to early 1970s marked the beginning of the end of the great post-war boom. Beginning in the mid-1970s and extending until the late 1990s, macroeconomic performance in the OECD economies was characterized by high and rising unemployment rates, greatly reduced growth in productivity and incomes and the spread of poverty.

In our view, the failure of the economics profession to foresee the events about to unfold in the mid-1970s was due to an inability to comprehend some important underlying institutional changes that were taking place; these were to have a strong negative effect on economic performance. This failure can be traced to two causes. First, the trend in macroeconomic theory had for some time been in the direction of greater formalization in modelling dynamic processes, a formalization increasingly devoid of attention to economic structures, especially institutions. Second, these economies had never before experienced prolonged full employment during a period of rising union strength. The impact of these events on institutions, eventually leading to strong inflationary pressures under full employment conditions, could not have been foreseen even had trends in macroeconomic theory followed a different path.

In view of this, the question arises whether the inability to predict future structural changes casts doubt on the value of our approach. We think not. For one thing, we believe that our framework provides a deeper explanation of past macroeconomic performance of the developed capitalist economies; it examines the historical record, viewing both exogenous and endogenous forces as potential determinants of economic performance. We also believe that, by pinpointing the structural features that lead to poor or superior performance, we are better able to make sound short- and intermediate-run forecasts than alternative approaches would allow. All forecasts are conditional but ours explicitly emphasize their conditionality on unchanged structures, and these are relatively stable features of most economies. Further, our approach involves examining economies for evidence of structural change, so that observed systematic trends can be used for forecast purposes; when change has no discernible pattern, it will be clear that no forecast will be reliable.

Its inclusion of structural change enables our approach to offer deeper understanding of the current difficulties of persistent high unemployment, and this opens new options for improving performance through policy. It emphasizes the need to look for structural changes as sources of the current difficulties. More ambitiously, by determining the structural causes of malfunction, we are able to indicate the kind of policy-induced structural changes that will foster recovery. This is not a claim that policies can always be found, or that they will achieve results quickly and accurately. There are still too many unknowns. But, rather than attempting short-run 'fine tuning' of the economy, we are suggesting that establishing which institutions stand in the way of recovery and seeking policies that will induce the needed changes offer hope for a longer-term solution to malfunction in economies that are clearly not self-regulating.

10 What can we learn from studying the long run?

The purpose of this study is to explain long-run macroeconomic development. Given current economic conditions, this raises the question of relevance. We live in an age of high unemployment now well in to its third decade; there is little indication of noticeable improvement in the near future. Accordingly it can be argued that the proper role of a macroeconomic model builder should be to tackle the unemployment problem. Certainly explaining macroeconomic performance over nearly a century is our stated aim, but it is done with the objective of shedding light on current problems and has been motivated in large part by a desire to find remedies for this malfunction. However, in order to provide a convincing explanation of today's problems we think it necessary to demonstrate that our framework has some claim to generality by offering an explanation of other historical periods. We wish to convince the reader that in earlier periods as well as today, whether performance can be termed superior or poor, the outcome has been the result of structural changes themselves induced by endogenous economic forces, and not simply caused by avoidable human error or other exogenous disturbances interrupting the otherwise seamless progress of a self-regulating system.

11 Looking ahead

The remaining chapters in part I develop the points summarized in this chapter. Here we have introduced the idea of the evolution of the economy's structural framework as a fundamental process of development. Chapter 2 concentrates on the economic variables, particularly trends in output and unemployment and the likely causes of these trends. This requires some evaluation of mainstream growth theories and of the adequacy of conventional unemployment measures. Alternative measures of unemployment are also discussed. We pay particular attention to the recent American experience because, as usually measured, its unemployment performance has been relatively good. The institutional features of the 'American model' are alleged to be responsible for this result and are widely cited as the proper goal of institutional reform. Chapter 3 is a critique of supply-determined equilibrium analysis in general and the neoclassical theory of unemployment in particular. Chapter 4 introduces an extended Keynesian model of demand-determined growth in which outcomes are attributed to the state of AD and not to forces on the supply side, not only when there are unemployed resources but also under full employment conditions. Chapter 5 discusses institutions and their functions, and considers both institutions and the distribution of power as determinants of economic performance. These ideas are illustrated by several well-known empirical studies, to which we add our own econometric investigation. Chapter 6 considers the long run, when institutions and the distribution of power vary. This completes our framework for modelling economic development. Chapter 7 compares our approach with other attempts to model long-term economic development.

2 The stylized facts

1 The stylized facts

Kaldor (1963) maintained that, in order to choose between competing theoretical approaches, it is first necessary to agree on the broad historical tendencies of macroeconomic development we wish to explain. These he termed the 'stylized facts'. We have chosen the alternating episodes of good and poor macroeconomic performance as the stylized fact of greatest interest, but include differences in the performance of economies that have shown this common historical pattern and the unbalanced nature of the growth process as additional aspects of development to be recognized and explained. In this chapter we briefly describe these tendencies as a background for discussion and evaluation of the mainstream analysis of the dynamics of output and unemployment, topics continued in chapter 3.

1.1 Unemployment and growth patterns

Table 2.1 records rates of unemployment and rates of growth of per capita incomes and GDP for 16 developed capitalist economies for which comparable data are available. Beginning with the 'boom' years of the 1920s, most of the economies experienced periods of low unemployment and rapid per capita income growth alternating with periods of high unemployment and slow growth. Notable exceptions were Germany and Japan, where rearmament programmes led to booms in the 1930s. Most other economies endured a marked deterioration of macro performance in the 1930s compared with the 1920s. The strong recovery during the golden age episode of 1955–73 stands out, as does the widespread poor performance of the post-1973 period. Since 1973, unemployment rates have risen and growth rates of GDP and per capita income have fallen compared with their golden age rates. As stated in the introduction to part I, determining the causes of these alternating episodes is a primary task of the study.

1.2 Comparative growth and unemployment performance in the golden age

While the general pattern of macroeconomic development was similar, there were differences between countries in their growth and unemployment records. For example, a notable feature of growth performance during the golden age was the very rapid growth of productivity in most of the developed capitalist economies. One of its sources in countries other than the United States (as industrial leader) has been traced to technology transfer. Economies starting late in the industrialization and modernization process have been able to borrow the most advanced technology. This source of rapid growth contributes to a negative correlation between growth rates of productivity over some period and per capita income levels at its beginning. Table 2.2 illustrates this correlation and the implied tendency for income levels in the group of developed capitalist economies to converge during the golden age. This convergence tendency had not existed prior to World War II (Abramovitz, 1986). Countries with relatively high initial per capita income, for example Canada, Switzerland and the USA, experienced relatively low rates of productivity growth (and therefore low rates of growth of per capita incomes), while the three economies with the lowest initial levels of per capita income, Ireland, Japan and Spain, were among the most rapidly growing economies.[1] Chapters 10 and 11 provide an explanation of differences in growth rates between economies and the role of technology transfer.

A second outstanding feature of the golden age episode was the bimodal distribution of unemployment performances. Three economies in table 2.1, Canada, Italy and the USA, experienced average unemployment rates during this period of approximately 5 per cent. The next highest rate was 2.8 per cent in the UK. If these four high unemployment economies are excluded from the sample, the average rate of unemployment of the remainder is 1.7 per cent. As we will show, countries with low unemployment rates did not achieve this enviable record at the cost of relatively high inflation rates. Indeed, there was little difference in inflation rates among countries in spite of pronounced differences in unemployment. Explaining these cross-country differences in performance will occupy our attention in later chapters.

1.3 Unbalanced growth

A conspicuous characteristic of capitalism's development is that growth is a typically unbalanced process (see chapter 10). Even at the lowest levels of

---

[1] It should be emphasized that our analysis deals with a group or 'club' of developed OECD economies that experienced rapid growth of income and productivity during the golden age.

Table 2.1 Unemployment rates (U), growth rates of real per capita income ($\dot{y}$) and real GDP growth rates ($\dot{Q}$) for 16 OECD countries: selected periods (%)

Country	1922–29			1930–37			1955–73			1974–98		
	U	$\dot{y}$	$\dot{Q}$	U	$\dot{y}$	$\dot{Q}$	U	$\dot{y}$	$\dot{Q}$	U	$\dot{y}$	$\dot{Q}$
Australia	5.7	−0.7	1.2	14.1	2.5	3.3	2.0	2.7	4.9	9.0	1.7	3.1
Austria	6.0[a]	3.7	4.0	13.4	−1.8	−1.7	2.1	4.5	5.1	3.2[f]	2.1	2.4
Belgium	0.9	1.8	2.8	8.8	−0.1	0.4	2.4	3.7	4.3	8.7	1.8	2.0
Canada	3.2	4.1	5.9	13.6	−1.0	0.1	5.1	3.1	5.0	9.9	1.5	2.7
Denmark	8.4	2.9	3.7	11.0	0.9	1.7	2.1	3.6	4.3	7.5	1.9	2.1
Finland	1.6	4.0	5.0	4.2	3.7	4.5	2.0	4.3	4.9	12.1	2.0	2.5
France	1.7[b]	3.9	4.5	3.4[e]	−0.1	0.0	1.9	4.1	5.2	11.2	1.7	2.1
Germany	4.4	2.8	3.5	9.7	3.0	3.6	1.4	4.0	5.0	6.3	1.9[h]	2.0
Italy	1.7[c]	2.3	3.2	4.8	1.9	2.7	5.2	4.7	5.4	10.8	2.0	2.2
Japan	n.a.	1.5	2.9	n.a.	3.3	4.8	1.5	8.1	9.3	2.9	2.3	3.0
Netherlands	2.4	6.8	4.6	8.5	−0.4	0.8	1.8	3.3	4.6	6.0	1.7	2.4
Norway	5.6	3.2	3.7	8.4	2.0	2.5	2.0	3.3	4.1	5.1	3.0	3.5
Sweden	3.0	4.2	4.5	5.6	2.5	2.8	1.8	3.6	4.2	7.3	1.3	1.6
Switzerland	0.4[c]	4.6[d]	5.2[d]	3.0	−0.2	0.3	0.0	2.9	4.4	1.4[g]	0.7	1.0
United Kingdom	7.8	2.5	2.9	11.8	1.9	2.4	2.8	2.5	3.0	8.5	1.7	1.9
United States	4.1	3.2	4.7	18.2	0.5	1.2	4.8	2.0	3.4	5.9	1.7	2.6
Unweighted average	3.8	3.2	3.9	9.2	1.2	1.8	2.4	3.8	4.8	7.4	1.8	2.3

Notes:
[a] Average for 1924-9. [b] Average for 1921, 1926 and 1929. [c] Unemployment rate in 1929.
[d] Interpolations for the years 1922 and 1923. [e] Average for 1931 and 1936.
[f] Average for 1974-89 and 1993-8. [g] Average for 1974-89 and 1991-1997. [h] Break in 1991.
Sources: Maddison (1991), Tables A.8, B.2 and C.6; OECD, *Economic Outlook, 66*, December 1999, Annex Tables 1 and 22; OECD, *Historical Statistics 1960-1997*, Tables 1.1, 3.1 and 3.2; OECD, *Labour Force Statistics 1978-1998*.

Table 2.2 *Correlation between per capita income and growth rates*

Country	Per capita income 1960 ('000 1980 international dollars)	Growth rate of GDP per person employed, 1960–73 (%)
Australia	5.2971	2.5
Austria	3.7263	5.0
Belgium	3.9490	4.3
Canada	5.7245	2.6
Denmark	4.9574	3.0
Finland	3.8179	4.7
France	4.1800	4.7
W. Germany	4.8739	4.1
Ireland	2.5642	4.3
Italy	3.3267	5.8
Japan	2.3095	8.2
Netherlands	4.9640	4.0
New Zealand	5.5371	1.8
Norway	4.4838	3.1
Spain	2.4085	6.4
Sweden	5.3448	3.5
Switzerland	7.3993	2.9
United Kingdom	5.3437	2.8
United States	7.8087	2.0
Correlation coefficient	−.819	

Sources: Per capita income data were provided by John Helliwell and Alan Chung, Economics Department, University of British Columbia; GDP growth data are from OECD, *Historical Statistics*, various issues.

disaggregation, continuous shifts in sectoral shares of output, as a result of differences in sectoral growth rates, was a historical tendency throughout the period covered in table 2.1 and earlier. For example, when the economy is divided into agriculture, industry and service sectors, output shares in all the economies shifted, tracing out a similar pattern over time. The relative importance of agricultural output fell continuously, industrial output as a share of GDP rose and then fell, while output of the service sector increased continuously, reflecting sizeable differences in rates of growth of sectoral outputs (OECD, *Historical Statistics 1960–1997*). The same transformational aspects of the growth process were displayed by persistent differences in growth rates of the components of final demand. For example, in the post-World War II period relatively high rates of growth of exports and investment exceeded the growth rates of other components of final demand.

And, within the consumption expenditure category, the relative importance of particular items shifted continuously from 'necessities' such as food and clothing to goods higher in the hierarchy such as consumer durable goods. Mainstream growth theory, with its focus on the long-run steady-state properties of its models, must work within a balanced growth format. A consequence of doing so is that it ignores the changing distribution of output and the resulting shifts in the distribution of labour inputs, both of which are important sources of growth in output and productivity. This stylized fact will also command our attention later in the study.

2 Modelling dynamic processes in the absence of structural change

Next consider the two mainstream models of economic growth, neoclassical and endogenous growth theory. Much of the literature in growth theory emphasizes the differences between these two approaches. Our position is that their similarities outweigh their differences, and in evaluating their ability to explain the historical record outlined in table 2.1, we treat both theories as examples of aggregate production function growth theories. This is to emphasize the pivotal role of aggregate supply in determining growth and their common (neoclassical) assumption of continuous full employment. In both theories, growth is explained in terms of its immediate causes, the inputs in the production function, as AD adjusts passively to the supply side. In both, the underlying preference and production possibility sets are exogenous, institutions are ignored and saving determines investment. However, to make clear their limitations in explaining historical growth processes, it is useful to first summarize separately the basic model for each of these two theories.

2.1 The basic neoclassical growth model

Consider the following constant returns to scale aggregate production function of neoclassical growth theory:

$$Q = (AL)^{1-a}K^a \qquad 0 < a < 1 \tag{2.1}$$

in which A is an index of technological progress assumed to grow at rate g, K is the capital stock and L is the available supply of labour measured in 'natural' units and assumed to grow at rate n. In this production function, technological progress augments the natural growth of the labour supply, and the supply of labour in 'efficiency' units grows at rate $(g+n)$. Transforming equation (2.1) into growth rates gives

$$\dot{Q} = (1-a)(\dot{AL}) + a\dot{K}, \tag{2.2}$$

where a dot indicates the geometric rate of growth of each variable. Next assume saving, S, is a fixed share of output, $S = sQ$, which automatically flows into investment, I, so that $S = I$ with $I = dK/dt$ and therefore $\dot{K} = I/K = sQ/K$. By definition, $\dot{Q}^* = \dot{K}^*$ in the steady state, and substitution gives

$$\dot{Q}^* = (\dot{AL})^* = (g + n) \tag{2.3}$$

and

$$\dot{q}^* = \dot{Q}^* - n = g. \tag{2.4}$$

Equation (2.3) is the long-run equilibrium rate of growth of output, $\dot{Q}^*$, and equation (2.4) gives the long-run equilibrium rate of growth of labour productivity, $\dot{q}^*$. As growth in the model is balanced, in the steady-state output, capital, investment, consumption and saving all grow at rate $(g + n)$. Since g and n are both assumed to be exogenous, the long-run growth rates of all these variables, as well as of productivity, depend solely upon forces outside the system. In particular, we note that, as in the Solow–Swan model, all long-run rates are independent of the rates of saving and investment ($s = S/Q = I/Q$).

2.2 The AK growth model

Consider next an example of the simplest of the new growth theory models, the AK model stripped of its 'micro foundations'. Write the aggregate production function as

$$Q = A'K^aL^{1-a}, \tag{2.5}$$

where A', K and L are an index of technological progress or knowledge, the capital stock and the labour force measured in natural units, respectively. Technological knowledge is treated as a kind of disembodied capital whose stock can be augmented through investment activities such as R&D efforts. Because of its dependence on the amount of capital in the economy, Frankel (1962) assumed technological knowledge to be a function of the stock of capital per worker:

$$A' = A(K/L)^b, \tag{2.6}$$

where A is a constant. Equation (2.6) expresses the level of technological knowledge in the aggregate; it is the result of an externality or spillover effect arising when the benefits from investing in knowledge cannot be totally appropriated by the investing firm, for example through patents. The greater is the level of 'development', measured here by the capital–labour ratio, the more advanced is the level of knowledge, and the more rapid will be the growth of productivity. Substituting equation (2.6) into equation (2.5) and assuming $a + b = 1$ gives

$$Q = AK. \tag{2.7}^2$$

The AK production function displays the major innovation of new growth theory, that there are constant returns to capital. The capital input in the production function of equation (2.7) is a composite variable that includes the stock of technological knowledge as well as physical capital goods. The critical underlying assumption is that knowledge automatically grows at a rate just sufficient to counter the effects of diminishing returns. In the steady state, $\dot{Q} = \dot{K}$ and, as the system is assumed to be at full employment, $S = I = sQ$. Then we can write

$$\dot{Q} = \dot{K} = sQ/K. \tag{2.8}$$

With the capital–output ratio constant, the long-run growth rate of output depends upon the saving ratio, and in this sense growth is said to be endogenously determined. From equation (2.8) it can be seen that any change in the saving (= investment) ratio permanently alters the long-run growth rates of capital and output. The importance of the saving and investment ratios arises from there being constant returns to capital in endogenous growth theory. This is its key difference from neoclassical growth models. However, this gain in explanatory power is at a great cost because of the model's lack of robustness. The exponent of capital in the production function must be exactly one (Chiappori, 1989; Solow, 1994). Even small deviations in either direction quickly lead to results quite contrary to the spirit of these endogenous growth models, i.e. the growth rate tends to zero or infinity. Aside from this major difference, in other respects the defining features of the two aggregate production function growth theories are the same.

2.3 Some shortcomings

With respect to their ability to explain the stylized facts of growth described in table 2.1, both growth theories contain serious errors of omission. These models are offered as explanations of the long run, yet they ignore institutional change, a prominent structural feature of capitalism's long-run development, as an influence on long-term growth. In addition, we question the value of any long-run theory of economic growth that ignores the changes in tastes, technologies and institutions that are induced by economic performance.

---

[2] More recent new growth theory versions of AK models incorporate micro foundations by including an intertemporal utility maximization function for a representative agent that determines saving and therefore investment. Our discussion of the weaknesses of new growth theory has little to do with these micro foundations.

We also have reason to question the explanatory value of these models because of their errors of commission. By choosing to model dynamic processes in a steady-state, balanced growth framework, mainstream growth theory ignores the shifting sectoral composition of output. And, because of this choice, transitions from one steady-state growth path to another, as well as differences in the steady-state growth paths between economies, cannot be explained within the model; they require appeal to exogenous forces. In neoclassical models, these differences must be attributed to changes in g or n, both exogenous variables; in new growth models, differences in growth rates must be attributed to unexplained changes in tastes, which determine the saving ratio. Finally, by assuming continuous full employment, production function growth theory must ignore another stylized fact, sustained periods of high unemployment.

3 Modelling unemployment

3.1 Attributing unemployment to shocks

Ignoring the frictional component of unemployment, production function growth theory assumes that capital and labour are fully employed at every point in time, a state ensured by some unspecified mechanism adjusting AD to the level of maximum output given by the production function. AD plays only a passive role. Treated as descriptive devices, mainstream growth models formalize the belief, currently widely shared among economists and political leaders, that capitalism has strong self-regulating tendencies. This conception of capitalism usually allows for shocks, including ill-conceived government interventions, and 'market imperfections' that may lead to temporary deviations from the economy's natural full employment state. But in their absence the system is either converging toward or moving along a full employment growth path. Therefore lapses from the full employment state would not necessarily undermine the explanatory value of full employment growth models provided that they are infrequent and short lived.

However, table 2.1 shows that when high unemployment has occurred it does not appear to be a random event, unrelated to earlier events. Historically, high rates of unemployment have occurred in episodes of considerable length, suggesting causal mechanisms that are sustaining high unemployment once it sets in. As a result, attributing episodes of poor macroeconomic performance to a series of negative shocks is no explanation, and we will show that explaining them as the consequence of pronounced deviations of markets from the competitive model is not consistent with the historical record. The historical record of lengthy periods of high unemployment alternating with episodes of low unemployment (as well as alternating episodes of slow and rapid growth) remains a stylized fact yet to be explained.

3.2 Voluntary versus involuntary unemployment

The history of macroeconomic thought over the past century shows wide swings in the economics profession's view of capitalism's ability to avoid periods of involuntary unemployment, that is, the presence of workers prepared to accept work at the going real wage or less, but unable to find jobs. Until the Keynesian revolution it was also widely assumed by economists (and political leaders) that, in some rather vague long run, full employment, i.e. the absence of involuntary unemployment, was a natural feature of capitalist development. In our view, the high unemployment periods shown by the data in table 2.1 were episodes of high rates of involuntary unemployment. This assumption reflects our acceptance of the revolutionary message of Keynes' *General Theory*: there are no inherent tendencies for the private sector of a modern capitalist system to generate a full employment level of AD. In addition to the existence of frictional voluntary unemployment, episodes of high rates of involuntary unemployment occur and these require stimulative fiscal programmes if the economy is to return to full employment.

With memories of the mass unemployment of the 1930s still fresh, this position was widely accepted by the economics profession throughout most of the golden age episode, but was challenged by reformulations of the classical view beginning in the late 1960s (Friedman, 1968). As in the earlier classical perspective, this neoclassical or 'new' view saw unemployment as (at worst) the result of frictions in the labour market. The long-run 'natural' position of the economy was full employment, an outcome achieved through a haggling process between individual buyers and sellers until markets cleared. In other words, markets were assumed to be competitive.[3] In such an economic system, interventionist policies were unnecessary. In an influential study supporting this view, Phelps et al. (1970) modelled frictional unemployment as a type of voluntary search activity. Characteristics of search unemployment included the activities of workers who voluntarily quit a job to search for a better one, spells of unemployment of short duration, and the absence of multiple spells of unemployment in any period. Understandably, the lengthy post-war success of capitalism in solving the unemployment problem during the golden age led to an easy and wide acceptance of the neoclassical view.

---

[3] At the same time as assuming this, Friedman (1968, p. 8), describing the properties of a capitalist system, also assumed there were all the 'market imperfections' of a modern, high technology economy, for example unions and large corporations!

3.3 Classical versus Keynesian unemployment

With the long upward trend of unemployment rates beginning in the mid-1970s, it became increasingly difficult to accept the argument that the increase could be accounted for by rising voluntary unemployment. Closer analysis of the data showed that most of the increase in unemployment could be attributed to workers being laid off and not to a higher quit rate, that a large share of the total weeks of unemployment experienced in any year could be attributed to workers unemployed for long periods (e.g. six months or more) and that multiple spells of unemployment within the year were common (Clark and Summers, 1979; Main, 1981; Hasan and de Broucker, 1982). These findings strongly suggested that much of the rising unemployment had to be considered involuntary and required an explanation that the new view could not provide.[4]

In response to the lack of empirical relevance of the original new view, a second generation of 'new' perspectives on unemployment emerged incorporating a new vocabulary (for example, Malinvaud, 1977) and subsequently an institutional framework for formally modelling wage bargaining.[5] Rather than distinguishing between voluntary and involuntary unemployment, the distinction adopted was between classical and Keynesian unemployment. By definition the latter could be reduced through stimulative AD policies whereas the former, although it may contain an involuntary component, could not. Instead of modelling wage bargaining as a competitive haggling process between individual buyers and sellers of labour, outcomes were modelled as an optimizing process subject to institutional constraints. In an influential subgroup of these models, the system settles at an equilibrium unemployment rate at which the real wage rate is rigid downward and too high to justify employing all workers willing to work. As a result, employment could not be increased by stimulative AD policies. Policy measures to directly reduce the real wage were required. These models of the labour market gained wide acceptance and were used and continue to be used to attribute the high unemployment since the mid-1970s to the growth of involuntary but classical unemployment. This unemployment cannot be reduced by stimulating AD, the 'policy ineffectiveness argument', but allegedly responds to policies that reduce real wages. Empirical support for this argument relied heavily on the inferior unemployment performance of Europe compared with the USA since the early 1970s. 'Eurosclerosis' was the term given to the alleged

---

[4] In 1969, the unemployment rate in the USA was 3.5 per cent. Almost one-sixth of the weeks of unemployment in this year was experienced by people unemployed for 40 weeks or more and 35 per cent by people out of work for at least 6 months (Clark and Summers, 1979).

[5] For a full account of developments in unemployment theory, see Carlin and Soskice (1990).

labour market inflexibilities and rigidities in the European economies that were claimed to be the cause of higher unemployment. Unfortunately this argument runs up against the relatively superior unemployment performance of most European economies during the golden age, when the same 'inflexible' system produced full employment and low inflation (see table 2.1). A formal analysis and critique of mainstream unemployment modelling is taken up in chapter 3. Suffice it to say at this point that a great deal of unemployment needs to be explained.

4 Measuring unemployment

In this section we show that measured unemployment rates understate the potential gain in employment and output from stimulative AD policies. The reason is that measured unemployment does not record the full extent of the unemployment problem because of two assumptions underlying the official figures. These are that all employed workers are working the number of hours they wish to work, and that all workers not in the labour force do not want to work. As a result of these assumptions, the official unemployment figures fail to include sizeable amounts of two sorts of unutilized labour: part-time workers (working fewer than 30 hours per week) who are involuntarily working less than they wish to, and discouraged workers, persons omitted from the official figures because they had stopped looking for work for economic reasons.[6] Additional measures have been devised to include these two components, providing a better estimate of the extent of labour underutilization. These measures are also valuable for assessing differences in the two added components over time or among economies.

Among the reasons given for constructing broader measures of the underutilization of labour are their ability to provide a more complete measure of slack in the labour market, a better measure of the welfare losses due to inactivity and an improved measure of inflationary pressures in the labour market. For example, the standard measure of unemployment defines anyone working at least one hour in the survey week as employed, so that no distinction is made between full-time and part-time employment. One consequence is that a previously fully employed worker who is involuntarily reduced to part-time work does not affect the unemployment statistics as long as the minimum one hour is worked. Measures of underutilization or underemployment have been compiled since the early 1970s. They use various definitions of involuntary part-time and discouraged workers, and sometimes assign them different weights when computing the underemployment statistics. For example, an involuntary part-time

---

[6] Involuntary part-time workers and discouraged workers are defined in table 2.4.

Table 2.3 *Measures of unemployment in the United States: selected years, 1973–1999*

Measure	1973	1979	1989	1991	1993	1995	1997	1999
U	4.9	5.8	5.3	6.7	6.8	5.6	4.9	4.2
U^{PT}	2.6	3.2	4.0	4.6	5.0	3.4	3.0	2.4
U^{DW}	0.8	0.7	0.7	0.8	0.9	0.3	0.3	0.2
U^{T}	8.3	9.7	10.0	12.1	12.7	9.3	8.2	6.8
U^{T}/U	1.7	1.7	1.9	1.8	1.9	1.7	1.7	1.6

Notes:
U is the official unemployment rate. U^{PT} is involuntary part-time employment and U^{DW} is discouraged workers, each as a percentage of the labour force. The underemployment rate is $U^{T} = U + U^{PT} + U^{DW}$, and U^{T}/U is the ratio of the underemployment and unemployment rates. For additional definitions see table 2.4.
Sources: The State of Working America, various issues, Table 4.2.

employed person might be included as half employed and half unemployed. This causes some differences in the computed values, but these are small when compared with the difference between any of them and the official unemployment rates.

The earliest underemployment data and the longest series available are those for the USA, compiled by the Economic Policy Institute and based on Bureau of Labor Statistics data. Along with the official measure of unemployment, table 2.3 includes rates of involuntary part-time employment, disguised unemployment and their sum (U^{T}), the underemployment rate.[7] In this measure of underemployment, the involuntarily part-time employed and discouraged workers are counted as unemployed. Giving them a weight of 1 emphasizes the incidence of underutilization. The ratio of the underemployment rate to the official unemployment rate (U^{T}/U) of 1.7 is relatively constant, reflecting the positive correlation between movements in the two rates. A number greater than 1 indicates the extent to which the official unemployment rate underestimates the slack in the economy, in this case 70 per cent.

In the light of claims made regarding the superior unemployment performance of the USA, cross-country differences in underemployment rates are of some interest. Table 2.4 compares measures of slack comparable to those of table 2.3 for Canada, the UK and the USA for the period 1983 to 1993 using Bureau of Labor Statistics data. The most striking difference among

[7] We have used the civilian labour force as the denominator in the ratios, whereas the Economic Policy Institute adds the number of discouraged workers to this figure in calculating the denominator.

Table 2.4 *Measures of unemployment in the United States, Canada and the United Kingdom: 1983–1993 averages*

Country	U	U^{PT}	U^{DW}	U^{T}	U_7	U^{T}/U	U_7/U	U^{PT}/U	$U^{\mathrm{PT}}/U^{\mathrm{T}}$
USA	6.8	4.7	0.9	12.4	10.1	1.8	1.49	0.69	0.38
Canada	9.8	4.7	0.6	15.3	13.0	1.6	1.33	0.48	0.31
UK	9.9	2.3	0.8	12.7	12.3	1.3	1.24	0.23	0.18

Notes:
U is the official unemployment rate, U^{PT}, U^{DW} and U^{T} are involuntary part-time employment, discouraged workers and total underemployed persons as a percentage of the labour force, respectively; U_7 is the Bureau of Labor Statistics measure of the underutilization of labour. The ratios show the relative magnitudes of the measures.

Discouraged workers are those who "must explicitly want and be available for work and have searched for work in the prior year, even though they are not currently looking for a job because they feel their search would be in vain" (*Monthly Labor Review*, October 1995, p. 24).

Involuntary part-time work "comprises three groups: first, individuals who usually work full-time but are working part-time because of economic slack; second, individuals who usually work part-time but are working fewer hours in their part-time job because of economic slack; and third, those working part-time because full-time work could not be found" (OECD, *Employment Outlook*, 1995, p. 65).

Source: Monthly Labor Review, August 1995, Table 6.

these economies is the degree to which the underemployment rate diverges from the unemployment rate, as measured by their ratios, U^{T}/U. For example, in the USA, the official unemployment rate understates the broader measure of slack by 80 per cent; for the UK the figure is 30 per cent. The difference between these two countries is due primarily to the much greater incidence of involuntary part-time employment in the USA, which averages 4.7 per cent of the labour force, whereas the UK rate is 2.3 per cent. Table 2.4 includes a second underemployment measure, U_7. It differs from U^{T} in giving involuntary part-time employed workers a weight of only 0.5 when calculating the ratios and in including discouraged workers in the denominator.[8] Although this reduces the computed value of the underemployment statistic, it leaves the rankings of the countries unchanged.

The existence of several alternative measures of underemployment leads to the question of which is the most appropriate. Leaving aside the problem

[8] See *Monthly Labor Review* (August 1995, p. 33) for a discussion of these calculations. As noted in the text, the Economic Policy Institute underemployment measure gives full weight to involuntary part-time employed workers.

of which weights are best for the various components of underemployment, the general case can be made that the more comprehensive measures are better indicators of the amount of forgone output and the welfare costs of inactivity. Discouraged workers and those involuntarily reduced to part-time work are ready for full-time work should jobs become available; their full-time employment would increase output and total welfare. The same claim can be made for the broader measure as an indicator of relative inflationary pressures, other things being equal. For example, table 2.4 shows that the difference in inflationary pressure between the USA and the UK implied by their official unemployment rates is almost entirely eliminated when the underemployment measure U^T is used. In 1999, the official unemployment rate for the USA was 4.2 per cent, suggesting a much tighter labour market than the 6.1 per cent rate in the UK, other things being equal. However, when account is taken of the much higher rate of involuntary part-time employment in the USA, a rather different picture emerges. Although data for 1999 are not available, if we use the 1995 ratios of U^T/U from table 2.4, we can make a rough estimate of U^T for 1999 as 7.6 per cent for the USA, and 7.9 per cent for the UK. The implication is that inflationary pressures are close to being equal in the two countries, and AD stimulation would have comparable inflationary results in each of them.

5 Incarceration and the unemployment rate

Compared with many other OECD economies, the USA's official unemployment rate is low, and this has been used as evidence that the 'flexible' US labour market is a model for others seeking to lower unemployment rates. The previous section showed that these differences are not as great as the data suggest, owing to measurement problems. When discouraged and part-time workers are included, the effect is to narrow the gaps. Another dimension of measurement error, and a source of differences between the US unemployment figures and those elsewhere, is the effect of incarceration. The incarceration rate in the USA has been increasing rapidly over the past two decades. Katz and Krueger (1999) investigate the extent to which rising incarceration has contributed to declining official unemployment rates. For the period 1989–98, they attribute 20 per cent of the drop in US unemployment to this cause. In a comparative study of 14 OECD economies, Western and Beckett (1999) show the impact of incarceration by computing two alternative unemployment measures. The large disparity in incarceration rates between the USA at 519 per 100,000 and the remaining 13 economies' average rate of 80 per 100,000 proves to be a significant contributor to differences between the official unemployment rates of the USA and the other economies in the study.

Table 2.5 *Male incarceration and unemployment in the United States and Western Europe: 1995 (%)*

Country	Unemployment rate, u	Adjusted unemployment rate	
		u_1	u_2
Austria	3.3	3.3	3.5
Belgium	9.1	9.2	9.4
Denmark	6.2	6.3	6.4
Finland	17.7	17.8	17.9
France	10.1	10.2	10.4
Germany	7.1	7.2	7.4
Ireland	12.3	12.3	12.5
Italy	9.5	9.6	9.8
Netherlands	5.9	6.0	6.1
Norway	5.3	5.3	5.5
Sweden	8.4	8.5	8.7
Switzerland	2.7	2.8	2.9
United Kingdom	10.1	10.2	10.4
United States	5.6	6.2	7.5
Average excluding USA	8.3	8.4	8.5

Source: Western and Beckett (1999), Table 4.

The first Western and Beckett measure attempts to find the unemployment rate that would have obtained had there been zero incarceration. The numerator of their statistic includes both the conventionally counted unemployed and all prisoners who would have been unemployed if at large; in its denominator all prisoners are added to the labour force. This gives

$$u_1 = ((U + pP)/(U + E + P)) \times 100,$$

where U and E are the numbers unemployed and employed as usually counted, P is the number incarcerated, and p the proportion of inmates that would be unemployed if not in prison; all data are for males only. Using this measure and 1995 data for males gives a value of 6.2 per cent for the USA, which is 0.6 percentage points above the conventionally measured rate. For 4 of the remaining 13 countries there is no change in the rates and a change of only 0.1 percentage points for the rest. The USA's high incarceration rate reduces its male unemployment rate by half a percentage point more than the other countries, according to this measure. These results are shown in table 2.5.

This statistic understates the effect of incarceration in two ways. First, the numerator is too small, because of the implicit assumption that jobs previously held by the incarcerated will not be filled; that is the number of unemployed drops when some of them are put in prison but is unaffected if employed individuals are jailed. Instead, it seems more reasonable to assume that, when an employed person is imprisoned, his job is taken by one of the unemployed. Then, the number of unemployed is reduced when any member of the labour force is jailed, whether employed or unemployed. Second, the denominator is too large because of the implicit assumption that the participation rate of inmates was 100 per cent.[9] If these problems are corrected, assuming that the 84.3 per cent male participation rate for the USA in 1995 is applicable to the incarcerated population, we obtain

$$u^* = ((U + 0.843P)/(U + E + 0.843P)) \times 100 = 7.2 \text{ per cent.}$$

The second statistic that Western and Beckett use differs from u^* only in assuming the participation rate to be 100 per cent. It extends the definition of unemployed to include the incarcerated. This gives

$$u_2 = ((U + P)/(U + E + P)) \times 100,$$

where U, P and E are defined as before. This provides a 'loss of productive potential' measure, with strong parallels to the treatment of discouraged and part-time workers in the total underemployment measure (U^T) compiled by the Bureau of Labor Statistics. In this case the underutilized are prison inmates. Although the implicitly assumed participation rate is unrealistic, it does not alter the value for the USA by a large amount; it yields 7.5 per cent (compared with 7.2 per cent for u^*). This suggests that conclusions based on the data in table 2.5 are useful. The table shows that while u_2 for the USA is 1.9 percentage points above the conventional measure, it raises the rates by only 0.3 percentage points for 6 of the other countries, and by 0.2 for the remaining 7. Again, the far greater effect for the USA is clear, and it significantly reduces the difference between the USA and the remaining 13 countries. Using the conventional measure, their average male unemployment rate is 8.3 per cent, compared with 5.6 per cent for the USA. The use of u_2 raises the average for the 13 economies to 8.5 per cent, while the US measure rises to 7.5 per cent, a significant narrowing of the gap.

---

[9] A simple example may be useful. Assume no one is in jail and the labour force is 100 persons, with 10 unemployed, so that the unemployment rate is 10 per cent. Then assume that 2 of the unemployed are put in jail. U will fall to 8 and the labour force falls to 98. Next let 4 employed people go to jail. Then, 4 of the 8 unemployed can take their jobs, reducing U to 4. As well, the labour force will drop to 94, because 6 of its members are now in prison. The official unemployment rate is reduced to $(4/94) \times 100 = 4.3$ per cent. Imprisonment of persons not in the labour force will have no effect. The measure u^* reverses the effect of this example by adding all those who were members of the labour force at the time of incarceration to both the numerator and the denominator, i.e.

$$u^* = ((4 + 6)/(94 + 6)) \times 100 = 10 \text{ per cent.}$$

6 Conclusions

This chapter has recorded some of the key features of macroeconomic performance in the developed capitalist economies during the twentieth century. Among these were four lengthy periods of contrasting performance, beginning with the boom that preceded the episode of mass unemployment of the 1930s, the golden age with low unemployment and rapid growth of incomes and productivity, and the most recent period characterized by high unemployment, slow growth of income and productivity and high inflation until the 1990s. This was followed by a discussion of production function growth theory. Evaluation of this theory traced its inability to model the historical record to three key features. First, although it is a long-run model, it fails to take account of the economy's evolving structure. Second, its adherence to a steady-state, balanced growth approach prevents it from explaining historically observed growth patterns. Third, by assuming continuous full employment, it cannot explain lengthy periods of high unemployment.

The mainstream perception of the current high unemployment is that, although much of it is involuntary, it cannot be reduced by stimulative AD policy. This important topic is discussed in chapter 3, where the mainstream neoclassical theory of unemployment is considered in detail. The likelihood that official unemployment figures systematically underestimate the underutilization of labour has been examined here, and will be used in later chapters to re-evaluate the current view that the US unemployment record is to be envied and that it provides policy insights for reducing unemployment elsewhere.

3 The neoclassical analysis of unemployment

1 Introduction

Consider the two contrasting perspectives of the normal functioning of an advanced capitalist economy. The mainstream or neoclassical paradigm derives from a belief that the private sector of a capitalist economy is basically self-regulating in some undefined long run; our view is that capitalism is subject to economic and political conflict and to structural change that leads to periodic episodes of poor performance. Throughout the book we shall emphasize two connections: one between the mainstream conception of capitalism as a self-regulating system and its formalization in neoclassical equilibrium analysis and the other between the view of capitalism as a non-self-regulating system and the evolutionary-Keynesian framework developed in these pages. Which of these two analytical frameworks is better suited for modelling historical processes, in particular the unemployment record, can be determined only by a study of the historical record.

In neoclassical equilibrium analysis, long-run outcomes are modelled as interactions between endogenous variables constrained by a set of exogenous variables, usually tastes and technologies. The set of exogenous elements is customarily referred to as the 'supply side' or the 'structural framework' of the model. When neoclassical equilibrium analysis is used as a descriptive device for modelling capitalism's alleged self-regulating properties, it is assumed that there is a unique long-run equilibrium which depends only upon the values of the exogenous supply-side variables. Because of its properties, the equilibrium functions as an 'attractor', ensuring that in the absence of shocks a system in equilibrium will remain there. The absence of an independent long-run role for demand variables is an important defining feature of neoclassical equilibrium analysis. Its second essential feature is the stability of the equilibrium, necessary to ensure that the system is self-regulating. This requires mechanisms that automatically adjust aggregate demand (AD) to the supply side. For example, if a shock leads to deviations from the equilibrium, the system returns to the equilibrium whatever the cause or size of the disturbance and whatever the performance of the economy while it is (temporarily) out of equilibrium.

In some neoclassical models (for example production function growth models), adjustment is assumed to be instantaneous and continuous. In the absence of shocks, the system is always in equilibrium in the shortest of short runs. Since so few markets in the real world fit this description, especially the labour market, this type of equilibrium analysis is not considered further. The more usual type of supply-determined equilibrium modelling, and the one considered here, allows short-run deviations from the long-run equilibrium caused by incorrect information or shocks, but assumes that the adjustment mechanisms always ensure convergence to the long-run equilibrium. Clearly, the value of supply-determined equilibrium analysis as a framework for modelling historical processes depends upon whether real economies are endowed with mechanisms that ensure stability of the equilibrium. Specifically, these mechanisms must be sufficiently strong to dominate movements of AD, so that it adjusts to equal aggregate supply in the long run. Without such mechanisms, supply-side equilibrium analysis cannot explain macroeconomic processes in the real world.

2 The neoclassical theory of equilibrium unemployment

The mainstream analysis of unemployment is referred to here as either the neoclassical or the supply-determined equilibrium theory of unemployment. Its practitioners include members of both the monetarist and new Keynesian schools. While often treated as a theory of inflation, we find it more helpful to interpret it as a supply-determined theory of unemployment. There are several varieties of unemployment models within the supply-determined equilibrium framework, each defined by the special properties of its equilibrium unemployment rate. As in neoclassical equilibrium analysis in general, an independent role for endogenous demand variables in determining long-run outcomes is absent. Key defining features of all versions are an allowance for short-run disequilibria and stability of the long-run equilibrium through automatic adjustments on the demand side. For any given values of the exogenous supply-side variables there is assumed to be a unique long-run equilibrium unemployment rate which depends only upon those values. This set is usually more numerous and more specific than the traditional tastes and technologies in supply-determined growth theory cited earlier.

A model's relevance as a descriptive device is considered assured by the inclusion of the designated adjustment mechanisms. Starting from any set of initial conditions, the properties of the equilibrium are of such an 'attractive' nature that disequilibrium automatically sets in motion mechanisms that cause convergence to the supply-determined equilibrium. We maintain that in the real world the mechanisms assumed to stabilize the system at the unique equilibrium unemployment rate do not respond to disequilibria with sufficient speed and strength to make certain that AD adjusts to the supply-determined equilibrium even in some long run. This shortcoming makes supply-determined equilibrium analysis an inappropriate analytical framework for explaining movements in the unemployment rate.

3 Some simple models

Some simple textbook models bring out these points. Consider the basic expectations-augmented Phillips curve, which can be written

$$\dot{w}_t = a_0 + a_1 U^{-1} + a_2 \dot{p}_t^e + a_3 X_t \tag{3.1}$$

$$\dot{p}_t = \dot{w}_t - \dot{q} \tag{3.2}$$

$$\dot{p}_t^e - \dot{p}_{t-1}^e = c(\dot{p}_{t-1} - \dot{p}_{t-1}^e) \text{ and} \tag{3.3}$$

$$\dot{p}_t = \dot{p}_t^e \tag{3.4}$$

where the endogenous variables $\dot{w}$, $\dot{p}$, U, and $\dot{p}^e$ are the rates of growth of wages and prices, the unemployment rate and the expected rate of price inflation, $\dot{q}$ is the rate of growth of productivity and X is a vector of exogenous variables. The time subscripts describe the lag structure. Equation (3.1) is a standard short-run expectations-augmented Phillips curve for wage inflation, equation (3.2) assumes prices are a constant mark-up over labour costs, allowing wage inflation to pass though fully to price inflation, equation (3.3) describes how expectations are generated, i.e. adaptively, and equation (3.4) is the equilibrium condition. The inclusion of the expected rate of price inflation in equation (3.1) represents a concern by workers with protecting real wages and introduces a feedback effect from price inflation to wage inflation. The size of the coefficient a_2 measures the extent to which expected price inflation is built into wage demands, a value less than 1 indicating less than complete sensitivity to expected rates of inflation.

Consider first a Keynesian version of the inflation model. Assume $0 < a_2 < 1$ and for convenience $c = 1$, allowing equation (3.3) to be written as $\dot{p}_t^e = \dot{p}_{t-1}$ and equation (3.4), the equilibrium condition, to be written $\dot{p}_t = \dot{p}_{t-1}$. Substituting equation (3.3) into equation (3.1) gives the short-run Phillips curve for wage inflation:

$$\dot{w}_t = a_0 + a_1 U_t^{-1} + a_2 \dot{p}_{t-1} + a_3 X_t, \tag{3.5}$$

and the substitution of equation (3.5) into equation (3.2) gives the short-run Phillips curve for price inflation:

$$\dot{p}_t = a_0 - \dot{q} + a_1 U_t^{-1} + a_2 \dot{p}_{t-1} + a_3 X_t. \tag{3.6}$$

The long-run counterparts to equations (3.5) and (3.6) are found by setting $\dot{w}_0 = \dot{w}_t = \dot{w}_{t-1}$ in equation (3.5) (following minor substitution) and $\dot{p}_0 = \dot{p}_t = \dot{p}_{t-1}$ in equation (3.6) and collecting terms to give the long-run Phillips curves

$$\dot{w}_0 = (1/(1-a_2))\cdot(a_0 - a_2\dot{q} + a_1 U^{-1} + a_3 X) \tag{3.7}$$

and

$$\dot{p}_0 = (1/(1-a_2))\cdot(a_0 - \dot{q} + a_1 U^{-1} + a_3 X), \tag{3.8}$$

where $\dot{w}_0$ and $\dot{p}_0$ are the long-run equilibrium wage and price inflation rates, respectively. These equations are negatively sloped Phillips curves depicting unemployment rates and either the rates of wage or price inflation when the short-run feedback interactions have worked themselves out. They also indicate the relevance of Keynesian analysis and policies. Given a set of fixed values for the exogenous variables, there are multiple possible equilibrium values for $\dot{w}_0$ and $\dot{p}_0$, each depending upon an assumed value for U and, therefore, upon AD. The rate of growth of real wages is found by subtracting equation (3.8) from equation (3.7) to obtain $\dot{w}_0 - \dot{p}_0 = \dot{q}$. The rate of increase in real wages is independent of a_2, the effort by labour to protect real wages.

The neoclassical theory of unemployment can be described by a similar wage–price mechanism, together with adjustment mechanisms often rather casually grafted on to the inflation mechanism. The one significant difference from the Keynesian inflation mechanism is that the mainstream unemployment theory always assumes real wage bargaining, i.e. $a_2 = 1$. Again assuming $c = 1$ and making the appropriate substitutions, the short-run Phillips curve for price inflation is derived as:

$$\dot{p}_t = a_0 - \dot{q} + a_1 U_t^{-1} + \dot{p}_{t-1} + a_3 X_t. \tag{3.9}$$

Setting $\dot{p}_0 = \dot{p}_t = \dot{p}_{t-1}$ cannot be used to derive a long-run equilibrium rate of inflation since

$$\dot{p}_t - \dot{p}_{t-1} = a_0 - \dot{q} + a_1 U_t^{-1} + a_3 X_t = 0. \tag{3.9'}$$

Instead equation (3.9') is solved for U as

$$U_0 = a_1/(\dot{q} - a_0 - a_3 X). \tag{3.10}$$

U_0 is the unique equilibrium rate of unemployment in the sense that only at U_0 is the rate of price inflation constant and equal to the expected rate of inflation. At any other rate of unemployment the expected rate of inflation deviates from the actual rate of inflation, which then either accelerates or decelerates. This is a property of neoclassical unemployment models because they assume real wage bargaining.

As is well known, in the short run there may be a trade-off between inflation and unemployment as shown in equation (3.9). In the long run there is no trade-off, the long-run Phillips curve being vertical at the equilibrium rate of unemployment, U_0. Equation (3.10) reveals that in mainstream unemployment theory the long-run equilibrium unemployment rate is determined solely on the supply side, i.e. by $\dot{q}$ and the vector of exogenous variables, X. Endogenous variables reflecting an independent role for AD factors are entirely absent from equation (3.10). Corresponding to the equilibrium rate of unemployment, U_0, is a long-run equilibrium level of output, also determined on the supply side. However, in order to qualify as a full-fledged theory of unemployment, adjustment mechanisms must be grafted on to the inflation equations to provide stability to the equilibrium. Given unchanged values for the exogenous variables, this is to ensure that, if for any reason the actual unemployment rate deviates from the long-run equilibrium rate, AD will adjust automatically to the exogenously determined supply side until the discrepancy is eliminated.

4 Full employment rates of unemployment: an evaluation

In evaluating equilibrium unemployment analysis, the procedure is first to determine why it is an inappropriate framework for explaining periods of full unemployment, for example the golden age; its inability to explain high unemployment will then be more readily understood. The earliest exposition of the equilibrium unemployment rate doctrine and the long-run vertical Phillips curve was by Friedman (1968), who designated the equilibrium unemployment rate the 'natural rate' of unemployment. While his description of the properties of the natural rate allowed for various kinds of market imperfections, his analysis of how an economy converges to this equilibrium stressed competitive market-clearing processes. Following a disturbance, discrepancies arise between U_0 and the actual rate of unemployment and between the actual and expected rates of inflation. This initiates haggling between buyers and sellers of labour, which is assumed to continue until all markets clear, expectations are realized and a zero involuntary rate of unemployment is re-established. The natural rate of unemployment in this version of mainstream unemployment theory is the full employment rate of unemployment.

Subsequently, most model builders in the neoclassical tradition, unwilling simply to assume competitive 'flexprice' markets, allow that wages and prices are not perfectly flexible in the short run, but that in some long run these inflexibilities and frictions are overcome and the system moves to the full employment rate of unemployment.[1] However, even with this amendment there are difficulties with the neoclassical theory that question its value as a framework for modelling unemployment. This is particularly apparent when considering the behaviour of the system that is out of equilibrium. Assume the system is moving along its full employment growth path when it is disturbed by a negative real AD shock causing unemployment to rise above U_0. Because of the unique properties of the equilibrium unemployment rate, this is assumed to result in only a temporary deviation from equilibrium. The decline in rates of inflation of money wages and prices caused by the shock automatically sets in motion mechanisms stimulating AD that continue to operate until the economy returns to its full employment path. Specifically, with unchanged growth of the nominal money supply, the decline in the rate of price inflation leads to an increase in the growth of the real money supply and directly affects real consumption expenditures as real balances of households rise (i.e. the Pigou effect) and indirectly influences investment through a reduction in interest rates (i.e. the Keynes effect). As long as unemployment remains above U_0, this continues.

The assumptions of accelerating or decelerating rates of inflation whenever the system deviates from U_0, combined with Keynes and Pigou effects, provide the AD adjustment mechanisms assumed to ensure the stability of the equilibrium unemployment rate. However, supporters of vertical Phillips curve analysis have consistently failed to establish the usefulness of their supply-determined equilibrium framework for modelling unemployment in the real world. Three conditions must be met to establish its usefulness. First, when out of equilibrium the alleged exogenous supply-side variables must be truly exogenous. If they are not and depend on the behaviour of the economic variables, for example the actual unemployment rate, this raises the issue of how the so-called equilibrium unemployment rate can function as an attractor of the system. Even if this first condition is satisfied, there are two additional problems. Assuming that the equilibrium is exogenously determined, when out of equilibrium the speed of adjustment to equilibrium must be rapid relative to the rate at which the exogenous variables change. Empirical tests to determine whether this is true are

---

[1] Typically in this kind of analysis, the long run is simply defined as a period long enough to overcome year to year short-run stickiness of wages and prices. The length of this period in calendar time is not specified (see Mankiw, 1994; CEPR, 1995).

not available. However, even if this condition is met, there is a final condition and it is sufficient for our purposes to concentrate on it. Again assume the equilibrium is disturbed by a negative AD shock. Then, the mechanisms adjusting AD to the exogenously determined supply side must act with such force that they always offset both the impact of the negative shock and any shock-induced downward cumulative movements of AD, output and employment. When they do not, the way is open for disturbance-amplifying effects, for example the multiplier, that push the system further from the equilibrium. Convergence to the supply-determined equilibrium will not occur, so that the existence of such an equilibrium is of little interest or importance as a modelling device.

In fact there is little empirical or theoretical evidence to support the view that Keynes and Pigou effects act so quickly and forcefully in the real world that they dominate movements on the demand side of the market in either the short or the long run (Tobin, 1993).[2] And without a mechanism adjusting AD to the exogenous supply-side equilibrium, even if an equilibrium exists it is unstable, a situation reminiscent of the Harrod–Domar knife edge in growth theory. In the Harrod–Domar model, an equilibrium growth rate exists but it is unstable, as there is no adjustment mechanism in the model to ensure that the rate of demand growth is equal to the 'warranted' and 'natural' rates of output growth. Without such a mechanism, the system is liable either to continuous inflation or to continuous declines in output and employment.

Although the natural rate unemployment model assumes there to be mechanisms that provide stability to the equilibrium, we have argued that they lack plausibility. And, with no plausible adjustment mechanism, all that remains of the natural rate theory of unemployment is the concept of a unique equilibrium rate of unemployment. It cannot be considered a useful analytical concept because an economy would settle at this unemployment rate only by accident and once disturbed would show no tendency to return. Advocates of Keynes and Pigou effects as adjustment mechanisms merely resurrect arguments brought against the *General Theory* half a century ago, and evidence in support of their effective functioning as equilibrating mechanisms has remained scarce. As a result, the neoclassical theory of unemployment cannot account for historical episodes in which AD grows at the full employment rate of output growth, as it did in most economies during the golden age. Other adjustment mechanisms must be sought when attempting to formalize the self-correcting properties of a capitalist system.

---

[2] It is worth pointing out that Pigou did not believe in the curative powers of the real balance effect.

5 High rates of unemployment: an evaluation

Another difficulty with mainstream unemployment analysis is its unacceptable explanation of periods of high unemployment rates. The natural rate model of neoclassical unemployment theory, with its assumption that there is full employment at the equilibrium unemployment rate, is obviously not appropriate for explaining unemployment conditions such as those of the past 25 years. As recorded in table 2.1, advanced capitalist economies have experienced long periods of high unemployment, not short, mild spurts, suggesting that deviations from any full employment equilibrium would be due to something other than shocks, most likely a failure of Keynes and Pigou effects to fulfil their role as adjustment mechanisms. Furthermore, the lengthening episode of high unemployment since the mid-1970s has increased interest in the characteristics of the unemployed and other aspects of unemployment. Studies cited in chapter 2 focus on the reasons for being unemployed, on the duration of unemployment and on the rising proportion of long-term unemployment; they support the view that the secular rise in unemployment beginning in the mid-1970s can largely be accounted for by the rise in involuntary unemployment. These results raise additional doubts about the usefulness of supply-determined equilibrium analysis, as well as open up the issue of what forces are in fact determining unemployment.

Ironically, persistent high unemployment has not led to the rejection of neoclassical unemployment theory; instead the theory was modified in such a way as to lead to even wider acceptance. The updated versions came with a new terminology already introduced in chapter 2. Rather than refer to the equilibrium unemployment rate as the natural rate, the new attractor of the system was designated the non-accelerating inflation rate of unemployment (NAIRU), and the distinction between involuntary and voluntary unemployment was replaced by a distinction between classical and Keynesian (or cyclical) unemployment. Classical unemployment may be involuntary but by definition it is not affected by AD; only involuntary Keynesian unemployment responds to AD pressures.

However, it must be stressed that these versions of equilibrium unemployment analysis are fundamentally the same, and have the same policy implications, as natural rate theory. In spite of the admitted existence of involuntary unemployment, wage bargaining is always in real terms, i.e. $a_2 = 1$ as in equation (3.9) above, again leading to the long-run vertical Phillips curve with the same knife-edge inflation characteristics of natural rate theory. Only at the NAIRU, or more accurately the classical equilibrium rate of unemployment, is the rate of inflation constant. At any other unemployment rate, inflation accelerates or decelerates without limit. AD adjusts to exogenously given supply via Keynes and Pigou effects that alleg-edly ensure stability of the equilibrium. AD policy has no role in determin-ing the equilibrium level of unemployment; and trends in unemployment rates are explained not within the model but by recourse to exogenous forces.

What distinguishes NAIRU analysis from the natural rate theory of unemployment are the properties of the equilibrium rate of unemployment; involuntary unemployment may exist at the NAIRU in the long run but is absent at the natural rate. NAIRU advocates claim that persistent high unemployment, like that experienced since the mid-1970s, is evidence not necessarily that neoclassical unemployment theory is unable to account for high unemployment, only that the natural rate version of the theory cannot do so. Accordingly, the rising unemployment of the past 25 years is explained by an upward trend in the NAIRU. Even though large-scale involuntary unemployment may exist when the economy is at the NAIRU, it still reflects the natural tendency of the unemployment rate to settle at the minimum rate consistent with a constant rate of inflation. High unemploy-ment must be accepted unless policy changes on the supply side can be implemented to reduce the exogenously determined NAIRU, because involuntary unemployment at the equilibrium is classical.

Unfortunately, the adjustment mechanisms assumed to bring AD into line with the classical equilibrium unemployment rate are the same as those assumed in natural rate theory. These mechanisms must dominate move-ments on the demand side of the economy. There is little evidence that they do. Given their ineffectiveness in the real world, the newer versions of the neoclassical unemployment theory amount to little more than the substitu-tion of a unique classical rate of equilibrium unemployment for a unique full employment equilibrium rate. Whether designed to model a period of full employment such as the golden age or one of high unemployment such as the post-golden age episode, they hardly qualify as an acceptable way of modelling unemployment. Moreover, an additional problem with the clas-sical unemployment version of equilibrium unemployment theory is its assumption that involuntary unemployment cannot be permanently reduced by an increase in AD because of excessive real wage demands; that is, unemployment may be involuntary but it is classical.

6 Involuntary but classical unemployment

Very special and unacceptable assumptions are required to generate invol-untary unemployment that is also classical. There are two parts to our dissent and each challenges a basic assumption of the involuntary but classical explanation of unemployment. The 'involuntary but classical' description of unemployment assumes that (1) a stimulation of AD does not generate a permanent increase in employment because it cannot lead to a reduction in real wages, and (2) a reduction in the real wage is a necessary condition for an increase in employment. We argue that, when involuntary unemployment exists, neither condition is likely to be true and, as a result, rising involuntary but classical unemployment cannot be an explanation of recent unemployment trends.

6.1 Can the real wage be reduced?

The view that an increase in AD will not reduce involuntary unemployment because it is unable to reduce the real wage contains the implicit assumption that the real wage is determined in the labour market. This assumption has been shown to be unrealistic, the principal counter-argument being that the real wage is determined in the product market when firms set prices once the money wage is determined (Dow, 1990). In an affluent economy with flexible exchange rates, firms likely face low price elasticities of demand. Even if it is allowed that any additional workers hired have a lower productivity than the already employed, following an increase in AD firms can raise prices by enough to cover additional labour costs and the real wage will fall.[3]

Another form of the argument to support policy ineffectiveness shifts the emphasis from statics to dynamics and introduces a special case of a wage–price spiral process of inflation, that of complete indexation (with perhaps a short lag) of wage claims and settlements. The argument is made that, although in the first period of a dynamic sequence the increase in price may be sufficient to reduce the real wage, in the next period the upward money wage adjustment to protect real wages will restore the original real wage and the situation will repeat itself until AD returns to its original lower level. However, this example assumes the supply of labour is a function of the real wage, which is inappropriate when involuntary unemployment exists. Under conditions of involuntary unemployment, with workers willing to take a job at less than the going real wage, the complete indexation assumption is both arbitrary and unrealistic. Outcomes depend upon

---

[3] Although largely overlooked by the profession, an early advocate of modelling the labour market as a constrained optimization problem was Keynes (although he did not employ this language). In the *General Theory* he maintained there was no inconsistency in an unwillingness of involuntarily unemployed workers to take a money wage cut to gain employment, and a willingness to accept work at a lowered real wage following a rise in the price level induced by stimulating AD. Keynes argued that the charge by his critics that such behaviour was evidence of money illusion and irrationality on the workers' part could easily be refuted by the use of better economic theory. Workers included relative wages as well as the real wage as arguments in their utility functions (Trevithick, 1976).

general labour market conditions. With high unemployment rates the feedback effect of any price adjustment on money wage increases will be weak and real wages will fall. Weak feedback effects are likely to be true of the unionized sectors of the labour market as well. These considerations undermine allegations that labour controls the real wage.

Scrutiny of the behaviour of firms also suggests that these allegations are misplaced. During periods of prolonged high unemployment, such as that beginning in the mid-1970s, firms have reacted to the weakened bargaining position of labour in ways that clearly point to the dominance of employers in the determination of real wages. The forced early retirement of highly paid senior employees and their replacement by lower-paid newer entrants to the labour market has become a routine way for firms to control real wages. Perhaps even more prevalent is the practice of contracting out parts of the production process to foreign or domestic suppliers who pay relatively low wages; the threat of job losses gives employers the upper hand in wage negotiations. Indeed, in weak labour markets such as those of the 1980s and 1990s, business often adopted a 'take it or leave it' attitude in response to any wage demands. And, rather than strike, labour accepted the decline in real wages in order to stay employed. In general it is not appropriate to model labour supply as a function of the real wage when involuntary unemployment exists.[4]

6.2 Is a reduction of the real wage necessary?

The second part of our dissent is that a decline in the real wage is not a necessary condition for an expansion of output and an increase in employment. The view that the real wage must fall overlooks the possibility that there are constant returns to labour. With constant returns, additional workers can be taken on in the private sector without a need for firms to lower real wages. One explanation of constant returns to labour is that often firms can expand the amount of services extracted from physical capital already in place to accompany additions to the work force. In efficiency wage theories, firms will often maintain wages at rates above market-clearing rates when hiring additional workers, because doing so has positive effects on productivity through its impact on the quality of new hires, the level of labour's efforts and the rate of labour turnover (Salop, 1979; Shapiro and Stiglitz, 1984). Finally, frequently overlooked in this debate is that governments can act as employer of last resort and their decision of whether or not to expand job opportunities bears little relation to the real wage of the private sector.

---

[4] The same criticism holds for the 'bargained real wage' function used in imperfect competition models of wage and price setting (Carlin and Soskice, 1990, ch. 6).

All things considered, we must conclude that any attempt to attribute the rise of unemployment over the past 25 years or so to involuntary but classical unemployment that cannot be reduced by stimulating AD must be rejected. In Phillips curve analysis, the assumption of real wage bargaining (i.e. $a_2 = 1$ as in equation (3.9)) when there is involuntary unemployment is a misspecification. A necessary condition for reducing unemployment rates throughout this period has been an increase in AD. However, from a practical policy point of view, stimulating AD may not be sufficient to solve the unemployment problem. Prolonged periods of high unemployment with a large long-term unemployment component suggest there is a need to complement stimulative policies with additional measures that will reduce adverse side effects arising from problems such as a mismatch between the skills of the unemployed and those required for the new job vacancies. Nevertheless, given the high unemployment of the current episode, the discussion of this section strongly suggests that official unemployment rates do not overstate the potential permanent gain in employment and output from more stimulative AD policies.[5]

7 Measurement without theory

Neoclassical equilibrium unemployment analysis has fallen under a cloud recently, not so much because its theoretical underpinnings are weak but because of shortcomings revealed in econometric studies. For example, econometric estimates of the NAIRU vary appreciably with the sample period covered and with only minor changes in the specification of the model (Setterfield et al., 1992; Galbraith, 1997). An additional difficulty is that deviations of the actual rate of unemployment from estimates of the NAIRU have not been accompanied by accelerating or decelerating rates of inflation as the theory requires. In particular, recent studies indicate that the Phillips curve becomes horizontal at high rates of unemployment such as those experienced in the 1990s (Akerlof et al., 1996; Fortin, 1996). Further, during the 1980s and 1990s the supply-side determinants of the NAIRU 'improved' – for example, union density fell and unemployment benefits became less generous – but actual unemployment rates were not automatically attracted towards what should have been a lower NAIRU; they remained high. Finally, estimates of the equilibrium unemployment rate mimic actual movements in unemployment, evidence of hysteresis in the equilibrium unemployment rate.

Most econometric studies derive the classical equilibrium unemployment

---

[5] Sections 4 and 5 in chapter 2 show that they understate the potential gain in employment and output that stimulative AD policies would yield.

rate by using regression models to estimate the coefficients of a Phillips curve, such as equation (3.9), and then solving for U_0 as in equation (3.10). Because of growing dissatisfaction with the results of this method, economists have turned to more direct methods of 'estimating' the classical equilibrium unemployment rate. Rather than using regression analysis to estimate an equation such as (3.9) and solving it for U_0 as in equation (3.10), total unemployment in any year is arbitrarily decomposed into its equilibrium classical and Keynesian cyclical components by simply fitting a smoothly evolving trend to an actual unemployment series. It is then declared that the trend line measures the classical equilibrium rate over time and all deviations from trend measure the Keynesian or cyclical component (Mankiw, 1994, figure 5.1; CEPR, 1995, fn 20). Alternatively, it is said that the equilibrium rate of unemployment is the "rate that would be observed if the economy were durably operating at the normal level of activity, free from disturbances of one kind or another" (Wyplosz, 1994, p. 77).

Although we have been highly critical of neoclassical equilibrium unemployment analysis, the conventional method of deriving its value at least has some theoretical justification. The same cannot be said of these more mechanical methods which simply determine the equilibrium unemployment rate as a moving average of past unemployment rates. Even advocates of these models would acknowledge that the high unemployment record since the mid-1970s has been at least partly the result of restrictive AD policies. This means that estimates of the unemployment rate at which all unemployment is defined as classical, i.e. the equilibrium unemployment rate, are dependent upon the past stance of AD policies. No evidence is offered that these estimates measure the rate of unemployment at which wage bargaining is in real terms.

8 What remains of Phillips curve analysis?

No matter how it is defined, the equilibrium unemployment concept in supply-determined analysis is of little theoretical interest and little use for understanding movements in the unemployment rate. In the absence of well-designed AD policy, the economy would achieve the unemployment rate where wage bargaining is in real terms only by chance. We claim that the concept of a unique equilibrium unemployment rate based on real wage bargaining, combined with mechanisms alleged to adjust the economy to this rate in the long run, is not adequate to the task of modelling unemployment rates. Nevertheless, we do not conclude that Phillips curve analysis has no place in a theory of inflation or unemployment. Its place is re-established by dropping the assumption that $a_2 = 1$ from the analysis, certainly over the range of unemployment rates at which involuntary unemployment exists.

The analysis of section 5 shows this modification to have radical implications. Over the range of unemployment rates at which involuntary unemployment prevails, rates of increase of money wages are not completely sensitive to rates of price inflation, i.e. $a_2 < 1$. Within this range there will be a long-run trade-off between unemployment and inflation rates: corresponding to each unemployment rate there is a constant long-run rate of inflation. In short, there are multiple equilibria in the real world, each corresponding to a different level of AD; discretionary macroeconomic policy has a role to play in determining the equilibrium unemployment rate. However, we allow that at low rates of unemployment there will be no trade-off.

9 A variable-coefficient Phillips curve

To deal with these matters, we offer a modification for equation (3.1), the equation for wage inflation. The coefficient a_2 in equation (3.1) measures the amount wage earners add to their money wage increases to cover the expected rate of current inflation. We allow this to vary in order to take account of labour's greater concern with possible real wage erosion at high rates of price inflation than low, and of labour's greater market power when there are high inflation rates, which are associated with low rates of unemployment (Cornwall, 1994, ch. 8 and appendices; Duesenberry, 1991). The modification is accomplished by assuming that the expectations coefficient, a_2 in equation (3.1), is a function of $\dot{p}_t^e\,(=\dot{p}_{t-1})$. The new wage equation is

$$\dot{w}_t = b_0 + b_1\dot{p}_{t-1} + b_2(\dot{p}_{t-1} - b_3) + b_4 U_t^{-1} + b_5 X_t, \tag{3.11}$$

where $0 < b_1 < 1$, and $b_2 = 0$ if $\dot{p}_{t-1} \leq b_3$, otherwise $b_2 = 1 - b_1$, b_3 is the threshold rate of inflation, to be defined shortly, and X is a vector of exogenous variables. The remaining variables have their previous meanings. The restrictions on b_1 and b_2 assume that when expected price inflation is moderate, i.e. $\dot{p}_{t-1} \leq b_3$, the expected rate of price inflation is not fully built into wage demands, i.e. $b_2 = 0$ and $b_1 < 1$. But when expected inflation exceeds the threshold rate, i.e. $\dot{p}_{t-1} > b_3$, there is complete sensitivity of wages to the expected rate of price inflation as $b_1 + b_2 = 1$.

The dynamics of wage–price inflation require the inclusion of equation (3.2), $\dot{p}_t = \dot{w}_t - \dot{q}$, where $\dot{q}$ is the rate of growth of labour productivity as before. Substituting equation (3.11) into equation (3.2), we can write

$$\dot{p}_t = b_0 - \dot{q} + b_1\dot{p}_{t-1} + b_2(\dot{p}_{t-1} - b_3) + b_4 U_t^{-1} + b_5 X_t. \tag{3.12}$$

The long-run Phillips curve for price inflation when inflation is moderate is

$$\dot{p}_0 = (1/(1 - b_1))\cdot(b_0 - \dot{q} + b_4 U^{-1} + b_5 X). \tag{3.13}$$

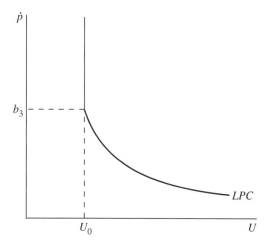

Figure 3.1 The variable-coefficient Phillips curve

Since $b_1 < 1$, there is a long-run trade-off between inflation and unemployment over the range where $U \geq U_0$. When $\dot{p}_{t-1} > b_3$, there is no long-run trade-off between price (and wage) inflation and unemployment, and equation (3.12) must be solved for U_0, giving

$$U_0 = b_4/(\dot{q} + b_2 b_3 - b_0 - b_5 X). \tag{3.14}$$

The long-run variable-coefficient Phillips curve for price inflation is shown in figure 3.1. At unemployment rates equal to or greater than U_0, there is a trade-off between unemployment and inflation, so that there are multiple equilibria; the actual unemployment rate is determined by AD. Once the unemployment rate falls to U_0 and inflation becomes severe, i.e. $\dot{p}_{t-1} > b_3$, rates of price inflation are completely built into wage demands. Any effort to keep unemployment at this low rate leads to accelerating rates of inflation. Finally, it must be noted that we do not rule out the possibility of shifts in the long-run Phillips curve but, by permitting a long-run trade-off over a range of unemployment rates, AD is restored to its original Keynesian role as a determinant of unemployment outcomes when involuntary unemployment exists.[6]

---

[6] The admitted instability of the NAIRU has led to a 'time variable NAIRU' model. It also makes the untenable assumption of real wage bargaining whatever the unemployment rate (Gordon, 1997).

10 Starting over

Neither the natural rate nor the NAIRU versions of equilibrium unemployment theory are adequate to the task of modelling unemployment. Changes in the actual rate of unemployment do not reflect passive adjustments to shifting equilibrium unemployment rates. Whether intended as an explanation of periods of low unemployment such as the golden age or of periods of high unemployment such as the current episode, mainstream unemployment theory cannot explain movements in the unemployment rate. Further, it provides no support for the view that AD policies are always ineffective, and none for the assumption that capitalism is self-regulating. We should dispense with it.[7] The intention of this chapter was to determine those features of mainstream unemployment analysis that undermine its usefulness and to find clues for constructing a more satisfactory approach. It should be apparent that the main source of the problems in neoclassical unemployment analysis, and in neoclassical equilibrium analysis in general, arises from the insistence that outcomes be modelled within a very special kind of equilibrium framework, in which AD is assumed to adjust passively and automatically to an exogenously determined 'supply side'. Explaining the unemployment record requires a radically different treatment of AD.

The challenge is to develop a theory of unemployment that explains what actually transpired over roughly the past 80 years. For example, why did the unemployment problem largely disappear during the golden age and why has unemployment since the mid-1970s reverted to conditions comparable to the 1930s? One conclusion seems inescapable: in order to explain unemployment trends in the real world, AD must play a key role. This raises two questions: in episodes of full employment, what is the adjustment mechanism that results in equilibrium between AD and aggregate supply and what is the cause of deficient levels of AD during high unemployment periods?

To examine the first question, consider the period following World War II. Table 2.1 shows that for approximately two decades most economies operated at what would today be considered over-full employment rates, and figure 5.1 shows they did so at politically acceptable rates of inflation. This certainly suggests the presence of a mechanism bringing a growing level of AD into line with a growing full employment level of output in this group of economies. The mainstream view that this was achieved by AD adjusting passively to the supply side has already been rejected. However, there are two other possibilities to consider. The first is that 'finely tuned'

---

[7] In correspondence, Tony Thirlwall has made the important point that the concept of a unique equilibrium unemployment rate loses all meaning when there are constant or increasing returns to labour in the aggregate.

AD policies were used to provide full employment levels of AD, no more and no less. This explanation must be rejected, because it implies an understanding of the economic mechanisms of capitalism bordering on omniscience. The second possibility, and the one that commends itself, is that an extended Keynesian account explains golden age unemployment performance in most economies. This account incorporates mechanisms that cause aggregate output to adjust to AD, not merely when slack exists in the economy, but even when the level of real AD rises above what would conventionally be considered its full employment level. In other words, Say's law in reverse operates over a (limited) range of growth rates of real AD. Outlining this demand-determined adjustment process is the concern of chapter 4.

The second question concerns the cause of deficient AD. The variable-coefficient Phillips curve was introduced to show that the immediate cause of periods of high unemployment is insufficient AD. Events in the golden age provide clues about why AD was insufficient. Most economies experienced full employment throughout this period. Others experienced comparable rates of inflation to the full employment economies, but could do so only at higher rates of unemployment. In these economies, deficient AD was induced by restrictive policy in order to keep down inflation. Why full employment levels of AD led to politically unacceptable rates of inflation in these economies but did not do so in others requires explanation. This is treated in chapter 5 where the discussion turns to the institutions that allowed inflation rates in most economies to remain low under full employment conditions.

4 An extended Keynesian model

1 Introduction

Chapter 2 provided data showing one of the most outstanding, yet largely unacknowledged, 'stylized facts' of modern capitalist development; over the past century, long periods of high unemployment have alternated with periods of low unemployment. A point stressed in chapter 3 is that neoclassical unemployment analysis is unable to explain these shifts because of its reliance on a very particular kind of equilibrium framework, in which aggregate demand is assumed to adjust automatically to an exogenously determined 'supply side'. This and the next two chapters develop an analytical framework that can explain these alternating unemployment episodes. This chapter focuses on the implications of reversing the neoclassical direction of adjustment. A model of demand-determined growth is outlined in which AD plays a causal role in determining the macroeconomic variables. Our attention is on demand-determined processes under conditions of full employment in order to highlight an extended Keynesian role for AD, that of generating adjustments on the supply side of the economy under full employment conditions. These adjustments act to bring real AD and full employment output into balance. The traditional Keynesian theory of AD explaining periods of high unemployment is treated only briefly at the end of the chapter.

2 Rapid growth and low unemployment: an extended Keynesian perspective

Table 4.1 shows average annual rates of growth for labour productivity and several components of GDP, and average rates of unemployment and inflation in the G7 economies for 1960–73 and 1974–98. These data suggest that the *immediate* cause of lower unemployment rates in the 1960–73 period was more rapid growth of AD, led by high rates of growth of exports and fixed investment. Table 4.1 shows clearly that relatively high rates of growth of AD and total output during the golden age were associated with

Table 4.1 *Macroeconomic performance in the G7: 1960–73 and 1974–98*

Period	$\dot{C}$	$\dot{G}$	$\dot{I}$	$\dot{Ex}$	$\dot{Q}$	$\dot{q}$	$\dot{p}$	U
1960–73	4.9	3.2	6.1	7.8	4.8	3.7	3.9	3.1[a]
1974–98	2.7	1.8	2.6	5.1	2.4	1.3	5.5	6.3

Notes:
$\dot{C}$, $\dot{G}$, $\dot{I}$, $\dot{Ex}$ and $\dot{Q}$ are annual average rates of growth of private consumption, government final consumption, gross fixed investment, export volume and GDP respectively, all measured in real terms; $\dot{q}$ and $\dot{p}$ are average annual growth rates of labour productivity and consumer prices, respectively, and U is the annual average standardized unemployment rate.
[a] 1964–73.
Sources: OECD, *Historical Statistics 1960–1993*, Table 2.20; OECD, *Historical Statistics 1960–1995*, Tables 3.1, 3.7, 4.1, 4.3, 4.7, 4.8 and 8.11; and OECD, *Economic Outlook*, 65, 1999, Annex Tables 1, 3, 4, 5, 9, 16, 20 and 22.

superior productivity growth and, although high AD lowered unemployment, low unemployment did not lead to higher rates of inflation. Instead, inflation rates were relatively low during the golden age, suggesting the presence of mechanisms bringing AD and aggregate supply into line at low rates of unemployment.

The questions at issue in this chapter concern the mechanisms that were maintaining balance between AD and aggregate supply at low rates of unemployment and acceptable rates of inflation, and how these adjustment mechanisms are to be modelled. As discussed in chapter 3, regardless of how the equilibrium unemployment rate is defined, periods of balance between AD and aggregate supply cannot be ascribed to the automatic adjustment of AD to some fixed aggregate supply. Nor is there historical evidence that balance can be attributed to the use of fiscal and monetary policy to fine tune AD, although the belief that governments were committed to using expansionary policy when required may have kept private sector spending high by reducing macro risk. Whether or not this was the case, an explanation of aggregate balance at full employment is required. To anticipate the conclusion of this chapter, a large part of the answer lies in there being processes that induce supply-side adjustments to AD not only when there is slack in the economy but also under conditions of full employment.

Although not all economies achieved full employment rates of unemployment in the golden age, most did and the rest had historically low rates. Therefore we will describe the process of adjustment in terms of full employment output adjusting to AD. A process of demand-determined long-run full employment growth can be outlined as follows. Assume a strong sustained boom in exports and fixed investment is in progress, sufficient to maintain full employment, i.e. involuntary unemployment is minimal. Allow a disturbance to raise both the level and growth rate of real AD. Whenever supplies of capital, labour and new technologies adjust to this higher aggregate demand growth, rather than AD adjusting to exogenous supply, as in neoclassical analysis, the long-run growth process will be designated demand determined.[1] Keynesian demand-determined modelling now becomes appropriate beyond the traditional Keynesian domain of periods of slack AD. It is applicable to periods of full employment when, over some range, growing AD determines a growing level of full employment output. In such instances, it is misleading to model growth with a conventional aggregate production function defining a unique maximum output at any point in time and a unique growth path of maximum output, both unrelated to the performance of the economy. Instead, in this reversed causation model, maximum output and its long-run growth rate vary, endogenously determined by demand.

Three caveats are in order before discussing the details. To establish the applicability of an extended demand-determined framework, it is not necessary to argue that 'Say's law in reverse' holds for any level and rate of growth of AD. What is essential is that there is a range of aggregate demand growth rates that induce similar growth rates of maximum output. Second, in the real world there may be constraints that limit real AD, keeping it below the full employment level. A key assumption of this purely demand-determined framework and the realization of full employment output is that the economy has institutions that relieve policy makers of any need to impose constraints on AD. As will be maintained, potential constraints on AD stem from institutions that fail to provide this relief, and instead lead to politically unacceptable rates of inflation, to rates of growth of exports relative to imports that are unacceptable to world financial markets, or to restrictions on government spending or budget deficits that keep AD below full employment levels. In developing the argument to support the extended Keynesian framework, it will be assumed in this chapter that there are no constraints on AD of the type just mentioned. By making this assumption, the process that adjusts aggregate output to different levels of real AD under full employment conditions can be isolated.

Third, while the emphasis throughout this chapter is on the role of aggregate demand in influencing long-run macroeconomic performance, this does not mean that AD alone determines long-run macroeconomic outcomes in the real world. For example, the rate of innovational investment

---

[1] Demand-determined models of growth were relatively common before the advent of neoclassical growth models. Two notable examples were Duesenberry (1958) and Kaldor (1957).

and the quality of 'entrepreneurship' can exert a strong influence on long-run full employment growth rates. Rather the case to be argued is that strong, sustained AD pressure is a necessary condition for rapid growth and low unemployment rates because of its impact on factors such as the amount of innovational investment and entrepreneurial activity.

3 Responses to aggregate demand when the capital stock and technology are fixed

To see the basic issues we distinguish between short-run and longer-term supply-side responses. This section considers the short run, when the capital stock measured in physical units is fixed; that is, there are so many machines with a certain set of characteristics in each sector, there is a given population with a fixed demographic composition, for example a certain age and gender distribution, and there is a given set of blueprints of available techniques defining the technology. Consider again an economy that has been growing steadily at low levels of involuntary unemployment when a sustained increase in the rate of growth of real AD occurs. According to Okun's law, a given percentage increase in AD and output reduces the unemployment rate by an appreciably smaller percentage. This discrepancy arises from three sources. Higher levels of aggregate demand and output lead to a reduction in part-time employment and increased overtime, an increase in the labour participation rate and an increase in productivity through a redistribution of labour within firms from low-productivity jobs to high-productivity production-line work.

Related studies of short-run responses outline the positive effect of an increase in AD on aggregate productivity and output as a result of the redistribution of jobs across industries (Okun, 1973). Define the sectoral elasticity of demand for labour as the ratio of the percentage change in employment in a sector to the percentage change in the overall employment rate and assume these elasticities vary appreciably across sectors. Given a positive correlation between sectoral employment elasticities of demand and sectoral levels of productivity, higher levels of aggregate demand (and therefore higher rates of employment) will generate increases in overall productivity and output. The underlying labour market process is a supply response to higher levels of AD in the form of a higher participation rate of labour. New entrants to the labour force tend to find employment in low-productivity jobs with low employment elasticity of demand, for example in wholesale and retail trade, that are vacated by the 'bumping up' of already employed workers to high-productivity jobs with high employment elasticity of demand, for example in durable goods manufacturing. In short, new jobs are created in the high-productivity occupations and sectors.

A counterpart to higher participation rates and labour reallocation to higher-productivity jobs in response to increasing aggregate demand is the higher rate of utilization of the existing physical stock of capital. This can be traced to additional production shifts, overtime and bringing into production standby equipment that would be unprofitable under less buoyant economic conditions. A final example of a short-run supply response to higher levels of AD is the presence of dynamic economies of scale, even in the absence of changes in the capital stock. According to this version of 'Verdoorn's law', higher rates of growth of demand lead to higher rates of growth of output due to these short-run responses. Faster output growth generates faster productivity growth through such influences as 'learning effects', which are a function of cumulative increases in output, and less 'down time' on the production line as longer production runs reduce the frequency of product changes (Boyer and Petit, 1990).

Even if these are no more than 'one off' responses, they play an important role in subsequent developments, illustrating a positive short-run elasticity of aggregate supply in response to increases in AD even under full employment conditions. There is also a long-run effect. The cumulative result of these short-run impacts is to provide the incentive for firms to engage in longer-term, riskier responses (for example greater investment outlays), the recruitment of more labour and the introduction of new technologies.

4 Responses to aggregate demand when the capital stock and technology are variable

The longer-run effects of aggregate demand on labour supply under tight labour market conditions treated in section 6. Here we consider the long-run effects of higher rates of growth of AD on investment and improvements in production techniques, as well as the more sustained effects on productivity and output growth that higher rates of investment generate. Again assume there is sustained rapid growth of aggregate demand leading to high growth rates of sales and output because of the short-run responses discussed in the previous section. There are a number of plausible theories describing the positive impact of these events on investment. Two of the more widely accepted are the accelerator relation, in which net investment is proportionate to the change in output, and various forms of the capital stock adjustment theory of investment of which the accelerator theory is a special case. Although the data in table 4.1 suggest that high rates of growth of investment (and exports) were driving the economies through their multiplier effects, it is also true that rapid growth of AD and output generates rapid growth of investment, and this leads to expectations of further growth of AD and output, creating a long-run positive feedback process.

Early neoclassical growth models treated investment and improvements in production techniques (i.e. technical progress or innovations) as separable determinants of output and productivity growth. Some subsequent models (Arrow, 1962; Phelps, 1962) assumed that the effects of investment and technical progress on output and productivity cannot be separated because technical progress must be embodied in investment. In this case, investment affects productivity and output by adding to the capital stock and also through technical progress. Since technical progress acts as a separate factor of production, investment has a double effect on output. Other models, while allowing that innovations may be embodied in investment, maintain that innovations that enhance productivity growth can occur independently of investment – for example, new managerial practices (Porter, 1990, ch. 9) and a more favourable attitude of labour towards restructuring work practices. Whatever the relative importance of these different views, the point to be made is that high rates of growth of AD are likely to stimulate higher rates of both kinds of innovations.

Lamfalussy (1961, 1963) provides further means to shed light on the link between the rate of aggregate demand growth and embodied technical progress. In his work, he postulates that the production processes available to a firm at any time are limited; for example, only highly capital-intensive and highly labour-intensive production processes are available from which to choose. The decision depends upon the principal objective of the investing firm. Choosing the capital-intensive technique indicates an 'enterprise' investment strategy aimed chiefly at expanding the capacity of the firm; the choice of the labour-intensive technique arises out of a 'defensive' investment strategy which aims to reduce costs. Enterprise investment includes innovational investment, frequently of the Schumpeterian type. It creates substantial dynamic scale economies under conditions of mass production, but also involves indivisibilities and the greater likelihood of excess capacity. In contrast, the defensive investment is cost reducing and does not suffer from the problem of indivisibilities, but it results in little in the way of scale economies.

Given these characteristics, other things being equal, the impact of different rates of growth of demand on investment strategies, productivity and capacity growth is straightforward. In economies where demand and output are growing relatively slowly, firms will adopt production techniques of low capital intensity, replacing old capital through piecemeal defensive investment projects. This enables them to reduce the risks associated with the high costs of lengthy periods of excess capacity that enterprise investment projects often generate, but the outcome for the economy is relatively slow growth in productivity and productive capacity. In an economy with rapidly growing markets, in contrast, mass production techniques will be adopted widely and enterprise investment strategies chosen because the risks of excess capacity are reduced. In comparison with the economy suffering from slow growth of aggregate demand, per capita incomes, productivity and capacity output will grow rapidly.

5 Aggregate demand and the transformation of output

In both the developed and developing capitalist economies, economic growth has been noticeably unbalanced, with rates of growth of output varying widely across sectors. This is true whatever the level of aggregation (e.g. agriculture, industry and services) or categories of consumption and investment output. In the process of growth and development, sectoral growth rates of demand and output not only vary across sectors at any point in time, but vary widely within a sector over time, tracing out a pattern of variable sectoral growth as per capita incomes rise. As a result, a fairly common sectoral growth pattern can be approximated by a logistic function. As well, there is evidence that different goods and collections of goods have a priority ranking in the budgets of consumers, allowing the growth process to be visualized as movement through a hierarchy of goods.

Together these findings lead to the following pattern underlying aggregate growth performance. Starting at a given point in time and at some initial level of per capita income, there will be sectors producing consumer goods with income elasticities of demand appreciably greater than 1, i.e. 'luxury' goods. These goods are affordable by only a relatively few consumers and their rate of growth of demand and output will be low. However, as per capita incomes rise further and the size of the market grows, goods produced in these sectors experience a rising rate of growth of demand. Accelerating demand causes investment strategies to shift towards enterprise investments, generating scale economies and a more rapid growth of productivity. Eventually, high and growing levels of income lead to declines in rates of growth of demand as the income elasticity of demand falls and consumers shift their demands to the next collection of goods in the hierarchy, and the demand and growth pattern repeats itself.

This scenario is not dependent upon unlimited economies of scale in any sector. Exploiting scale economies by adopting an enterprise investment strategy and gaining rapid growth of productivity corresponds to the high growth of demand phase of a sector's development. Once the market for a good becomes relatively saturated and the growth of demand slows down, both the desire and the ability to exploit scale economies will recede, and firms will shift to a defensive investment strategy. What a higher rate of growth of aggregate demand and output accomplishes is to accelerate rates of growth of investment and productivity in each sector, so that the overall rates of investment and productivity rise relative to an economy experiencing less buoyant AD conditions. Clearly, higher rates of AD shorten the time taken for any sector to go through a phase of its variable income elasticity growth pattern and, therefore, shorten the time required to move the economy through its hierarchy of goods.

These complexities stem from the unbalanced nature of economic growth. Recognition that growth is an intrinsically unbalanced process, and of the consequences of this lack of balance for economic performance, provides insights for modelling economic growth. First, the aggregate production functions of neoclassical or new growth theory cannot be used. The technology for each good varies with its demand, which determines investment strategy, and the proportion of each good as a share of total output changes as per capita income rises. Only coincidentally would the underlying sectoral production functions described above aggregate into the static fixed-coefficient production function of mainstream theory. If a functional form describing the technology must be specified, a flexible and rather complicated relation between rates of growth of output and investment is an appropriate beginning (e.g. Scott, 1989). Second, the notion of a steady-state equilibrium of a dynamic system is quite inappropriate for modelling economies in which the distribution of output is constantly changing as incomes grow.

6 Aggregate demand, supply elasticities and the redistribution of capital and labour

Our emphasis on unbalanced growth gives special importance to there being elastic supplies of capital and labour. These must respond to increases in the rate of growth of AD if high overall growth rates of productivity, per capita incomes and output are to be achieved. Given that most of the stock of plant and equipment capital is neither malleable nor mobile, a high rate of growth of new capital goods is essential for a rapid redistribution of capital between sectors and for the installation of the new technologies required for rapid overall growth of output and productivity.

Similarly, high overall growth rates of full employment output and productivity require that labour supply responds to high growth rates of aggregate demand. When growth rates of demand relative to growth rates of labour productivity vary among sectors, a continuous redistribution of labour among sectors is necessary. For example, sectors experiencing high rates of growth of demand and output relative to productivity growth require a relatively large growth in labour. In contrast, slow-growing sectors with high productivity growth may be shedding labour. Such developments are illustrated dramatically by similar movements in all the advanced economies over the past century. For example, relative rates of growth of demand and productivity in agriculture have been such that agriculture has experienced an absolute decline in employment, providing 'surplus labour' for the expansion of the workforce in the industrial and service sectors.[2] But it is also worth noting that, during the golden age period, the expansion of AD was so rapid that the labour released from agriculture was inadequate in most economies to satisfy the growing labour demand in the industrial and service sectors. The induced response on the supply side was immigration.

This suggests that economic growth must be modelled as a radical transformation of the economy, involving not merely continuous change in the distribution of output, but a continuous redistribution of capital and labour. Recognizing growth to be an unbalanced process in the real world adds force to the position that, without high rates of investment, sustained high rates of growth of productivity and per capita income are not possible; 'investment is important' for growth. Similarly, in this scenario labour supply is not one of the 'givens' but is endogenous, and high overall growth likely requires high rates of growth of the labour force (or initially a large pool of 'surplus labour' in agriculture) to overcome problems of labour immobility.

7 The elasticity of supply of inventions and innovations

The last point to be made in support of the reversal of Say's law and the rejection of neoclassical adjustment mechanisms concerns the supply of inventions and innovations. When economic growth is unbalanced, higher demand can create a sustained increase in supply under full employment conditions only if new process and product technologies are available, allowing production to expand rapidly in the new growth sectors. In an economy with no opportunity to borrow technology from abroad, the supply of inventions and innovations may be very inelastic. If so, when demand is shifting towards new sectors, output response will be weak because the necessary modern technology is absent or available only at a very high cost. In this case, the rate of growth of supply will show a more limited response to an increase in the growth rate of demand. A stronger supply response must await favourable but as yet undiscovered technological and perhaps scientific developments.

---

[2] The importance of the rate of growth of AD in this process is brought out clearly by the interruption of this trend during the Great Depression. During the 1930s, stagnating demand conditions led to a net migration of labour into agriculture in many countries.

In spite of this possibility, during the golden age most OECD economies in fact faced a very elastic supply of both inventions and innovations. The industrial leaders, particularly the United States, made a large stock of technology available to other economies, transferring it by means of licensing agreements, patent sales and the establishment of multinational subsidiaries. Consequently, there was no supply constraint for countries prepared to borrow these technologies. Borrowing was a continuous process. Once started, it contributed to rising incomes; rising per capita incomes shifted the composition of domestic consumer demand, creating markets for new products. Borrowing extended to the technologies needed to produce them. Variation in initial levels of development across the OECD influenced the timing of this process in individual economies, but broadly similar development patterns ensured that the later-developing OECD members repeated this process as their incomes rose. For all except the technological leader, from the point of view of an individual economy the supply of inventions and innovations, like the supply of labour, was endogenous. In each case, the development of effective demand and a reasonable effort to locate supply were sufficient to ensure that supply would be found.

8 Externalities

A general theme of this chapter is the central role of investment in the growth process. Investment not only adds to the capital stock but is often a source of new knowledge embedded in human and physical capital. Furthermore, because economic growth involves a transformation of output and sectoral shifts in the distribution of capital inputs, new investments are the means of overcoming problems of non-malleability and immobility of the existing capital stock. But, as Lachman (1947, 1948) pointed out half a century ago, in any economy undergoing transformation the changing structure of the capital stock must be considered for an additional reason. Conventional marginal productivity theory treats the capital stock of an economy as a collection of homogeneous units that compete with one another and with new capital goods; this is the basis for the doctrine of diminishing marginal product of capital. However, emphasis on the changing composition of demand and output owing to rising per capita incomes suggests that the capital stock is better treated as a collection of qualitatively different units. Because of this, many of these units of capital will be complementary to each other, as well as to units yet to be produced. As a result, higher rates of growth of investment generate externalities because of the technological interrelatedness of elements of the capital stock; this can further increase the productivity of existing capital, offsetting any tendency towards diminishing returns to capital.

Lachman's idea has been used more recently by new growth theory, which emphasizes investment as a source of new knowledge. For example, investment in R&D generates new knowledge with economic benefits that are only partially appropriated by the investing firm, say in the form of a patent (Romer, 1986; Lucas, 1988). The remaining 'non-excludable' benefits constitute a free good which can be appropriated by other firms. In the aggregate, spillover effects of this nature keep the marginal product of capital from declining as investment expands the capital stock. Additions to the capital stock do not compete with but are complementary to the existing units of capital.[3]

Our position is that new growth theory is on sound ground in its emphasis on spillover effects as a source of capital productivity and growth (and the related assumption that the investment ratio affects long-term growth), but neither neoclassical nor new growth theory is an acceptable framework for modelling economic development. This is partly because of their supply-determined full employment framework, but also because we reject the view that any fixed-coefficient aggregate production function is a useful tool for modelling unbalanced growth processes (Cornwall, 1977, ch. 6).

9 Explaining macroeconomic malfunction

Part II will show that the actual performances of the developed capitalist economies during the golden age can be modelled as demand-determined growth processes. For most of the OECD economies, it was a period of sustained full employment growth, with all the characteristics of induced adjustments on the supply side discussed above. Certainly forces other than sustained rapid growth of aggregate demand were contributing to superior macroeconomic performance compared with performance in the 1930s and since the mid-1970s; these will be discussed in chapter 10. But strong sustained demand pressures were a necessary condition, not only for low unemployment but also for high growth rates of productivity, per capita incomes and output, primarily because of their impact on the rates of investment and the adoption of new technologies.

An explanation of high unemployment and low growth is easily derived from the low unemployment/rapid growth scenario. Just as a sustained, strong growth rate of AD is the immediate determinant of rapid growth and low unemployment, the immediate cause of episodes of low growth and high unemployment is an absence of strong AD pressures. The additional

---

[3] Alternatively, some new growth models posit a relationship whereby investment in R&D generates new capital goods of a higher quality or a different variety which are complementary to existing units of capital. Since the new units do not compete with existing units, they do not bring down the marginal product of capital (Romer, 1990).

unfavourable effects of sustained low AD growth need be only briefly summarized. High unemployment rates will persist and the growth rates of output, investment, productivity and per capita incomes will be low or even zero, as will the rate at which the economy transforms itself. As the traditional textbook Keynesian models have long argued, prolonged weak aggregate demand is a key factor in accounting for poor macroeconomic performance.

From our Keynesian perspective, the high unemployment of the 1930s and following the golden age represented episodes of prolonged high rates of involuntary unemployment, raising the question of why low AD persists. Keynes provided one answer by observing that automatic mechanisms ensuring that the private sector will always generate a full employment level of AD do not exist. But this raises the further question of why, in periods of deficient private demand, the authorities do not intervene to compensate for the private sector's deficiencies. The discussion in section 2 suggested that the presence of insufficient AD and high unemployment might result from something other than an uncritical acceptance of an invisible hand. Thus there may be circumstances in which the authorities are aware that stimulative AD policies would be effective in reducing unemployment, but they are unwilling to act because of undesirable side effects. As a result, the level of AD is constrained below full employment output. We suggest that these circumstances are the result of institutions, which at full employment either cause or fail to prevent side effects such as unacceptably high rates of inflation, unsustainable payments positions or large budget deficits. This issue will occupy our attention in part II and will be the basis of a recurring theme throughout the remainder of the book. For the moment we must emphasize that, by accepting institutions as possible constraints on AD, we are not resurrecting the supply-side equilibrium framework. Institutions are social constructs and society can change them. They are also subject to change by the performance of the economy.

10 Conclusions

In this chapter we have examined the effect of AD on other economic variables in both the short run, when technology is fixed, and the long run, when it is variable. Before leaving this chapter, we reiterate its central message. Keynes understated the role of AD in influencing macroeconomic outcomes. AD not only determines the level of output and employment when there are involuntarily unemployed resources, the usual view associated with Keynes, but, over a limited range of growth rates, also determines the rate of growth of maximum output. Demand-determined adjustment processes are the core of any explanation of macroeconomic performance, whatever the unemployment rate. Influences on performance other than AD have been left for later consideration. In chapter 10 an econometric study supports our claims for AD, and shows other variables to be significant determinants of growth. Confining the discussion here to AD has allowed us to stress by direct contrast the limited usefulness of mainstream supply-determined models.

The next two chapters introduce institutions, which we include with technology as part of the economic structure. As in this chapter, we examine the short run, marked by stable institutions, and the long run, when they change. In the first half of chapter 5 we define institutions and examine their functions in the context of two theories of the origins of institutions. This lays the groundwork for the remainder of chapter 5, which contains the next stage in the development of our framework. That is to indicate how, in the short run, institutions 'matter' because they may act as constraints on AD, adversely affecting the unemployment and growth records. Chapter 6 expands the analysis to include the long run.

5   Institutions and power

1 Introduction

An increasing number of economists have come to recognize that institutions affect economic behaviour and performance and must be treated as part of the structural framework. Microeconomists have led in this trend, enriching their formal models by including institutions as determinants of behaviour, often as constraints in optimization models. Macroeconomics has lagged behind; the inclusion of institutions has been concentrated in empirical studies that explain cross-country differences in macroeconomic performance. In spite of these developments, markets and market behaviour devoid of institutional characteristics remain the primary focus of mainstream neoclassical economics; there is little or no reference to the social context that shapes behaviour, to 'the macrofoundations of micro' (Colander, 1996). Not only are the social values and customs that influence preferences ignored, so are those preferences that reflect anything beyond the individual's self-interest; 'economic man' is not a social being. In pursuing this paradigm, economics divorced itself from the other social sciences. These have continued to emphasize the central place of social values in guiding behaviour, so that institutions are accepted as necessary to the analysis. But in economics the inclusion of institutions requires justification, and an introduction to ideas unfamiliar to many readers. A fundamental viewpoint of this book is that real world macroeconomic processes can be adequately modelled only if institutions are included, along with technology and tastes, in the structure of an economic system. Instead of the neglected, unexplained role mainstream economics gives to the traditional structural variables, they are fundamental to our explanation of capitalist development, not only influencing, but influenced by, economic performance.

A second element of social organization, equally unfamiliar to economic analysis, is the distribution of power. In economics, the expression of preferences in making choices is stressed at the most elementary level, but the emphasis is on individual choice and preferences; social choice is assumed to be the aggregate effect of the individual pursuit of self-interest. In reality, choices are made at the macroeconomic level, and their impact is not universally beneficial. We can, however, be confident that a large share of the benefits will accrue to those who have the power to make the choice and impose their preferences on the broader society. Policy choices are the clearest example of the exercise of power by coalitions pursuing their collective interest, and these choices will certainly affect economic performance. Like institutions, the distribution of power is an integral element of our framework. This chapter introduces the impact of power and some of the links between power and institutions. Its main task is to incorporate them into the analysis and to show how they affect economic performance.

Although both institutions and power are largely neglected in mainstream economic analysis, they are dealt with in other work, some of which has been very influential. We begin by discussing some of the divergent views expressed in this work, selected to provide both context for and contrast with our own analysis. One broadly held view is that institutions, other than perhaps a system of property rights, are no more than impediments to efficient economic performance; this view is rejected in sections 3 to 5. Sections 6 and 7 deal with a contrasting view (associated with 'new institutional' economics). It claims institutions originate from the optimizing responses of private agents to changes in technology, so that they are most 'efficient' and therefore universally 'beneficial'. Section 8 examines shifts in the distribution of economic and political power as sources of changed institutions and economic performance. It is concluded that institutional change can be designated as efficient or beneficial only with respect to specific effects on the economy, for example on the unemployment or inflation rates, or on specific groups within the economy, for example organized labour or the financial industry.

The balance of this chapter turns to empirical studies that have incorporated measures of power and institutions to assess their effects on macroeconomic performance as they influence policy choices or alter constraints on AD. One conclusion from these studies is that macroeconomic performance depends upon institutional characteristics. But, contrary to a widely accepted view, institutional change leading to a more competitive type of capitalism does not necessarily improve performance, and can worsen it. This is borne out by the post-war record, which shows that during the golden age economies with institutions that created the greatest divergence from the competitive norm were actually among the best performers, largely because of externalities.[1]

---

[1] Schumpeter took the same position in attributing greater innovative capability to monopolies than to competitive firms.

2 Institutions and organizations

Institutions can be defined as the beliefs, customs, laws, rules and norms that guide the behaviour of individuals and groups within society.[2] They are not mechanistic determinants, but act as guideposts defining what is acceptable behaviour, the rights and responsibilities of individuals and groups, and the rewards and penalties that induce compliance. Institutions are intrinsically collective in nature, reflecting the culture and traditions of the society and a desire for orderliness in social relations. In the broadest sense, they 'legitimize' actions, including the exercise of power by individuals and groups. Institutions can be classified as social or legal (Elster, 1989). Social institutions are the unwritten rules of conduct that are enforced by members of the society. Legal institutions include the laws of a country, or its constitution, or the constitution of a group within the country (for example a labour union); these are enforced by specialists for reasons of self-interest. Taken together, they form the institutional structure for social interactions.

To define beliefs, customs, laws, rules and norms as institutions is not controversial. Although they are always included, other definitions are broader, including entities such as firms and government agencies. True of much of the older institutional economics literature (e.g. Commons, 1950; Ayres, 1962), this can lead to a loss of clarity, particularly regarding the nature of institutional change. The problems stem, at least partially, from common usage in which firms, churches, labour unions and other such bodies are routinely referred to as institutions. These are not institutions as defined here, but organizations. An organization is a group of individuals systematically organized to pursue particular goals; a set of rules governs its structure and the methods used to achieve its objectives (Bromley, 1989). North (1990) expresses this distinction most succinctly by referring to institutions as 'the rules of the game'; organizations and their members are the players. Thus labour unions, firms and churches are organizations, each with a set of rules that determines their internal operation and relations with other organizations and individuals. Not only do their rules depend upon the institutional structure of the larger society, but so do the types of organization that arise. The goals organizations choose, as well as the ways they pursue them, are conditioned by the institutional structure; they reflect the incentives, opportunities and rewards that it provides.[3]

---

[2] This and the following sections include topics selected to give context for the development of our model. There is no attempt to survey institutional economics, which is composed of several schools with different research agendas and vocabularies. For a comprehensive survey, see Rutherford (1989).

[3] North (1994, p. 361) writes: 'if the institutional framework rewards piracy then piratical organizations will come into existence; and if the institutional framework rewards productive activities then organizations – firms – will come into existence to engage in productive activities.'

3 The impact of institutions

In this study, the relevance of institutions lies in their impact on economic behaviour and performance. Consequently we are less concerned with categorizing them as 'economic' or 'political' than with the nature and extent of their influence on economic performance. Even institutions that serve specific economic functions embody social norms and reflect social aspirations. However categorized, society's institutions influence the type of organizations that are formed, the goals of organizations and individuals, and how these goals are pursued. In doing so, they shape economic processes (for example how wages are determined and how individuals and groups interact) that influence economic outcomes. For example, the economic system is itself a set of institutions, with feudalism and capitalism just two of the many possible variations. Among the institutions that form an economic system, property rights play a defining role, whether private or communal rights; private property rights are fundamental to capitalism. Just as there is variation among economic systems, there is variety within capitalism. Examination of their corporate, labour, tax and environmental laws will demonstrate differences among countries. These laws may encourage or discourage trade and strengthen or weaken labour unions. Similarly, different systems of education can assist or hinder the acquisition of marketable skills, and religious beliefs can increase costs (for example Sunday closing laws which leave capital equipment idle).

These laws are part of the broader set of institutions comprising the institutional framework. This includes the most fundamental norms and beliefs of the society, and these guide economic behaviour just as they guide behaviour in other spheres. Examples include whether behaviour is cooperative or competitive and what is regarded as fair or just, both of which influence the way the economy operates. Institutions affect the economy relatively directly, through the laws that are enacted, but they also have less direct effects. First, social aspirations are reflected in policy goals and targets, for example the priority attached to full employment. Second, and central to understanding the profound part played by institutions, they affect how, and how successfully, these goals are pursued. In both cases, institutions affect economic outcomes. The availability as well as the usefulness of economic policy tools depend upon the institutional framework. Since this differs among economies, their policy 'choice sets' will also differ, as will the effectiveness of any individual policy under consideration.

4 The cognitive function of institutions

This and the next section consider the basic functions of institutions. Here, we draw upon institutional economics, noting that this is anything but a unified field. The various schools not only specify and emphasize different ways in which institutions affect economic activities, but also use different language to describe essentially similar effects. However, there is widespread agreement regarding two basic functions of institutions. First, as cognitive devices they reduce uncertainty by providing information about the likely behaviour of individuals and groups. They are the shared beliefs which supplement conventional 'instrumental rationality', i.e. behaviour guided by means–end optimization (Hargreaves Heap, 1994). Second, by defining acceptable behaviour and the penalties for non-compliance, institutions provide social cohesion and orderliness to an economy (and the society of which it is a part). This includes legitimizing power and mediating conflicts, roles essential to the survival of a society or economy. Some studies stress other functions, but our view is that how an economy's institutions provide information and mediate conflict and how well they perform these functions show most clearly their impact on economic performance.

In the real world the task facing a participant in economic activity is the acquisition of the relevant information to make decisions, and effective participation encounters several difficulties. First, it has long been recognized that no decentralized decision-making economy can be effectively organized solely on the basis of 'primary' information – a common knowledge of price signals cited in competitive theory for determining what is to be produced, how it is to be produced and for whom; additional 'secondary' information describing the likely behaviour of other market participants is necessary (Richardson, 1959). Second, some of the relevant information is unknowable, owing to radical uncertainty. Here, uncertainty refers to ignorance about the future, so that it is impossible to attach a probability to a particular outcome, even if one can envisage the outcome itself. Third, of the information that can be had, some will be irrelevant and some will be erroneous or misinformation. This will exacerbate the final possibility – that the amount of available information may well exceed the computational capacity of the human mind.

This combination of radical uncertainty, misinformation and information overload prevents agents from making decisions solely by rational means–end calculations, i.e. by instrumental rationality. As Hodgson (1988, p. 205) points out, without institutions 'an uncertain world would present a chaos of sense data'. The concept of 'bounded rationality' has been adopted to characterize such situations in which decision makers must fall back on 'rules of thumb' in their deliberations. Rules of thumb are a familiar example of institutions as sources of secondary information that reduce information problems. In fostering behavioural regularity, institutions reduce uncertainty about the actions of others, replacing it with a substantial measure of predictability. Knowledge of the beliefs, laws and norms that guide behaviour provides this secondary information.

As sources of information, institutions are essential in organizing a market economy, but in some quarters their inclusion in the analysis has assumed a decidedly negative character. In mainstream macroeconomic theory, the significance of institutions has been interpreted in a very special and misleading manner. This interpretation treats institutions as market imperfections that create distortions preventing the realization of efficient outcomes and reducing the available choice sets. This widely accepted but mistaken view held by mainstream economists derives from the strong influence of the institutionless Walrasian competitive model, with its assumptions of perfect information, and the traditional belief of the Austrian school of economics that, for efficiency, a decentralized decision-making economy requires only price information. In fact it is precisely their cognitive function in a world of uncertainty that allows institutions to do the reverse: in many situations they increase the number of available choices by providing information about the behaviour of others, which reduces uncertainty and improves the functioning of markets. Most market transactions would be cumbersome if not impossible unless exchanges were guided by rules and norms of behaviour. Markets function because of, not in spite of, institutions.[4]

5 Legitimizing power and mediating power conflicts

Adherence to a common set of norms, laws and rules based on shared beliefs generates and reinforces an individual's attachment to a group. Institutions guide behaviour when conflict within the group threatens social cohesion. Their function in this context is to legitimize power and provide the mechanisms for conflict mediation. When power is not sanctioned by underlying institutions, the result, as North (1991, p. 11) remarks, is 'the law of the jungle'. We consider only legitimate or sanctioned power in this study. We are interested in power because it may be used to alter institutions, and in the distribution of power because it is a central determinant of the kinds of institutions that arise. In this section, attention is confined primarily to defining power and to showing why it cannot be ignored in economic analysis. Section 8 takes up the relation between power, institutions and performance.

Power has been variously defined in the social sciences. Indeed, a vast literature exists describing strongly asserted but differing views on the 'true' meaning of the term, stretching from simple slogans, e.g. 'power is whose interest counts', to careful and detailed definitions. Since definitions are

---

[4] Hodgson (1988, p. 174) defines the market as 'a set of social institutions in which a large number of commodity exchanges of a specific type regularly take place, and to some extent are facilitated and structured by those institutions'.

neither true nor false but only useful to the purposes at hand, we can forgo lengthy discussion of the alternative uses of the term and the kinds of refinements common in the literature. Wartenberg (1990, pp. 17–27) provides a simple two-part definition in which power refers both to the ability to do something and to the ability to control or command others. It is the second part of this definition that best suits our purpose, that is, power as the ability of dominant individuals or groups in economic relationships to make subordinate individuals or groups act in the former's interest. When institutions legitimize a power relationship, they simultaneously legitimize the economic outcomes that flow from it. In economics these outcomes are often, although not exclusively, concerned with income distribution, as are many of the conflicts that arise.

Although our main interest lies in the relation between power and the economy, it is useful to categorize two different kinds of power. We distinguish between economic and political power in terms of the means that enable individuals or groups to exercise power, and not for what particular purpose power is used. Consider two situations in which power is used to alter economic activity, for example working conditions. A unionized workforce exerts economic power when it uses collective bargaining to achieve improved safety conditions. The exercise of political power is illustrated by labour's ability to induce their political representatives to pass legislation with the same purpose. The connection between political and economic power is very close. In general, when private groups are dissatisfied with market-determined outcomes, they will organize against the market and redress their grievances through political channels. These are cases where the economic power of private agents is insufficient to secure their objectives. Examples are employers seeking legislation to curtail union activities, and labour seeking legislation to limit the power of employers.

We have noted that reliance on the competitive equilibrium model has led mainstream economists to treat institutions as harmful market imperfections, denying their cognitive function and its positive impact on economic mechanisms. Similarly, the mainstream neglect of power removes any need to consider the role of institutions in legitimizing power and mediating conflict.[5] However, unlike the world envisaged in the competitive model, the real world is populated with organized interest groups that have

---

[5] In most economics textbooks, the word 'power' occurs in one of only two contexts: in the discussion of monopoly, and in the case of electricity generation. Rothschild (1971, p. 11) attributes this lack of interest to two sources, the unwillingness to forgo the elegance and determinacy of competitive equilibrium models and the economics profession's wish 'to avoid the detailed occupation with facts which powerful social groups prefer to keep under a cloud of uncertainty'.

the power to influence economic and political events, including the establishment and maintenance of institutions favourable to their causes. This is also a world to be contrasted with public choice theory, where collective decision-making is the result of competition between individuals rather than arising from the activities of organized groups; this neoclassical choice theoretic foundation ensures that power is of no consequence.

Here we follow the lead of social scientists outside of economics and focus attention on the power of organized interest groups, its distribution among these groups, and the institutions that dominant groups use their power to establish. Because of this focus, we redefine the term 'tastes' and alter its role to distinguish it from traditional consumer demand theory in two ways. First, since we are focusing on organized interest groups, our attention is on the preferences of coalitions within society. Second, instead of the effect of individual tastes on consumption expenditures, our interest is in how the preferences of interest groups influence institutions. Whether exercising these preferences leads to the desired institutional change will depend on the relative power of the group in question, and on the characteristics of the existing institutional framework.

6 Efficiency theories of institutions

Having noted that mainstream analysis usually ignores institutions, or at best accords them only a negative role, we now turn to theories that take an equally extreme but opposing view. These theories not only include institutions, but claim that they are efficient, always improving economic performance. There are several versions, falling into two main categories: the transactions costs and imperfect information theories. These theories are concerned with costs in addition to the payments for labour, capital and raw materials that make up the usual list of production costs; examples are the costs of negotiating, monitoring and enforcing agreements, including legal contracts, and the costs of acquiring information. The transactions costs and imperfect information theories differ primarily in the costs they choose to emphasize, but their similarities outweigh their differences. They share a common methodology and stress the cognitive function of institutions. Both assign to institutions in the private sector (but not the public sector) the role of increasing economic efficiency and entrepreneurial profits by reducing transaction costs. This allows us to combine them under the single heading of efficiency theories.

The early works of Douglass North bring out the main themes of this approach and provide a useful comparison with our treatment of institutions later in the chapter. North (1981, 1987) is concerned with the impact of private sector institutions on macroeconomic performance, especially

economic growth and development, within a transactions costs framework.[6] In his view, sustained growth and development require the continuous adoption of modern technologies to obtain the efficiency gains
available from specialization, division of labour and scale economies.
However, modernization and industrialization increase the size of the
market and increase mobility. These trends increase anonymity, weakening
the personal ties of loyalty and friendship and the mutual trust developed
by individuals engaged in repeated exchange. In the absence of formal rules,
the likelihood of cheating, shirking and opportunism is greatly increased
and the enforcement of agreements becomes more difficult and costly. The
result is that, in order to exploit gains from modern technologies and reap
the benefits of affluence and modernization, elaborate institutional structures must be developed to control transactions costs. These take the form
of precisely specified legal agreements and guarantees, with effective monitoring systems and third party enforcement mechanisms (i.e. a well-speci-
fied system of property rights enforced by governments) to reduce the
uncertainties that would otherwise arise in an impersonal, interdependent
society.

Efficiency theories claim that the responses of entrepreneurs to technological change result in the establishment of efficient institutions (Alchian,
1950; Friedman, 1953). In his early writings North maintained that in the
private sector 'competition in the face of ubiquitous scarcity dictates that
the more efficient institutions, policy or individual action will survive and
the inefficient ones perish' (North, 1981, p. 7). Institutional change is a 'survival of the fittest' selection process applied to a menu of options generated
by individual entrepreneurs seeking to reduce transactions costs. In the
long run, recognition spreads that natural selection has shown one of these
options to be better than the rest; it is adopted and becomes the new
institution.

7 An evaluation

The assumption that choice made at the micro level by individual firms will
lead to macroeconomic improvement leaves several problems unaddressed.
First, it overlooks the possibility that the micro-level choice most widely
adopted might be not the best, but merely the best known. Second, even if
we can assume that firms adopt the best available option, there is still the
possibility that there will be external costs borne by society that outweigh

---

[6] At the micro level, imperfect information theory and much of the transactions costs literature treat the firm and especially the large hierarchical corporation as institutions designed
to enhance efficiency and increase profits by reducing transaction costs in response to an
evolving technology. See Coase (1937).

the private gains of firms. The literature overlooks these possible welfare costs, and is generally unclear about the definition of 'efficient'. The general implication is that there will be improved performance in the long run, but there is no exploration of the short run or of the distribution of the gain. These views have been replaced more recently, as in the later writings of North (1990, 1994), by the position that attempts to reduce transactions costs at the micro level are unlikely to translate into improved macroeconomic performance even in the long run.

We agree that institutional change in the private sector cannot always be assumed to be beneficial to the whole economy even in the long run. This raises the issue of what criteria to adopt in evaluating institutional change. Evaluating any particular institutional change in the real world by the criterion of its impact on transactions costs is too general to function as a policy guide and probably impossible to test empirically. However, two important clues for formulating criteria are implicit in the previous section. First, as it is almost inevitable that changes in institutions such as new laws have redistributive effects, i.e. their impact will be beneficial to some and harmful to others, any useful criterion for evaluating institutional change must explicitly recognize that redistributional issues are involved. Second, the excessive generality of the transactions costs concept suggests that a useful criterion for evaluating institutional change must be formulated in terms of specific impacts on the economy (for example the creation or removal of constraints on aggregate demand). In this way, beneficial or harmful changes in institutions must be defined simply as those that enhance or detract from the achievement of some designated measure or goal of macroeconomic performance, in this example higher or lower unemployment. Winners and losers are the groups that gain or lose from the institutional change, for example those who gain employment and those who suffer from high inflation because of the stimulation to AD. This brings the analysis to theories that link power to institutional change and explicitly recognize its redistributional impacts.

8 Power and institutions

Far from the idea of efficient institutions arising at the micro level to ensure the best economic outcomes, other theories consider power, exercised at the macro level, to establish institutions that improve outcomes for specific groups. That interest groups use economic and political power to gain control of economic activity in pursuit of their own objectives is well recognized in the social sciences, including non-mainstream economics. In contrast, mainstream economics confines its interest in power to the impact of existing market structures on the economic variables, for example the ability of monopolies and unions to affect prices (Rothschild, 1971, pp. 15–16). This ignores the dynamics of power and its capacity to alter the market structures and institutions that in large part determine economic outcomes.

The view that society's institutions reflect the underlying distribution of economic and political power has its roots in Marx's theory of economic development. Recent treatments of the links between power, institutions and economic performance by political scientists include the party control theory of economic policy (Cameron, 1984; Hibbs, 1987) and Lindblom's (1977) theory of the natural dominance of capital over labour under capitalism. Contributions by economists include Kalecki's theory of the political business cycle (Kalecki, 1971) and partisan theory (e.g. Alesina et al., 1997), as well as Régulation theory and social structure of accumulation theory, which are discussed in chapter 7.

These power theories share the view that institutions established by the exercise of power rarely favour all groups. There is generally a welfare trade-off, as some benefit while others are harmed. This is the approach of the party control theory of economic policy, recent versions of which are usually called partisan theories. These theories focus on the effect of power on economic performance, as the government uses its political power to change legal institutions, i.e. to enact laws that put its policies into practice. A basic premise of the theory is that political parties and their policies represent a society's economic and social divisions. A second premise is that, in any trade-off between unemployment and inflation, labour will accept higher inflation to achieve low unemployment, whereas capital's preferences reverse these priorities. Accordingly, a powerful labour movement will produce strong left-of-centre political parties that will pursue its interests, seeking to enact laws and regulations that foster full employment and extend the social safety net, if necessary at the cost of higher inflation. Given a democratic political process, these trade-offs are manifestations of the effective use of labour's political power.

A parallel approach is to consider the use of economic power to create institutions, for example the introduction of 'fairness' considerations in wage settlements (Hicks, 1974) or 'restructuring' the workplace (Kalecki, 1971). But whether institutions stem from economic or political power, there will be redistributional effects. This view is in sharp contrast with efficiency theories, which rely on individual optimization behaviour in conjunction with a 'survival of the fittest' selection process to ensure that the most efficient institutions prevail. Here, the exercise of power determines which institutions are established and whose goals they will favour.

Unlike efficiency theories of institutions, power theories have been the subject of empirical tests. Typically, party control theories of economic policy use the strength of left-of-centre political parties that represent labour to measure the distribution of power. The measures used have included the proportion of parliamentary seats or cabinet posts held by left-wing parties or the percentage of left-wing votes cast at national elections. The hypothesis is that the distribution of power determines the policies that will be enacted into law. For example, an increase in labour's political representation, however measured, is expected to increase the likelihood of institutional change to support a more stimulative AD policy stance.

This relationship is tested in cross-country studies by calculating the correlation coefficient between the average unemployment rate, assumed to measure the strength of stimulative AD policies, and various measures of labour's political power. Based on the usual statistical criteria, these relationships are found to be rather weak (Cameron, 1984; and Hibbs, 1987). Alesina et al. (1997, ch. 6) and Hibbs also use regression analysis to test this relationship for individual countries, using quarterly data. Very large R-squares result from their inclusion of lagged dependent variables among the regressors. Disappointingly, there is little left for the power variable to explain; even when its coefficient is statistically different from zero, it is so small that its effect is negligible. A consistent shortcoming of party control theories is their tendency to ignore influences on the current unemployment rate other than power and past unemployment rates. In effect these theories assume that the strength of demand for AD policies determines which economic policies are implemented. They overlook the possibility that stimulative AD policies may have adverse side-effects that restrict their use, so that even the most powerful labour movement may be unable to persuade governments to enact low unemployment policies. This leads to a body of empirical work claiming that differences in labour market institutions may explain different unemployment performance because of their ability to create or remove constraints on the use of AD policy. These studies have also been tested empirically but, like the power theories, they also omit variables that influence unemployment performance.

9 The structure of collective bargaining

An outstanding feature of the golden age was the ability of most OECD economies to reduce unemployment to full employment levels without experiencing unacceptable rates of inflation. However, it is because a small number of economies during the golden age were subject to constraints on AD, and therefore had relatively high unemployment rates, that the period is a fruitful source of information.[7] Annual average rates of unemployment

---

[7] As we will see in chapter 9, in most economies full employment was also consistent with an acceptable balance of payments position and there were no budget constraints on AD.

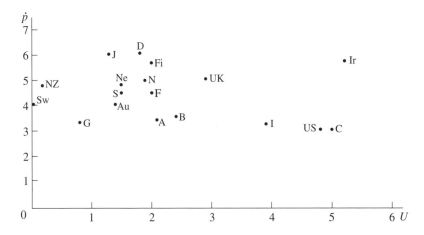

Figure 5.1 Average inflation rates ($\dot{p}$) and unemployment rates (U), 1960–73
Note: A = Australia, Au = Austria, B = Belgium, C = Canada, D = Denmark,
Fi = Finland, F = France, G = West Germany, Ir = Ireland, I = Italy, J = Japan,
Ne = the Netherlands, NZ = New Zealand, N = Norway, S = Sweden,
Sw = Switzerland, UK = the United Kingdom and US = the United States.
Sources: OECD, *Historical Statistics 1960–1997*, Table 8.11; Layard et al. (1991),
Table A3.

and price inflation for 18 OECD economies for the years 1960–73 are
shown in figure 5.1. The scatter of points indicates a bi-modal distribution
of unemployment rates. There are five economies with relatively high unemployment – Canada, Italy, Ireland, the United Kingdom and the United
States, with an average unemployment rate of 4.4 per cent. The remaining
13 countries have an average rate of only 1.5 per cent. Of special note is the
small difference in inflation performance between the high and low unemployment groups, which have averages of 4.4 and 4.6 per cent, respectively;
the range of values is virtually the same for the two groups. Most of the
economies were able to reduce unemployment rates to what would be considered full employment, and in some cases to rates lower than the full
employment rate, without generating rates of inflation appreciably higher
than those experienced in the high unemployment economies.

The search for an explanation of this ability has led economists to
examine institutional differences as the possible cause of differences in
unemployment performance. Assume that the observation for each country
in figure 5.1 is a point on its Phillips curve. The question is what institutions
account for the variations in Phillips curves that cause different inflationary pressures at low unemployment rates in the two groups and lead to

differences in their AD policies and unemployment rates. The usual procedure of studies seeking to answer this question is to hypothesize a relationship between certain institutions and the inflation costs of any
unemployment stance (i.e. the position of the Phillips curve) and to derive
an unemployment–institution relationship which is then tested empirically.[8] These studies tend to confine their attention to a particular institutional feature of the labour market as the determinant of differences in
unemployment rates among countries.

A well-known and widely discussed example is the work of Calmfors and
Drifill (1988). They assign each country in their sample to one of three
groups depending upon whether formal collective bargaining takes place at
the company, industry or national level. The degree of centralization is used
as a measure of how well wage bargaining is coordinated within a country,
coordination being assumed greatest when formal bargaining is at the
national level and least when at the company level. They argue that the level
of centralization affects a union's market power and the extent to which it
internalizes the social costs of its wage demands, and influences unemployment through a wage–employment relationship. Calmfors and Drifill then
examine the data for evidence of a relationship between the level of centralization and the rate of unemployment. They find a hump-shaped relationship: lower unemployment is associated both with highly centralized
bargaining and with decentralized bargaining and poor performance with
the intermediate case. The policy implication for an economy with bargaining at the industry level is that improved performance requires either
breaking up the industry-wide unions or working towards their consolidation into one large confederation.

Soskice (1990) has challenged these results, claiming that the relevant
measure of coordination is not the location of formal bargaining that
Calmfors and Drifill use (i.e. the level at which union and employer representatives meet), because in the cases of decentralized and intermediate
formal bargaining there may be informal coordination across companies
and industries via employer networks. Soskice argues convincingly that, by
ignoring this route for coordination, Calmfors and Drifill have underestimated the effective degree of bargaining coordination in several economies.
When the unemployment figures for each country in Soskice's sample are
related to its overall 'degree of effective coordination', the hump-shaped
relation disappears, replaced by a negative relation; the greater the degree
of coordination, the lower is the unemployment rate. The policy implica-

---

[8] Under the assumption that the Phillips curve is vertical, the unemployment rate is more or
less determined. If a long-run trade-off between unemployment and inflation is assumed,
as in this study, the rate of unemployment associated with any institutional form is still indeterminate.

tion is clear: improved performance needs increased coordination, and, contrary to the Calmfors and Drifill view, splitting the union movement will worsen performance.

These results and others are reviewed and their ideas tested with more recent data in an exhaustive study (OECD, *Employment Outlook*, 1997, ch. 3). For the period extending from the golden age until 1996, its authors find very little evidence of significant statistical relationships between alternative measures of economic performance (including unemployment and changes in unemployment) and collective bargaining institutions (including measures of centralization and coordination). As with the earlier studies, its main weakness lies in the lack of explanatory variables other than measures of the collective bargaining structure. The OECD study attempts a more sophisticated test by including in its regressions several variables designed to capture different dimensions of the collective bargaining structure; the results remain weak. These results are not surprising. One problem in the studies of this relationship lies in the theoretical base. This stresses the links from bargaining structure to wage inflation and employment, so that implicitly these studies are estimating the position of the Phillips curve. The weak results can be interpreted as the consequence of the exact position on the Phillips curve remaining indeterminate.[9] Even if the institutional (and other) variables included uniquely determine a negatively sloped Phillips curve, the unemployment rate associated with that particular institution is not determined because there is a set of inflation–unemployment positions from which to chose.

Careful evaluation of both the labour market institution and power theory explanations of unemployment leads us inevitably to the conclusion that each is looking at only part of the complete model. The power theories are examining the preferences of political parties for particular unemployment outcomes, while the collective bargaining structure models are implicitly establishing what is possible. In brief, one considers only the preference function of the party in power, while the other considers only the restrictions; together they define a constrained optimization model.

10 Avoiding class warfare

Clearly, these approaches have a serious specification problem that in each case is almost certainly connected to the lack of a well-defined theoretical model. There are also subsidiary problems caused by omitted variables. For example, the measures of political power in tests of party control theory

[9] Here we assume a downward-sloping Phillips curve, which is not controversial in the short to medium term. Chapter 3 made the case for a downward-sloping long-run Phillips curve.

make no distinction between what right-wing means in Switzerland (which has a high degree of participatory democracy) and what it means in the United States. This right–left dichotomy needs qualification based upon other dimensions, such as tradition and historical experience, that also help form preferences. Similarly, measures of the structure of collective bargaining are far from being the only variable that determines the position of the Phillips curve; other institutional variables as well as economic variables are relevant.

But the point to which we now turn concerns the choice of the collective bargaining structure as the prime characteristic of the industrial relations system. This variable cannot explain unemployment.[10] Although there can be little doubt that labour market institutions influence unemployment performance, they do so as part of a broader set of institutions that establishes the environment for relations between labour and capital. It is this 'bargaining climate', not the bargaining structure, that is a strong determinant of unemployment outcomes. A more profound determinant of unemployment is the extent to which there is an institutional environment of social consensus between labour and capital.

The studies cited in section 9 centre on particular institutional characteristics of the labour market assumed to determine the domain over which synchronized wage settlements are enforceable. This is alleged to influence a union's perception of the impact of its wage demands on employment and on other negative externalities of wage increases. According to the Calmfors–Drifill and Soskice analyses, the broader is the bargaining coverage the more a union internalizes the negative impact of its wage demands.[11] In fact, all that can be concluded is that the broader the bargaining coverage, the less likely is wage–wage inflation to be a problem; it cannot be assumed that labour will be willing to internalize the costs of wage–price inflation. Coordinated wage bargaining is a necessary but not sufficient condition for wage restraint under full employment conditions. It allows easier recognition of the adverse effects of large wage settlements, but does not produce wage restraint. This requires other institutions to be in place (Cornwall, 1994, ch. 5; McCallum, 1983; Crouch, 1985). The failure to incorporate these institutions in their work is the second major weakness of the studies discussed in section 9.

This shortcoming is most clearly illustrated by the strongest example of coordination, when bargaining is coordinated at the national level, with all labour represented by one national union and all employers represented by

---

[10] For a similar view, see Freeman (1988).
[11] Soskice comes to this conclusion even though he uses worker 'pushiness' as an additional influence on unemployment.

one employers' association. Here the problem of wage–wage inflation is eliminated; the crucial issue that remains is the impact of this concentration of market power on the wage–price inflationary mechanism. The mere existence of national coordination of wage bargaining under full employment conditions is likely to exacerbate class tensions and lead to unacceptable inflation.[12] This means that, before low inflation rates and full employment can be realized simultaneously, other institutions are needed that provide incentives for labour and employers to forgo unrestricted collective bargaining. This is true whatever the level of coordination of collective bargaining. Only to the extent that both sides restrain their demands will wage and price inflation at full employment be moderated. Something is missing in accounts that attribute superior performance to complete coordination of collective bargaining.

The missing element is an agreement between labour and employers to forgo unrestricted wage bargaining, an institutional arrangement in which each side attempts to increase its share of income at the expense of the other. In its place, institutions based on trust and cooperation are needed, which induce labour and employers to restrain wage and price increases in exchange for the long-run benefits of low inflation, such as full employment and growing profits, productivity and real wages. Such institutions were to be found in many economies during the golden age.

11 Institutional features of the golden age

A brief summary of the far-reaching institutional changes that occurred following publication of Keynes' *General Theory* provides perspective. The hardship endured during the Great Depression and World War II had led to the widely held belief that the benefits of the post-war recovery must be shared equitably. Chapter 9 discusses the efforts made by capital, labour and government to establish institutions that would make this possible. Two distinct industrial relations systems developed from these efforts, one best characterized as cooperative, the other as adversarial. The cooperative industrial relations systems reflected a substantial degree of trust between capital and labour. This allowed negotiation to begin from the position that there is always a large area of agreement that must be preserved by compromise and consultation. The adversarial industrial relations systems arose in

---

[12] This problem is captured in prisoner dilemma games. The dominant strategy on the part of the participants, in this case a national union and its employer counterpart, is not a cooperative solution in which both sides benefit; instead each tries to increase its share of national income. The result is accelerating rates of wage and price inflation, ultimately inducing restrictive AD policies and rising unemployment.

economies lacking trust between labour and capital, leaving conflict as the dominant force in negotiations.[13]

All economies experienced a shift in relative economic and political power to labour, which, together with the impacts of World War II and the depression of the 1930s, caused radical changes in labour market institutions. Wage setting by employers on a 'take it or leave it' basis was no longer accepted; labour could now obtain 'fairness' in wage settlements, fairness being defined as achieving a target rate of growth of real wages and the protection of relative wages, and more generally as an acceptable share of the national income. A major effect of including fairness as an element of wage settlements was the creation of a potential inflationary bias, i.e. politically unacceptable inflation rates at full employment. If labour should choose to exert its market power fully to support money wage demands, this bias would be activated. A notable feature of the golden age was that in most countries labour chose not to do this; low rates of unemployment did not necessarily lead to relatively high rates of inflation. This is illustrated most vividly by the horizontal cross-country Phillips curve implied in figure 5.1.

Labour's choice regarding its use of market power depended on the strategy adopted to institutionalize fairness in labour markets. One strategy allowed full employment with politically acceptable wage and price inflation; the other failed to do this.[14] The latter, called a 'market power strategy', used unrestricted collective bargaining between labour and management to reach wage settlements. Economies which chose this strategy had no machinery in place routinely to coordinate wage setting with national goals; occasional attempts to do so were weak or inconsistent. Their governments had failed to exercise leadership in establishing the institutions that would allow coordination. The lack of coordination or common goal left the money wage as the only available target of bargaining. Maximizing the money wage, with the cost of living and wage settlements in other sectors of the economy as guides, was seen as the best means of securing real wage gains. Market power strategy stemmed from and perpetuated the conflict typical of adversarial industrial relations systems.

Since labour's market power increased when unemployment fell, this strategy generated a negative long-run relationship between rates of unemployment and money wage inflation, i.e. the Phillips curve. Further, the record of these economies shows that full employment was not consistent with politically acceptable inflation rates; that is, an inflationary bias

---

[13] 'When we say we trust someone or that someone is trustworthy, we implicitly mean that the probability that he will perform an action that is beneficial or at least not detrimental to us is high enough for us to consider engaging in some form of cooperation with him.' Gambetta (1988, p. 217).

[14] This is treated in greater detail in Cornwall (1994, chs. 5–7).

existed. Policy-induced high unemployment became their only means available for containing inflation; in the 1960–73 period these were the high unemployment economies in figure 5.1.

During the golden age the principal actors in the remaining OECD economies entered into what will be referred to as social bargains.[15] These were the economies with cooperative industrial relations systems. In cooperation with capital and government, labour accepted the need for money wage restraint in the interest of achieving national goals such as wage and price stability and international competitiveness. In return, labour was promised full employment and other rewards, depending upon the country. Among the incentives were rising real wages as full employment boosted productivity growth, cooperative industrial relations, and a role in organizing the workplace, at least as a junior partner. The institutional forms comprising the social bargain differed among countries, largely because of differences in the economic and political power of labour. For example, in countries in which labour was particularly strong there were more generous welfare benefits and a greater role in developing, implementing and monitoring the social bargain. Labour in Japan and Switzerland was not very strong, but these countries nevertheless adopted social bargains. Labour's right to fair treatment was secured in Switzerland by the democratic empowerment of individual citizens achieved by recourse to referenda, and by organized labour's representation in advisory groups and coalition governments. In Japan, longstanding traditions governing social rights and obligations supported the development of institutions of cooperation and codetermination at the company level. In all these economies, after-tax and transfer income differences were small, relative to those in the market power countries.

The social bargain proved to be a successful instrument for restraining inflation even at full employment during most of the golden age. Restricted levels of AD and high unemployment were not necessary to keep down inflation in most OECD economies, allowing them to achieve both low unemployment and low inflation. In this period most economies were free to pursue a relatively independent AD policy largely because they were relieved of unacceptable inflation problems at full employment. The horizontal cross-country Phillips curve in figure 5.1 shows the success of social bargains in achieving low rates of inflation and unemployment simultaneously. Points close to the vertical axis depict economies that had a favourable trade-off between unemployment and inflation rates, while the USA and Canada are examples of economies where inflation could be restrained

---

[15] The term 'social bargain' is used throughout the text rather than 'incomes policy'. The latter term is often associated with policies in which the authorities unilaterally impose money wage norms on labour. The term 'social bargain' is meant to suggest programmes in which the wage norms were the outcome of consultation and agreement with labour.

only by high unemployment. Whereas inflation rates varied very little between the two groups, average unemployment rates were almost three times higher in the economies that sought to control inflation by creating unemployment. These collective bargaining strategies reflect the bargaining environment (i.e. whether industrial relations were cooperative or adversarial) and determine how favourable is the inflation–unemployment trade-off. It is the bargaining environment that matters, not the structure of bargaining. In the next section we discuss how this is to be modelled.

12 Institutions and power as determinants of unemployment

Earlier in this chapter we criticized other work for omitting either institutions or power. Our contention is that both act together to determine economic outcomes – unemployment in our example. Among the relevant institutions are those that determine the degree of trust and harmony in industrial relations. Social bargains are manifestations of harmonious industrial relations, while market power strategies are evidence of an adversarial system. The level of industrial harmony is a crucial determinant of the position of the Phillips curve. The distribution of power decides the political party whose preferences will be furthered. However, the pursuit of these preferences is limited by what is possible, in this case by the existing institutions that govern the position of the Phillips curve.

The model introduced here consists of a political preference function, which is to be optimized subject to the prevailing Phillips curve. The Phillips curve is assumed to be downward sloping, so that there is an inflation–unemployment trade-off to be exploited. The curve may be very steep at low rates of unemployment, but there is evidence that it is relatively flat at high unemployment rates (Akerlof et al., 1996; Fortin, 1996; McCallum, 1986). The price inflation Phillips curve is written as

$$\dot{p} = f(U; \mathbf{V}_1), \tag{5.1}$$

where $\dot{p}$ and U represent the inflation and unemployment rates, and $\mathbf{V}_1$ is a vector of variables that influence its slope and position. This vector includes institutional as well as the more usual economic variables.

The political preference function measures the disutility (M) of pairs of unemployment and inflation rates, and is to be minimized subject to the existing Phillips curve.[16] It is assumed to be strictly convex, so that it yields strictly concave indifference curves. The preference function can be written as

[16] This model was originally used by Lipsey (1965) and later by Trevithick (1976) to provide a definition of full employment that is consistent with other objectives of economic policy.

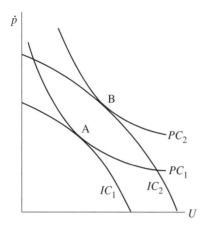

Figure 5.2 Optimizing political preferences

$$M = M(\dot{p}, U; \mathbf{V}_2) \ M_p, M_u > 0, \tag{5.2}$$

where $\mathbf{V}_2$ is a vector of political and institutional variables that determine its parameters. For example, we expect the parameters to depend on the political party in power, with left-leaning governments attaching a greater weight to unemployment than right-of-centre governments, leading to steeper indifference curves.

Each observed unemployment rate is interpreted as the result of a government acting to optimize its preference function subject to the existing Phillips curve. Because the preference function measures disutility, indifference curves closer to the origin are preferred. Any observed (optimal) unemployment rate is a tangency point between the existing Phillips curve and the left-most achievable indifference curve. This is shown as point A in figure 5.2. The figure also shows that if the Phillips curve shifts from PC_1 to PC_2 the new optimum at B has greater disutility. Figure 5.3 shows the effect of different political preferences. Indifference curve IC_L depicts the relatively lower tolerance of unemployment expected from a left-wing government. The optimum at A shows higher inflation and lower unemployment than the tangency at B, where IC_R represents right-wing preferences.

Since our objective is to examine power and institutions as determinants of unemployment outcomes, we use the structural equations (5.1) and (5.2) to derive the reduced form equation

$$U = U(\mathbf{V}_1, \mathbf{V}_2), \tag{5.3}$$

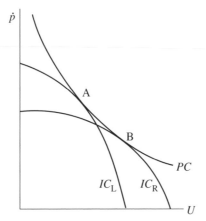

Figure 5.3 Alternative political preferences

where the vectors $\mathbf{V}_1$ and $\mathbf{V}_2$ include variables that measure power and institutional characteristics. Estimation of this reduced form using data for a group of OECD economies allows us to assess the contributions of these variables to unemployment outcomes. To avoid problems associated with business cycle fluctuations, we use data averaged over the cycle. The first step is to specify the variables to be used and relate them to our theoretical model.

Recall that the vector $\mathbf{V}_1$ is from the political preference function, so that it must include variables that determine the slope of the indifference curves. We have already suggested that left or right political leanings will affect the slope, as shown in figure 5.3. We use the proportion of left-of-centre votes cast in the period as a measure of effective political preferences. Others (e.g. Hibbs, 1987; Alesina et al., 1997) have relied on simple dummy variables that merely distinguish left-wing from right-wing governments by assuming values of plus or minus one. Using left-of-centre votes allows a finer distinction, providing a measure of the extent to which any government hoping for re-election must moderate its ideological preferences. A strong left vote will temper the policies of a right-wing government, or strengthen a left-wing administration's ability to resist the claims of powerful business and financial interests. The simple left–right classification cannot distinguish between high unemployment countries such as the United States and Canada, and low unemployment ones such as Japan and Switzerland, since they all consistently elect right-wing governments. But their voting patterns show marked differences, with the average percentage of left votes being 38 per cent for Japan and 26 per cent for Switzerland, compared with zero for the United States and about 15 per cent for Canada. The use of left votes also avoids some of the measurement problems for multi-party states that often have coalition governments. In general, the higher the proportion of left votes, the greater the tolerance for inflation and the stronger the preference for low unemployment.

Political preferences also depend on the history and institutions of a country, so that even countries with identical voting patterns cannot be expected to have identical indifference curves. One source of variability is the level of aversion to inflation, proxied here by an index of central bank independence.[17] Lastly, because membership in the European Monetary System (EMS) was voluntary, it also represents political preferences; a dummy variable is used to capture its effects. The monetary policy of EMS members was affected by exchange rate coordination, lowering inflation rates (Jenkins, 1996). Consequently, EMS membership is an additional measure of a preference for lower inflation.

The vector V_2 contains variables that determine the parameters of the Phillips curve, which in turn defines the set of possible outcomes. The position of the Phillips curve is expected to be strongly influenced by the degree of industrial conflict, measured here by the volume of strikes; this is lagged to allow time for changes in industrial relations to exert their influence. Harmony in industrial relations depends upon trust, particularly in wage bargaining. When management's assessments of costs and productivity are believed, wage claims will take them into account, reducing conflict and the likelihood of strikes, and improving the inflation–unemployment trade-off.[18] The volume of strikes is a more direct and more sensitive measure of the wage bargaining environment than the structure of collective bargaining used in the work discussed in section 9 of this chapter. In addition to this institutional variable, the position of the Phillips curve responds to changes in economic conditions. The international economic environment is an example. To account for the external demand conditions we use unemployment in each country's trading partners' economies, weighted by its exports to GDP ratio. This weight allows for differences in openness that determine the degree of exposure to external demand. Lastly, we include lagged inflation as a determinant of the position of the Phillips curve, but in this case it is the average inflation rate in the previous business cycle. Therefore it is not a simple inflationary expectations variable; instead, it measures the cumulative effects of past inflation on the position of the Phillips curve. These effects can be traced to institutional changes in the post-war era, especially the increasing power of labour. Backed by this

---

[17] We support the proposition that central bank independence is caused by aversion to inflation, whether this is 'grass roots' aversion (Debelle and Fischer, 1994) or the view of powerful financial interest groups (Posen, 1995).

[18] McCallum (1983) and Paldam (1980) provide further discussion of these points.

Table 5.1 *Definitions of the variables used in the unemployment equation*

Variable	Definition
U	Average unemployment rate over the period
LV	Left-of-centre votes as a proportion of total votes cast in elections during the period
CBI	Index of central bank independence
EMS	Dummy variable for membership in the European Monetary System
STR	Logarithm of man days lost to strikes per thousand workers, lagged one period
WU	Weighted average unemployment rate of the other 17 countries in the sample, scaled by the country's own exports to GDP ratio
$LINF$	Average inflation rate, lagged one period

Sources: voting data, Mackie and Rose (1991); central bank independence index, Cukierman et al. (1992); strike data, *ILO Yearbook of Labour Statistics*, various issues; OECD data are used for the remaining variables.

power, labour's claim to 'fairness' in wage settlements induced employers to accept the protection of real wages as a legitimate objective (Hicks, 1974; Perry, 1975). Past inflation can also affect the Phillips curve via the restrictive policies it induces, in a hysteretic process. In addition, more familiar economic variables such as productivity growth and import price inflation are potential determinants of the position of the Phillips curve.[19]

Our model was tested using a sample of 18 OECD countries, with four observations for each, for the years 1960–7, 1968–73, 1974–9 and 1980–9, which approximate the business cycles of the period.[20] The variables used are defined in table 5.1. In table 5.2 we list the countries included in the sample, and report regression results for the reduced form unemployment equation (5.3).[21] The equation was tested to see whether there were changes in any of the coefficients after 1973. The tests showed the estimated coefficients to be very stable, with one possible exception. The Hocking specification test suggests that a break occurred in the lagged inflation variable, reported in equation 2. The coefficient of lagged inflation was not significantly different from zero prior to 1974, but afterwards shifted to a significant positive value, implying that lagged inflation played no part in

---

[19] Our tests showed these to have coefficients that are not significantly different from zero, probably the result of data averaged over the business cycle.

[20] More recent data are not included, partly because there is not a complete business cycle, and partly because of the inconsistencies created by the unification of Germany.

[21] For a full treatment of the model, the variables used for estimation and additional estimation results, see W. Cornwall (1999).

Table 5.2 *Regression results for the reduced form unemployment equation*

	Equation 1	Equation 2
Left-of-centre votes	−4.877	−4.535
	(4.02)	(3.77)
Central bank independence	3.046	2.810
	(2.64)	(2.47)
Membership in the EMS	3.016	3.149
	(4.60)	(4.87)
Strikes	1.005	1.001
	(8.05)	(8.17)
'World' unemployment (WU)	0.944	0.794
	(4.04)	(3.27)
Lagged inflation	0.195	−0.037
	(3.43)	(0.28)
1974–89 dummy × lagged inflation		0.198
		(1.88)
Constant	−2.7337	−2.0652
	(2.27)	(1.68)
Adjusted R^2	0.8222	0.8289
Hocking test critical value	2.0317	
Hocking Sp	3.5445	

Notes:
The figures in parentheses are the absolute values of the t-statistics. The 18 countries are: the United States, Japan, Germany, France, Italy, the United Kingdom, Canada, Australia, Austria, Belgium, Denmark, Finland, Ireland, the Netherlands, New Zealand, Norway, Sweden and Switzerland. There were four observations for each, for the years 1960–7, 1968–73, 1974–9, 1980–9.

determining unemployment during the golden age, but came to do so only after its end. This result is consistent with a change to greater intolerance of inflation and the acceptance of higher rates of unemployment to combat it. It is also consistent with the widespread use of restrictive policies since the mid-1970s. The coefficient of the external demand variable (WU) is significant, with a value of about 1. This is expected, given the extent of trade among these countries and sufficient time in each period to allow the transmission of changes to take place. The coefficients of the institutional and power variables are all of the expected sign, and significantly different from zero at the 5 per cent level.

The strong partial correlations of these variables with unemployment and the high overall explanatory power of the estimates support the view that power and institutions play a significant part in determining unemployment rates. Stemming from our rejection that power is the sole determinant of outcomes, or that the structure of collective bargaining (also alone) can adequately explain unemployment performance, we have developed a model that includes both, giving our results a firm theoretical base. This model allows us to trace the effects of power and institutions on both political preferences and the constraints on economic outcomes embodied in the Phillips curve, with observed outcomes the result of a constrained optimization process. For the econometric tests, the use of a reduced form of the model links unemployment outcomes directly with power and institutions; the test results yield strong support for our contention that both are needed to explain economic outcomes fully.

13 Conclusions

This chapter took as its starting point the failure of mainstream macroeconomic analysis to incorporate institutions as part of the economy's structural framework and to recognize both institutions and the distribution of power as vital determinants of economic performance. To support our view, we first examined other treatments of institutions, beginning with the mainstream approaches of either ignoring them or regarding them as market imperfections that should be removed to create a more competitive system. A second influential view is that institutions are beneficial to performance to the extent that they correspond to some competitive norm. Both of these views run contrary to the historical record of the golden age. Among the best performers during this episode were Austria, Germany and the Scandinavian economies, all of them characterized by extended welfare states, high taxes, high union densities and highly regulated labour markets. In contrast, economies with institutions that more nearly approximated a competitive norm (for example Canada and the United States) were among the poorest performers. Figure 5.1 shows the large differences in unemployment rates and small differences in rates of inflation among these economies in the golden age.

As 'rules of the game', institutions govern how an economy works, affecting its performance often by circumscribing what is possible. Differences in institutions are therefore expected to play a large part in accounting for differences in performance among economies. To test these ideas, others have chosen very specific labour market institutions, such as the structure of collective bargaining, to explain unemployment performance. Instead, we have argued that the essential requirement of labour market institutions is not to define the structure of bargaining but to foster harmonious industrial relations, and that to do this they must be embedded in a broader institutional framework of cooperation, trust and social consensus.

We have further argued that institutions affect performance both by acting as constraints on the set of available outcomes, but also through their influence on the policies chosen from this set of possibilities. However, the final element in the choice of policy is power. Our view that left-wing governments will make 'labour-friendly' choices, preferring low unemployment to low inflation, and right-wing governments will do the reverse echoes the views of party control theory. But they consider only power, where we also recognize constraints imposed by institutions and economic conditions.

Our cross-country econometric study has allowed us to trace a large share of the variation in unemployment rates to institutions and power. Such cross-section studies provide clues for explaining changes in unemployment performance over time within an economy. For example, the discussion in section 11 suggests that, if labour shifts from a social bargain to a market power strategy, an inflationary bias will develop and the government will respond with restrictive AD policies leading to higher unemployment rates. We shall argue in part II that historically this has been the case. In this way, cross-country analysis can help to establish the linkages between the alternating episodes of good and poor performance in the post-World War II period. This shift in emphasis from relating performance and institutions at a point in time to determining their relationships over time is the subject of the next chapter, as we continue assembling the pieces needed to construct our framework for modelling economic development.

6 Evolutionary and hysteretic processes

1 Introduction

A central theme of this study is the role of changing economic structure in macroeconomic performance, specifically its role in generating alternating periods of good and poor macroeconomic performance. Beyond this, we examine the interaction between structure and performance which causes endogenous change in each, often by means of evolutionary processes. Chapter 6 brings together some of the main ideas of the previous three chapters to construct an evolutionary Keynesian framework for studying economic development. Before embarking on a detailed discussion of this framework, a brief review of the main points of the previous few chapters is helpful.

Chapters 2 and 3 discussed serious shortcomings of the supply-determined neoclassical equilibrium approach, including its inability to explain long-run outcomes within the model. Chapter 4 reversed the neo-classical direction of causation, and outlined a model of demand-determined dynamic processes. Chapter 4 also emphasized the unbalanced nature of economic growth, a 'stylized fact' completely overlooked by neo-classical and new growth analysis. Taking account of the changing composition of output emphasizes the changing allocation of factor resources as an inevitable accompaniment of economic growth. While recognizing that factors other than demand pressures affect macroeconomic performance, chapter 4 concentrated on demand as the primary endogenous force driving long-run performance. It did so by assuming a structural framework with no institutional constraints on aggregate demand and with substantially eased technology constraints. This led to an extension of the traditional Keynesian direction of causation. Not only does AD determine the level of output when there are idle resources but, even under initial conditions of fully utilized capital and labour, further increases in demand pressures lead to an expansion of output through an expansion of production possibilities.

As pointed out in chapter 4, this does not imply that 'Say's law in reverse' always holds in the real world; there are limits to the ability of demand to induce changes on the supply side. However there are good reasons for including an early chapter on extended Keynesian demand-driven processes. First, chapters 9 and 10 propose that capitalism's 'golden age' is appropriately modelled as a demand-driven process made possible by the absence or attenuation of constraints on AD in most of the developed capitalist economies. Second, in the closing section of chapter 4, we suggested that extended periods of weak AD, high unemployment and low rates of growth could be explained by constraints on AD. In chapters 11 and 12 it is argued that structural changes led to constraints on AD and poor performance in the episode since the golden age. Third, a major theme of chapter 4 is that AD pressure is important in determining the supplies of capital, labour and entrepreneurship. The responsiveness of supply-side variables is essential to our analysis of economic development.

Demand-driven dynamic processes will play a key role in our long-run economic development framework; so will changes in economic structures and in the distribution of economic and political power. Chapter 5 illustrated some of the benefits of incorporating institutions, a structural feature neglected in so much of mainstream macroeconomics. Cross-country analysis showed how differences in institutions during capitalism's golden age influenced relative economic performance by creating different constraints on AD. Using pooled cross-section and time-series data our study indicated that both institutions and power affect unemployment. In this chapter, these findings are recast in a dynamic form to illustrate the impact of institutional change. Then the impact of economic performance on institutions is added to the model. This final dynamic element completes one version of the endogenous core of our basic framework. Its usefulness in understanding the dynamics of change is taken up in chapters 9–12, which examine two episodes in economic development since World War II. With only minor changes, this kind of dynamics can be used to portray interactions between performance of the economy and its technology. This version of our framework is presented in chapter 8, which discusses economic development before WWII. Each version traces a process of interaction between performance and economic structure, central to our explanation of performance in a historical episode. The remainder of the chapter presents these ideas in terms of an interaction between performance and institutions.

This chapter proceeds as follows. Sections 2 to 4 discuss systems in which institutional change is explained within the model (i.e. it is induced by the actual performance of the economy) and compare our evolutionary process with others. We are aware that institutional change must often be attributed largely to exogenous forces and, even when endogenous forces are prominent, exogenous influences may also be at work. The discussion in chapter

5 of the impact of technology and power on institutions illustrated possible sources of exogenous influence.[1] We discuss processes initiated from outside the system in section 5, arguing that, whether institutional change is attributed to exogenous or endogenous forces or to a combination, the focus on institutional change leads to a deeper understanding of economic performance and development. It also leads to a history-dependent or hysteretic explanation of economic events. Section 5 concludes with a basic taxonomy of concepts. Section 6 presents a diagram that depicts our approach, and sections 7 and 8 introduce new concepts and refine earlier ones in preparation for part II of the book, where the framework is applied to historical events. Some of the advantages of our approach compared with the more conventional ones are also discussed in section 9. The conclusions follow in section 10.

2 Modelling capitalist development: institutions in the short and long run

The first step in fitting together the various pieces of our approach is to clarify the role of institutions. When treating the impact of the institutional framework on macroeconomic performance, two seemingly opposing considerations must be kept firmly in mind. Chapter 5 noted that the institutional framework, unlike the economic variables, is not a free-moving phenomenon quickly responding to fluctuations in economic variables. It is a structural feature that changes, but at a relatively slow pace compared with the economic variables it influences. As rules of the game, institutions require general acceptance, so that significant changes in the institutional structure tend to take place slowly, for example as new beliefs undergo a process of diffusion until they become widely accepted. Also, since the institutional structure comprises numerous rules and norms, change is likely to be achieved over time as the cumulative effect of changes to many individual interrelated customs and rules.

However, although institutions change relatively slowly, economic historians have reminded economists that, in the long run, institutional change is a common feature of economic development. At the very least we are warned and encouraged to 'update' our analysis, recognizing that, over time, rules and customs evolve and present new structural effects on economic performance, altering outcomes. As a result, failure to incorporate institutional change can lead to false explanations of economic events and harmful policy recommendations.

Taking into account the arguments of the institutional economists as well as the reminders of the historians, we adopt the following treatment of

---

[1] Changes in the distribution of power may also be attributed to endogenous causes.

institutions in modelling economic development. First, although the institutional framework certainly changes, in an orderly society significant changes must be gradual, as time is needed for the new rules and norms to become generally accepted. As a result, change to the institutional framework must be included in the analysis, but its gradualness relative to movements in the economic variables suggests treating it as occurring over a long run, with the accumulated change at some critical point producing a functionally different institutional framework viewed as 'punctuation' of a short-run stable institutional configuration.[2] This emphasis on the relative gradualness of institutional change will allow us to define the short run as an episode in capitalist development in which the system is functionally in an institutional state of rest. As the prevailing institutions either foster or hinder the achievement of economic goals, each episode will be characterized by a certain performance record (for example high or low unemployment, slow or rapid productivity growth) and the institutions responsible for these outcomes.

As demonstrated by the work discussed in chapter 5, the choice of institutions to study flows from our special interest in explaining the unemployment record. Given our assumption that AD is the immediate determinant of unemployment (and of other dimensions of macroeconomic performance), the focus is on institutions that determine whether high and growing AD will prevail or whether it is weak or stagnant. A law forbidding fiscal deficits is an obvious example of an institution constraining AD. Of equal note are institutions that enable or thwart the realization of other policy goals under full employment conditions. For example, if labour market institutions that reduce or eliminate inflation at full employment are weak or absent, full employment will not be achieved, as governments have consistently given priority to a low inflation target.

Second, satisfactory modelling of economic development requires more than the simple inclusion of institutions and a description of their evolution. To the greatest extent possible the analysis will explain institutional change in terms of endogenous economic forces, that is, as part of an evolutionary process. Also, seeking out and identifying these instances of performance-induced change in institutions that affect AD conditions shed

---

[2] This terminology is borrowed from the literature on technology innovation, a major innovation being referred to as a source of 'punctuated equilibrium' (Mokyr, 1990). There are several similarities in the processes of technological and institutional change. These include processes of selection, adoption and diffusion of a new technology/institution, the possibility of making a sub-optimal choice, and the likelihood of being locked in to an unfavourable technology or institution. Generally speaking, those thinking in terms of periods between one punctuated technology equilibrium and the next have a longer historical period in mind, e.g. the advent of the age of the railroad, than we envisage in our institutional analysis.

light on the processes of interaction between the economy's institutional structure and its macroeconomic performance. Institutions influence economic performance in the short run and economic performance induces changes in institutions in the long run. This is the economic system transforming itself, moving from one episode to the next by means of endogenously generated change. Economic development is modelled as an evolutionary process without any necessary appeal to unexplained outside forces.

3 The process of interaction

3.1 A Keynesian mechanism of institutional change

Essential to the process of interaction is a mechanism generating institutional change. This involves a second relation between institutions and performance, one that reverses the direction of causation between institutions and performance illustrated in the cross-section studies in chapter 5. Rather than treating institutions as short-run structural features affecting economic variables, the impact of macroeconomic performance on institutions in the long run is examined. More particularly, Keynesian AD forces and their direct impact on other macroeconomic variables are treated as sources of institutional change, a further extension of the previously extended Keynesian model of chapter 4.

Recall the causal chain sketched in chapter 4. Booming AD conditions, such as those of the golden age, induce low unemployment, rapid growth rates of output, productivity and per capita incomes, rapid and pronounced shifts in the sectoral composition of output and employment, and a radical structural transformation of the economy's stock of capital and technologies, as output and employment shift from agriculture to industry and eventually to services. The point to be made here is that rapid and sustained growth of AD and its induced effects on other economic variables are also among the forces generating radical institutional changes in the long run, partly reflecting shifts in the distribution of economic and political power.[3] These include new forms of industrial relations and legal systems and greatly altered financial networks, dominated by new organizational forms, for example labour unions and large corporations. In this process, rapid growth in per capita incomes and prolonged periods of full employment lead to a shift in power to labour and with it the institutional features of fairness in wage settlements and potentially strong cost-push inflationary

---

[3] This illustrates an earlier comment in footnote 1 that shifts in power may have endogenous origins. Recall we do not consider endogenous changes in technology in this chapter.

pressures discussed in chapter 5. Conversely, periods of stagnating AD as experienced in the 1930s bring the growth and transformation process to a halt (Svennilson, 1954). The resulting sustained high unemployment rates, decline in innovation investment and retardation in productivity and per capita income growth are sources of new institutional forms. Among these are an industrial relations system that reflects labour's economic and political weakness relative to capital, including 'take it or leave it' attitudes in wage negotiations, the restructuring of jobs by capital and the reduction of the welfare state.

3.2 Feedback effects

The assumption that institutions act as part of the economic structure, yet are responsive to economic conditions, raises the possibility of proposing an evolutionary system in which institutions are simply lumped together with the usual economic variables to produce a more encompassing long-run endogenous mechanism. Although such an approach is a theoretical possibility, it fails to take account of the different relative rates of change of the institutional framework and economic variables; consequently it neglects the structural impact of any existing set of institutions on the economic variables. Instead, motivated by the slow pace of institutional change, a satisfactory framework for modelling evolutionary processes must incorporate the distinction between short run and long run made earlier, with the short run defined as an episode in which the relevant characteristics of the institutional framework are fixed and are key determinants of macro performance, and the long run defined as a period subject to significant institutional change.

Consider an evolutionary process incorporating the distinction between long and short runs. An initial set of institutions shapes and structures the movements of the economic variables, leading to a specific pattern of macro performance in the short run. Over a longer historical period significant changes occur in the institutional framework, induced by the actual performance of the economy. When they occur, these institutional changes act as new structural features, influencing the performance variables as the economy moves through a new episode. The long-run implication of this interaction is that the economic variables do not converge to an unchanging equilibrium position determined solely by some initial fixed set of institutions, since the institutional framework is changing in the long run. By taking account of differences in rates of change of the underlying institutional framework and the economic variables, the role of institutions as slowly changing forces influencing short-run performance is clarified, and a more informative picture emerges of the underlying evolutionary processes of economic development. What is crucial in justifying this approach is that certain aspects of the institutional framework of the economy remain sufficiently stable for long enough to reveal their structural impact on the behaviour of the economic variables.

An earlier point is worth repeating: in the real world there are institutional changes occurring that are largely or totally independent of the performance of the economy. Nevertheless, we maintain that much is gained by first modelling economic development as the outcome of an interaction between institutions and performance and then introducing exogenous determinants of institutional change. When development is the result of an endogenous, evolutionary process, capitalism is not static, even in the absence of all exogenous change, but continues to evolve. The formulation of such endogenous processes provides a benchmark for a more realistic analysis that allows for exogenous disturbances as well as, rather than instead of, evolutionary endogenous forces. This can provide information about how economies respond to shocks and how these shocks are incorporated into the process itself. It also helps to explain why a given exogenous shock has different effects in different economies – because a different institutional structure can 'cope' differently. Since our object is to explain the causal processes underlying the alternating historical periods of high and low unemployment, eventually we must consider both sources of institutional change that alter AD conditions.

4 Evolutionary processes: some comparisons

Chapter 7 compares our evolutionary-Keynesian approach with some related theories of economic development. In this section we compare features of our interaction process with other non-neoclassical dynamic models in which change is also generated endogenously. Models of cumulative causation associated with Kaldor (1985) are notable examples. In these models of long-run growth, an interaction of purely economic variables generates a self-reinforcing process based on dynamic economies of scale (Verdoorn's law). Where we have stressed institutions interacting with economic variables, cumulative causation models are devoid of institutions. In addition, the feedback effects in Kaldor's model are always positive, hence over time the economic impact of change is cumulative. Although positive feedback effects in real world dynamic processes are recognized in our work, here they are given less formal emphasis than negative feedbacks. Our purpose is to explain alternating historical episodes of good and bad performance, rather than possible self-reinforcing developments within these episodes.

Kaldor's positive feedback mechanism and our interaction mechanism have a common characteristic. The long-run behaviour of the system cannot be determined by reference only to the given exogenous variables as in neoclassical growth theory; reference to the system's history is required. But even here there is a significant difference between our approach and Kaldor's with respect to the source of hysteresis or path dependence and therefore how it is conceptualized. By ignoring the institutional features of the system and assuming dynamic scale economies, the final outcome of Kaldor's system 'can be deduced without reference to the subsequent adjustment path' once the initial conditions are specified (Setterfield, 1995, p. 530). Within the interaction framework, the final outcome depends not only on the initial conditions but also upon the features of the historical adjustment path. In models of cumulative causation, the system '*select(s)* between otherwise predetermined final outcomes on the basis of initial conditions'. In our interaction framework, the system '*(creates its)* own set of possible final outcomes in the course of (its) evolution' (ibid., p. 530) through induced changes in institutions.

This distinction between systems that select one from a set of predetermined final outcomes and those that create their own final outcomes lies at the heart of the distinction between hysteretic and evolutionary systems adopted here. Like institutional economics, there are several schools that are commonly designated evolutionary economics. The most widely known is that associated with Schumpeter (1934, 1942) and his disciples (Dosi et al., 1988). Here the system is driven by new technologies embedded in investment, leading in the aggregate versions to long cycles. These are discussed in the next chapter. However, evolutionary mechanisms of change encompass more than endogenous processes driven by technology. In his discussion of evolutionary economics, Witt (1992, 1993) lists three conditions for a theory or system to qualify as evolutionary. First it must be a dynamic system. Second, the processes generated must be 'irreversible' in the sense that the system has no steady-state equilibrium. Kaldor's model of cumulative causation satisfies these two conditions, but it does not describe an evolutionary process. Instead it describes a history-dependent or hysteretic process. To be evolutionary (as well as hysteretic), a third condition must be met: 'novelty' and 'innovation' must be the source of endogenously generated change. 'In the domain of economics . . . novelty is the outcome of human creativity and of discovery of new possibilities for action. If the newly discovered possibility of acting is taken up, this action is called an innovation' (Witt, 1992, p. 406). In Witt's usage, structural change in the form of institutional change as well as changes in technology qualify as innovations, so that the interaction mechanism constitutes an evolutionary process, with changes in institutions as the source of endogenously generated change. By way of contrast, in Kaldor's model of

cumulative causation the endogenous source of change is dynamic economies of scale.[4]

Rosser (1995) defines evolutionary systems or processes similarly and
locates them within the broader field of complex dynamics. More specifically, dynamic systems are defined as complex if they are non-linear and can
be characterized as possessing at least one of the following features: discon-
tinuities in the structural variables over time; dependence upon initial conditions; or erratic fluctuation patterns. But most importantly the
non-linearity must arise endogenously from within the system and not as a
result of random shocks. The dynamics of our interaction model possess all
of these characteristics.

In its reliance on induced changes in economic structure the interaction
framework bears a close resemblance to the non-linear dynamic models of
Goodwin (1990). In these models economic performance induces change in
the structural parameters of the model, thereby radically altering the performance of the system. In our approach, performance induces radical change
that punctuates the institutional structure and radically alters performance.

5 Hysteretic processes with exogenous origins

The interaction of economic performance and institutions as a mechanism
of endogenously generated change brings out evolutionary processes very
clearly. This may often be the appropriate framework for modelling historical processes. However, even a cursory study of historical events reveals
that institutional change is frequently attributable to exogenous causes,
alone or in combination with endogenous forces. To emphasize this point,
it is useful to describe two types of sequences initiated by exogenous forces
which affect those institutions determining the state of AD and unemployment. Let this exogenous influence take the form of a 'once over' change,
for example in technology or in the distribution of power, that directly
alters these institutions. In this case a new episode is initiated solely by an
exogenous change, rather than induced by previous performance. Such
dynamic processes lead to outcomes dependent upon the history of the
system because the shock-induced change in institutions subsequently
affects performance (recall there exists no long-run steady-state equilibrium). This is an example of institutional hysteresis but not of an evolutionary process, as the 'first round' of institutional change is not generated
within the system. To be evolutionary as well as hysteretic, the process
requires that the once-over disturbance first affects performance, which
then affects institutions (and therefore future performance). Of course, sub-

---

[4] For similar reasons, models emphasizing 'network externalities' generate hysteretic but not
evolutionary processes.

sequent rounds of induced institutional change can make any hysteretic process into an evolutionary one; for example, a non-evolutionary institutional change alters performance, which then affects institutions.

At this point, a basic taxonomy of concepts and the manner in which they are related is useful. Each concept describes a dynamic process with specific relationships between the performance variables and the economic structure, whatever the structural feature. Our intention is to provide a useful reference point for this chapter and the balance of the book. To clarify the usefulness of the classification scheme and its essential points, we continue to concentrate on institutions and therefore outline only interactions between performance variables and institutions and how they are related. We begin with a distinction between ahysteretic and hysteretic processes or systems.

When the long-run performance of an economic system is independent of any prior adjustment path, the process or system is ahysteretic.

When the long-run performance of an economic system depends upon the path taken to reach it, the process or system will be referred to as hysteretic.

However, prior adjustment paths can be of two types, those that depict endogenous adjustments of the system, and those that depict exogenous events impinging on the system from the outside. Hysteretic outcomes can be the result of either or both types of events, so a further distinction is needed between evolutionary and non-evolutionary processes.

An evolutionary process is one in which the *immediate* source of institutional change is a response to the past performance of the system itself, and hence future performance depends upon past performance.

A non-evolutionary process is one in which the *immediate* source of institutional change is an external event.

Note that the distinction between an evolutionary and a non-evolutionary process is defined in terms of the immediate source of institutional change. Thus, if a shock affects performance which is the cause of structural change, that process is also evolutionary. Also note from the above definitions that: traditional neoclassical models as in chapters 2 and 3 are strictly ahysteretic and non-evolutionary; an evolutionary process must be hysteretic; and our processes are always hysteretic, but can involve both evolutionary and non-evolutionary change.

6 Three routes of institutional change

We have acknowledged that institutional change and economic development are often driven by a combination of exogenous and endogenous

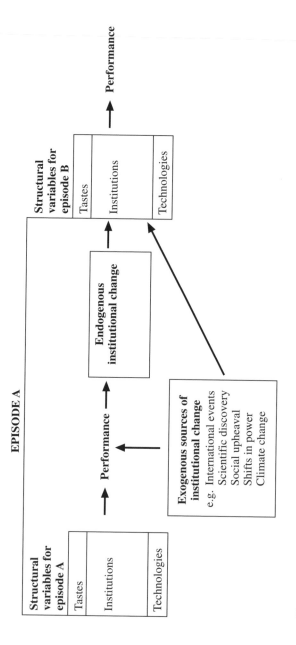

Figure 6.1 Three routes for institutional change

forces. When a process of institutional change is endogenously driven within the first round, it is evolutionary as well as hysteretic. Evolutionary-hysteretic sequences should be seen as complementary to hysteretic (but non-evolutionary) processes initiated by exogenously induced institutional change. A combination of these two processes forms the essential core of our framework for studying economic development since World War II. Its adequacy will be tested in chapters 9, 10 and 11. Here we use a diagram to summarize these ideas. For simplicity we assume the economy has only two goals, full employment and a politically acceptable rate of inflation.

Figure 6.1 illustrates the framework of economic development discussed in the previous sections. Episode A is the initial period, characterized by a set of structural variables represented by the left-hand box. In keeping with the emphasis in this study, these include institutions, collective tastes and technology. It is given that a specific Keynesian endogenous mechanism (not shown in the diagram) determines the *detailed* macroeconomic performance of episode A as described in chapter 4. It is represented by the left-most of the horizontal arrows.

However, it is the initial set of institutions that determines the *general* characteristics of macroeconomic performance of the period which is of interest in this version of our framework. It determines whether or not full employment levels of AD are consistent with acceptable rates of inflation. When they are consistent, strong AD pressures develop and low unemployment performance results in episode A. The alternative sequence of poor performance is easily formulated by the reader. The period of low or high unemployment will prevail as long as the relevant institutions prevail.

The three routes of institutional change are also shown. First, the performance in episode A can induce institutional change, a process represented by the horizontal arrows. Second, exogenous factors can affect performance in episode A, shown by the vertical arrow, and the changed performance induces institutional change. These are the two types of evolutionary process. In each case, economic performance induces institutional change, and this alters performance in episode B. Since our concern is to model alternative episodes of high and low unemployment, we necessarily concentrate attention on those performance-induced changes in institutions that result in a radical reversal of economic performance, i.e. those that generate negative feedback. For example, assume episode A is a period of full employment; negative feedback results when performance eventually induces changes in institutions which lead to an episode of poor macroeconomic performance. Moving further from left to right across the diagram, developments from one episode to the next are portrayed by the two middle horizontal arrows ending at the right-hand box. The right-hand box depicts the set of structural variables (which includes the new institutions) for episode B, and the beginning of a period of poor performance.

The third way in which institutional change occurs is as the direct result of exogenous events in episode A that move the system to episode B. This is indicated by the diagonal arrow running from the lower box to the institution segment of the right-hand box. This illustrates hysteresis but not evolutionary change. Although performance in episode B depends upon events in episode A, change is not generated by economic performance. However, the result in each of the three cases is to establish a new institutional framework, initiating a new episode.

It should be emphasized that figure 6.1 is concerned only with changes in institutions that, by affecting the state of AD, reverse performance. While structural change is a continual process, changes in the distribution of power, technology or institutions become relevant only if they lead to a reversal of AD conditions. In this chapter the analysis is confined to processes having institutional change as the catalyst that creates a new episode. Hence the horizontal and diagonal arrows end at the institution panel of the right-hand box. We do not preclude the possibility of positive feedback whatever the source. This may occur within an episode, but we restrict the analysis to negative feedback because we are modelling a historical record of alternating episodes of high and low unemployment.

7 Concepts

This discussion ignores some rather obvious practical problems involved in modelling historical processes. Chief among these is the need to establish which institutions matter in determining performance. Conceptually the short-run exogeneity and long-run endogeneity treatment of institutions is easily stated. As the short run or episode is defined, the evolutionary and hysteretic properties of the long-run model are temporarily suppressed in order to isolate the impact of a given institutional structure on macroeconomic performance. Obviously an institutional structure is composed of a large number of institutions, only some of which are relevant when considering macroeconomic performance and the changes in institutions that move the system to a new episode. Therefore we consider only those institutions that permit or preclude the continuous high levels of AD that are a necessary prerequisite of a full employment level of unemployment. In order to better appraise the internal structure of our analysis and the benefits it provides in explaining historical developments, the procedure for selecting the relevant institutions, i.e. those that ultimately determine unemployment performance, must be formulated.

We need spend little time discussing the obvious examples of laws or rules explicitly limiting stimulative AD policies, such as balanced budget rules or Maastricht criteria. More complex are those situations in which there are trade-offs between full employment and other macroeconomic goals, with the terms of the trade-off being set by the prevailing institutions. In these cases, the procedure to identify relevant institutions is as follows. First, a macroeconomic goal of special interest is specified, in our study full employment. Next, we determine other goals whose attainment may be jeopardized by strong AD pressures and full employment conditions, such as politically acceptable rates of inflation or external balance. Finally, we determine the institutions that allow or prevent the simultaneous achievement of these other goals. These are the relevant institutions.

The sections in chapter 5 relating differences in performance during the golden age to differences in certain institutions are again instructive. Differences in unemployment records depended upon whether or not institutions permitted the realization of other goals under full employment conditions. For ease of exposition, we assume that an inflation rate equal to or less than some maximum rate is the only goal that might be jeopardized by full employment, and that it is the adopted labour market strategy that alone allows or prevents the simultaneous achievement of acceptable rates of inflation. Under these assumptions the adopted strategy becomes the relevant institution in determining the inflation costs associated with the full employment rate of unemployment. As discussed in sections 11 and 12 of chapter 5, there were two broadly defined labour market strategies – a social bargain and a market power strategy. Following the argument of that chapter, economies in which labour adopts a social bargain strategy experience AD levels consistent with full employment because this institution restrains inflationary pressures at full employment. As long as a social bargain strategy prevails, low rates of unemployment and inflation are realized simultaneously. Superior macro performance is a manifestation of the presence of an institution (in this example a social bargain strategy) that allows full employment levels of AD. Since our efforts are directed towards explaining as well as demarcating unemployment episodes, we do not merely characterize episodes in terms of some average unemployment rate. We also describe such episodes in terms of the institutions whose presence permits or disallows the simultaneous realization of low unemployment *and* low rates of inflation. The low inflationary implications of the social bargain strategy fit in with full employment levels of AD.[5] In contrast, in economies where labour adopted a market power strategy, the inflationary implications of prevailing institutions are unacceptable and the full employment goal is abandoned.

---

[5] In Tinbergen's design of policy terms, the two goals of full employment and politically acceptable rates of inflation can be achieved simultaneously because there are two instruments available for achieving these goals, AD policies and a social bargain.

8 Intertemporal analysis

A maintained hypothesis in this study is that the institutional features that are relevant in explaining cross-country differences in unemployment and inflation rates are, when occurring as institutional change within an economy, those responsible for changes in macroeconomic performance over time. For example, a shift within an economy from a social bargain to a market power strategy or vice versa will initiate a new short-run episode. Consider the former shift. An institutional change of this particular kind is relevant, since it leads to an episode of high unemployment, as the authorities respond to the new inflationary tendencies by a reduction in AD.

In keeping with the earlier analysis, the institutional change within the economy could be induced by the performance of the economy or it could be the direct effect of an exogenous change. In either case the economy moves to a new episode characterized by new institutions that lead to a reversal of macroeconomic performance. Consider again a shift from a social bargain to a market power strategy induced by the performance of the economy. This describes an evolutionary process with negative feedback; the previous episode of superior performance is causally linked through induced institutional change and policy response to a succeeding episode of poor performance. There the system remains as long as the new labour market strategy prevails. To escape this high unemployment trap, the precondition is that institutions must change so as to allow full employment with acceptable inflation. Since institutional change is unpredictable, with regard not only to its timing but also to the type of change that occurs, it cannot reasonably be left to chance. Only a well-designed policy is likely to achieve the needed institutional change in a timely manner, and only when this is accomplished can stimulative AD policies be used to secure full employment. In this example the government must use policy to create the inducements for labour and capital to adopt a new social bargain strategy.

9 Application

9.1 Interpreting changes in performance

As is true of mainstream economics, the predictive power of our approach is limited. Nevertheless, we judge its limitations to be somewhat less severe, mitigated by the inclusion of institutions as crucial determinants of economic performance. As a start, we claim that this gives our approach the superior *ex post* explanatory powers and greater ability to identify the appropriate remedial measures in the event of malfunction. In explaining historical processes the central and difficult practical issue is how to interpret whether a marked change in performance is due to shocks, with no permanent effect on institutions, or to a change in institutions (whether exogenous or performance induced) and, if it is the latter, to identify the institutions that are involved. The question is which theoretical framework is the most likely to interpret events correctly, and we believe it is here that our approach, by emphasizing institutions, proves superior.

We take the position that alternating episodes of poor as well as superior macroeconomic performance are related to structural change and are normal outcomes of capitalist development. For example, periodically institutions may emerge that lead to unacceptably high rates of inflation at full employment and restrictive policy responses. In contrast, believers in capitalism's self-regulating properties argue that any search for causes of a significant deterioration in performance, such as a marked acceleration in inflation rates, should focus on outside disturbances, including policy errors, or on market imperfections.[6] If the problem is attributed to temporary disturbances, conditions will soon improve, if not automatically, then with the introduction of available conventional policies to counter the influence of disturbances. If attributed to market imperfections, on *a priori* grounds malfunction is the effect of institutional changes that have led to a further deviation of the system from the competitive model, for example the introduction of a minimum wage law.

The case in support of our approach as the more likely to interpret events correctly rests on its predisposition to study the institutional prerequisites for successful performance as well as for macro malfunction, in other words a continuous engagement in a research agenda relating economic performance to underlying institutional structures. When performance deteriorates in an economy, an inspection of institutions prevailing before the deterioration in performance, or in economies currently not experiencing the malfunction, is of immediate assistance. For example, when inflation rates accelerate in an economy previously experiencing low rates of inflation at full employment, an early diagnosis of the underlying causes may be possible by examining events in the labour market before and after the change in the inflation record. An absence of evidence of increased labour discontent in the form, say, of wildcat strikes, of rank-and-file challenges to union leadership and of excessive money wage demands would suggest that the acceleration of inflation rates was due to shocks, for example increased oil prices. If so, conventional policy measures to offset the impact of shocks

---

[6] As illustrated in chapter 7, a wide number of diverse studies of long-run economic development of capitalist economies have adopted the view that capitalism is not self-regulating. It is only in the more recent period that economists have chosen to model the dynamics of capitalism as a process dominated by convergence to the steady-state, full employment outcome.

would likely be sufficient to restore the previously favourable economic conditions.

On the other hand, a sharp increase in strike volume, in challenges to union leadership and accelerated money wage demands, followed by an acceleration in the rate of wage inflation, would be evidence of increased worker discontent and militancy, indicating a shift from a social bargain to a market power strategy (Soskice, 1978). Underlying the accelerating price inflation are changes in labour market institutions. However, accurate diagnosis requires information about institutions, and such an inventory of information is not likely to be available or to be considered of value to believers in self-regulating capitalism. In contrast to the mainstream equilibrium approach, we find much to gain from studying an economy's institutions and its history. An awareness of the role institutions play in determining performance reduces the likelihood both of failing to intervene to alter institutions when such policies are appropriate, and of intervening when no intervention is called for.

9.2 Institutional change and policy

This raises a related point and an additional gain from adopting an evolutionary-Keynesian approach. Not only is a continuous focus on institutions as underlying determinants of macroeconomic performance more likely to lead to an early and accurate analysis of the causes of malfunction, but, in those cases in which institutional change has been properly diagnosed as the underlying cause of malfunction, the necessary remedial polices are more immediately and clearly recognized. Assume that it is generally accepted by economists and policy makers that a significant institutional change is responsible for an acceleration in inflation rates. To those who perceive capitalism as subject to periodic malfunction, having diagnosed the cause of malfunction as a shift in labour market institutions from a social bargain to a market power strategy, the obvious remedial measure is to use policies to effect changes in institutions. The analysis of chapter 5 indicates that the reintroduction of a social bargain strategy, hardly a move towards more competitive conditions, improves performance.[7] In contrast, when malfunction is attributed on *a priori* grounds to some form of deviation from the competitive model, the policy measures that are advocated will be quite different, for example elimination of minimum wage laws, or a reduction in union powers.

Economists promoting the self-regulating view of capitalism have led the movement for institutional change toward more competitive markets, par-

---

[7] Assuming the goals of policy are still only full employment and low inflation.

ticularly toward more 'flexible' labour markets. They have profoundly influenced the political debate for almost three decades. An example is the programme of those who have attributed the malfunction since the mid-1970s to 'Eurosclerosis'. Unfortunately their programme for a return to full employment *and* acceptable inflation rates will be disturbance amplifying. Once in place it will intensify conflict as long as full employment conditions persist, eventually requiring the implementation of restrictive AD policies.

10 Conclusions

Among the assumptions underlying the analysis of part I, the most important is the view that capitalism is not self-regulating but is subject to lengthy episodes of malfunction, in particular high unemployment. The inability of neoclassical equilibrium analysis to provide a basis for understanding the unemployment issue has been a major reason for our rejection of this framework and for our effort to formulate an alternative. Basic to the development of our framework is a view that macroeconomic malfunction of the severity and persistence experienced since the mid-1970s can be understood only in terms of structural change, and then only when structural change is understood to include institutional change. The same case can be made for understanding the underlying forces leading to superior macroeconomic performance. More specifically, what we have outlined is a general framework, equally applicable to periods of good or poor performance. It distinguishes between and encompasses evolutionary and hysteretic approaches, both of which we believe are necessary to model historical processes accurately and to identify appropriate remedial programmes.

Part II is an application of the evolutionary-Keynesian framework, explaining episodes covering about a century of economic development in the developed capitalist economies. Before undertaking this task, other theories of economic development are summarized to provide a comparison with our evolutionary-Keynesian framework.

7 Theories of capitalist development

1 Introduction: the political economy tradition

The objective of this chapter is to provide the context for our proposed analytical method and its explanation of economic development in the twentieth century. To this end, we examine several well-known schools of thought that treat structural change as an integral feature of capitalist development. Abstracting from the detail, we focus on the broad characteristics that distinguish them from each other. Of greatest interest are the causes and mechanisms of change, and the extent to which each can explain periods of good and poor economic performance as a continuous process. These characteristics are then compared with those of our approach.

The central place of structural change, which typifies the development of capitalism, has a long and respectable pedigree within economics. For many early economists, structural change was capitalism's overwhelming characteristic, making capitalist development incomprehensible except in its historical context. This emphasis on structural change persists in several fields within economics, some of which are discussed later in this chapter. However, in the recent past economists have shifted their attention to those aspects of macroeconomic dynamics that are amenable to mathematical modelling. These models, which include both neoclassical and Keynesian formulations, describe the interactions of purely economic variables, and ignore structural change even while professing to model long-run outcomes. This has created a dichotomy between the currently conventional macrodynamics and those treatments of the subject that continue in the political economy tradition. The latter have, for the most part, developed independently of this trend toward formal modelling, and, while broader in scope, have too often been content to rely on rather loose generalizations. This dichotomy has raised a barrier to deeper understanding of long-run development processes in mature capitalist economies.

A common theme of the political economy tradition is that periods of economic malfunction are inherent to capitalist development. This is a fundamental difference from conventional macrodynamics, which either ignores malfunction completely or treats it as a temporary aberration, attributable to correctable market imperfections or to exogenous shocks. Arguably the most influential among these early writers was Marx, who envisaged a process driven by the central need of capitalism to amass capital. What is of interest here is not whether Marx correctly predicted the fate of capitalism, or even whether he provided a complete theory, but that he recognized within capitalism the inseparability of economic from structural (including institutional) change, influenced by endogenously generated periods of serious malfunction. These insights have inspired many other theories of long-run economic development, all of which stress structural change. Most envisage an evolving capitalist system dominated and transformed by radical changes in technologies; others highlight institutional change.

To gain a better understanding of the framework adopted in this study, particularly its treatment of structural change and the prominent role it assigns to institutions, some of the more influential of these theories are discussed briefly in the next sections. They fall into three groups. The first includes theories that focus on technology as the driving force behind economic development, with only a passing interest in institutions. Theories in the other two groups include institutional change as an integral part of the analysis. In the first of these, institutional change and economic performance are essentially responses to exogenous forces. These theories incorporate dynamic processes that are hysteretic but not evolutionary. In the third group of theories, technology plays an important but largely exogenous role, These theories stress evolutionary mechanisms of the type discussed in chapter 6.

2 The long cycle school

The first group of theories includes various versions of long cycle theory. The very existence of long cycles is controversial, but the methodology used by its proponents is of interest. Their objective is to explain what they see as fairly regular long-run swings in economic activity with special emphasis on rates of growth of GDP.[1] The driving force underlying these swings is the pattern of investment initiated by technological change, which is treated as exogenous. This work is most directly related to the ideas of Kondratiev (1925), who originally proposed cycles of some 50 or 60 years, generated by investment in long-lived capital, primarily infrastructure. This claimed regularity led Kondratiev to reject random causes and to express

---

[1] Much of the evidence used to support the long cycle hypothesis in periods before the twentieth century is very weak, utilizing price and not output data.

the opinion that 'long waves arise from causes which are inherent in the essence of the capitalistic economy' (*ibid.*, p. 115). Also in the early part of the twentieth century, van Gelderen (1913) proposed cycles of similar periodicity, driven by the establishment of new technologies, for example the introduction of electricity, or by opening up new territories, either of which would initiate a surge in investment.

Kondratiev outlines the development of a long cycle as beginning with an investment boom of substantial duration as productive capacity is increased and new technologies brought into commercial use. The process slows as demand for inputs pushes up prices and interest rates, reducing profitability, and contraction eventually follows. During the downswing, interest rates and input prices fall, and the search for new production techniques intensifies as firms seek to cut costs. These trends are claimed to lead inevitably to the next upswing as the newly discovered techniques are put into use.

The notion that waves in economic activity are an inherent feature of capitalist development was developed more fully by Schumpeter (1939). Earlier he had identified the innovative activities of the entrepreneur as the engine of development (Schumpeter, 1912, trans. 1934). This idea was now applied to cycles of various lengths, including the Kondratiev long wave. In each case, the wave was caused by a cluster of innovations, followed by imitation, which created a surge in investment. The cyclical movements were intrinsic to capitalist development, with innovating entrepreneurs the impelling force, supposedly giving rise 'to a purely economic theory of economic change which does not merely rely on external factors propelling the economic system from one equilibrium to another'.[2] Although this description may fit the shorter cycles, the innovation clusters of the long waves were clearly linked to radical shifts in technology, with the building of the railways initiating a long wave in the mid-1800s, and chemicals, electricity and the motor car triggering another at the end of the nineteenth century (Schumpeter, 1935). A Schumpeterian cycle eventually came to an end for reasons similar to those advanced by other long cycle theorists. However, the ensuing recession was interpreted as a benefit to the development process. Put simply, the exhaustion of profitable opportunities was the natural consequence of the cycle itself and, far from qualifying as a crisis, recession heralded the onset of the 'creative destruction' essential to capitalist development. The forces reversing the downswing were not well developed; and thus the timing of the next bunching of innovations was poorly explained.

More recent formulations of long cycle theory include a Marxian version

[2] Quoted in Cheng and Dinopoulos (1992) from the preface to the Japanese edition of *Business Cycles*.

by Mandel (1964, 1980) which identifies changing profitability as the driving force. Rostow and Kennedy (1979) and Rostow (1978, ch. 2) reinterpret the Kondratiev cycle theory in terms of changing relative prices of basic goods (raw materials and foodstuffs) and industrial (manufactured) goods, arguing that changes in these relative prices, rather than in the price level, reflect underlying economic conditions. These changes stem from the long lags associated with the large investments needed in basic goods industries compared with the short lags in manufacturing. The upper turning point occurs when large investments are complete in the basic goods industry and supply overshoots demand. The lower turning point occurs when a secular increase in demand causes relative prices to shift once more, and a new wave of investment occurs. Van Duijn (1983) proposes a version with three components: innovation, innovation life cycles and infrastructural investment. The first two are the long wave engines on the output side of growth, the third reinforces the upswing. Responding to these over the cycle are dependent variables, including the money supply and the functional distribution of income. The upper turning point is attributed to volatile investment due to changed expectations, for whatever reason, although anticipated overinvestment and market saturation are probable causes. Like Rostow, van Duijn also assumes secular demand growth, and the lower turning point arrives when demand eliminates excess capacity.[3] Freeman (1983) proposes that there is a swarm of new product innovations in the early upswing, followed by process innovations as a new technology system is established; the boom ends when supply outgrows demand.

In these theories good times alternate with bad, the initial expansionary phase of the cycle coming to a close as overexpansion of capacity, market saturation and reduced profitability lead to the downturn. Although each proposes an endogenous process of decay, there is no agreement about how the upturn originates, and none provides a convincing explanation. In spite of claims of its endogenous generation, early explanations of the upturn relied upon the ad hoc introduction of exogenous events, whether scientific discovery or discovery of new territories, which are met with a burst of entrepreneurial activity.[4] More recent versions simply assume there is an underlying steady growth in demand that eventually eliminates oversupply.

---

[3] Solomou (1987) argues that these cycles can be explained by the timing of wars over the period.

[4] For example, there is no satisfactory explanation of why entrepreneurs should embark upon investment projects in the midst of a slump. Mensch (1979) claimed that depressions make entrepreneurs more adventurous, out of desperation. Freeman (1983) argued that Mensch was wrong in fact, there being no evidence of innovation clusters during depressions. Further, given that there is always an inventory of unexploited scientific knowledge available, there is no explanation of why canny entrepreneurs wait for a recession in order to use it.

In each case, this marks the beginning of a new long phase of growth, which ends with the next downturn as the pattern inevitably repeats itself. The reliance on exogenous events seriously weakens the claimed regularity of the cycles, and reduces them to a series of disjointed phases. This lack of connection between cycles is the greatest obstacle to any claim that these are coherent theories of capitalist development.

Although our concern is with historical phases of development, that is, the observed episodes of good and poor performance, the explanation we offer differs from long cycle theory in several respects. First, ours is not a theory of cycles. There is no *a priori* reason to claim that an episode will be of any particular length. Nor can it be said that a sequence of two such episodes of good followed by poor performance is nothing more than a long cycle. The negative feedback that links episodes explains both the shift from poor to good performance, as well as the reverse, so that to identify either as the first in a sequence is entirely arbitrary. Second, the shift from good to poor performance in long cycle theory is a simple exhaustion of the current boom; in our approach the shift is the result of structural change, as is the reverse shift. Third, the engine of change need not be constant from one episode to the next; each episode has its own unique combination of forces effecting change. In tracing the linkages between episodes to structural change, we include technological change, but open up other components of structure, institutions in particular, as potential causes of changed performance. Institutions are given no place in long cycle theory.[5] It is precisely this expansion of structure beyond merely technology that permits us to explain both upturns and downturns, by providing the linkages between episodes of good and poor performance that long cycle theory fails to provide.

Although long cycle explanations of the downturn ultimately rest on the notion that supply eventually outstrips demand, this deviation from Say's law does not lead to anything more than a passive role for demand, which at most displays a secular trend. These remain fundamentally supply-side theories. Indeed, more recent formulations have stressed that stimulative aggregate demand policies cannot, by reducing macro risk and improving profit conditions, initiate an upturn; this depends solely upon such exogenous phenomena as an accumulation of inventions. Van Duijn (1983) argues further that such policies would crowd out private sector investment, delaying the upturn. This argument is consistent with the inevitability of the cycles implied throughout long cycle literature. This treatment of aggregate demand is a point of direct contrast to our approach, which introduces

---

[5] Schumpeter deliberately excluded any consideration of institutions in his business cycle theory, but he clearly recognized their importance elsewhere, see e.g. Schumpeter (1942).

a dynamic Keynesian aggregate demand mechanism as the primary generator of change in advanced capitalist economies.

One last point of comparison with our approach is noted here. Long cycle theory gives a central role to exogenous events in securing cyclical upturns; not only do exogenous events perform this function with remarkable regularity, but they have apparently no significant effect within the 50- or 60-year duration of the cycle. We include two routes for exogenously initiated change, one having a direct effect on institutions, the other an indirect effect by first altering performance, which then induces institutional change. Either of these can occur at any time and will influence the duration of an episode.

3 Theories with variable institutional structures

This section considers models that include institutions as part of the changing structure that typifies capitalist development. While the processes of change they propose exhibit path dependence, they are not evolutionary. Evolutionary theories are left for the next section.

3.1 'Old' institutional economics[6]

One of the most forceful critics of mainstream analysis in the early part of the twentieth century, Thorstein Veblen, inspired what came to be called 'American Institutional Economics'. Veblen viewed institutional change not as merely accompanying capitalist development but as an integral part of that development (Veblen, 1899, 1919). Consequently institutions could not be ignored, nor could the institutional framework be treated as a static 'given'. As part of capitalist development, institutional change must be incorporated into economic analysis. For Veblen, as for his contemporaries in other disciplines, a point of overwhelming significance was that the rise of industrial capitalism wrought sweeping changes in all spheres of life, not simply in economic matters. In fact, Veblen's view was that economic activity was firmly embedded in broadly defined social activity, and could be understood only in that context. In particular, he believed the essence of modern capitalism to lie in its continuously changing structure, rather than in the quantitative growth that is the subject of mainstream growth models.

The initiator of change is advancing technology, which changes economic performance, but not by simply accelerating growth. It alters the way

---

[6] This term is used to distinguish institutional economics within the political economy tradition from 'new' institutional economics, which pursues a neoclassical methodology in which institutions are spontaneously formed and reformed as outcomes of individual optimization behaviour.

production is organized, leading to the rise of big business and eventually of big labour unions. The rise of big business redistributes both income and power, causing economic instability and political conflict as the power of vested interests is undermined. Institutional change is forged from this conflict, as different habits and values are established. The resolution of conflict depended upon the institutions that formed. Veblen believed that the new institutions needed to overcome conflict and allow the full benefits of technology to be realized were unlikely to emerge. Instead, the growing political power of big business would ultimately ensure the state's protection for its interests; acquisitive capitalist values would prevail over social values, preventing the full realization of the benefits of technology. Veblen predicted that capitalism, in failing to mediate conflict, would be sustained by military dictatorship.

The work of J.R. Commons was similar to Veblen's in its proposal that economic and political institutions influenced each other's development (see, for example, Commons, 1950). Like Veblen, Commons emphasized the role of the state but, where Veblen saw it as the tool of the wealthy and powerful, Commons viewed it as the agent of collective action, with the tasks of resolving conflict between capital and labour and promoting economic progress. He was rather more optimistic than Veblen in his assessment of future developments, believing that political solutions would be found that would replace class conflict with class collaboration. Although profoundly influenced by Veblen, Clarence Ayres was far from pessimistic and put even more faith than Commons in the ability of the state to resolve conflict (see, for example, Ayres, 1962). Ayres advocated economic planning by a democratic state to ensure that social decision-making would replace private decision-making. This would allow greater exploitation of the advances of science and technology than was possible under private enterprise.

In the work of Veblen, Commons and Ayres we find the theme that technological change causes conflict, that this conflict causes change to political institutions and that political institutions influence the way the economy works. Depending upon the writer, the exact outcome differs, because the political institutions that emerge are different; but in each case these institutions determine the extent to which advancing technology can be exploited for the material benefit of society. Although Veblen claims this to be an evolutionary process with neither trend nor end point, there seems to be a very definite end point, whether we are looking at the planned economy of Ayres or Veblen's military dictatorship. In each case capitalism has been replaced by a new economic system imposed by the new political institutions. In contrast, our analysis deals only with recognizably capitalist systems. Furthermore, we would regard these processes of institutional change as hysteretic, but not evolutionary. They are described by Veblen as arising directly from the conflict between new technology (always assumed to be exogenous) and existing institutions, which act to delay or block its application. The nearest thing in our analysis is the case of institutional change directly caused by exogenous forces, which would include exogenous technological change.[7] In order to qualify as evolutionary in our framework, the effect of an exogenous technological change must be to alter economic performance; the changed performance would then induce institutional change, and this would lead to a new episode. This has no counterpart in American institutional economics. Instead, existing institutions act to resist the adoption of the new technology, so that this route is ruled out as a possibility.

3.2 The régulation school

The harmony of interests envisioned by Adam Smith yields benefits as a by-product of individual self-interest; no effort is needed because no conflict exists, market and political power being absent from the analysis. To the contrary, the achievement of harmony in the American institutionalist writings is possible only if the appropriate institutions can be established. This is a difficult process with an uncertain outcome, a struggle for progress against the inertia of vested interests, and for social values against capitalist ones. The notion that the 'wrong' political and social institutions impede economic progress, and that the right ones must be found to allow economic progress to proceed smoothly and yield its benefits to society, is to some extent echoed in the ideas proposed by the Régulation School (e.g. Aglietta, 1979; Boyer, 1988a).

Régulation theory combines Marxian with Kaleckian or Keynesian macroeconomics to form the basis for an institutionalist analysis of capitalist transformation in the twentieth century. As a result, demand is an important component, particularly as it affects the balance between consumption and investment spending. Periods of severe malfunction lack this balance. Like the long cycle theorists, régulation theorists emphasize technological change but, true to their Marxian roots, their main concern is with how it alters the way production and investment are carried out. They view capitalism as a series of episodes, each with a different technological base which determines the internal organization of firms, including the

---

[7] This is to be distinguished from endogenous technological change, induced by the performance of the economy. This affects future performance, making it evolutionary; it is the mechanism that resulted in the depression of the 1930s. In general, induced technological change provided the evolutionary engine prior to World War II, a role assumed by institutions since that time.

organization of work itself.[8] To realize the potential of this technical base, there must be a compatible institutional superstructure. If the technology changes, a new institutional superstructure is needed. Whenever there is a mismatch between the technology and the institutional superstructure, crisis follows, and persists until appropriate institutions are established. These are economic crises, identified as periods of stagnation and/or large instabilities (Boyer, 1988a), not the social crises of Marxian economics, and social (i.e. institutional) reform occurs within capitalism rather than leading to revolution. For example, assembly-line mass production needs institutions that enable mass consumption. These were not developed in the early part of the twentieth century, leading to the Great Depression. By the end of World War II they were established, allowing the rapid growth and increasing prosperity of the golden age.

The régulation school's account of the Great Depression bears a resemblance to ours, as does their view that the golden age depended on the institutions that arose after World War II, such as the labour–capital accord and the Bretton Woods Agreement. There are some clear differences, however. Like us, régulation theorists stress the importance of institutions. They trace out an endogenous process of breakdown as a cumulative process in which technology changes but institutions fail to change, creating a mismatch that eventually reaches a critical point; instability, crisis and poor economic performance follow. In broad outline this agrees with our account of the Great Depression (in chapter 8) as being the result of induced technological change. But their story of decay cannot be used to explain the advent of the golden age. Resolution of the crisis 'depends on innovations, social and political struggles, trials and errors, and chance' (Boyer, 1988b, p. 628), none of which we would disagree with as possible initiating causes of structural change, but this explanation fails to make a connection between one episode and the next. What is missing, and what we have proposed, is a theory of endogenous institutional change that provides a clear link between episodes.[9]

This difference is clearer in the régulation view of the advent of the current episode of decline, which again emphasizes technology, this time the exhaustion of economies of scale, causing slowing growth and declining profits. Increased globalization allowed firms to resist wage claims by

---

[8] We note that the régulation 'episode' is defined by the prevailing technology, and refers to a sequence of good followed by poor economic performance. Because we define episodes according to whether performance is good or poor, we would regard the régulation sequence as two episodes.

[9] Perez (1983) has provided a synthesis of long cycle and régulation theories, which Tylecote (1992) has further developed. The direction of this work has been to analyse in greater depth the causes and types of crises; neither author provides a clear advance in explaining the formation of new institutions that resolve the crisis.

threatening to export capital, weakening the unions and undermining the labour–capital accord. This eroded the stability of the system established after World War II, when the welfare state and increased union power increased labour's share of income; this provided the essential balance between wage income and profits, and therefore between consumption and investment. In contrast, we stress induced institutional change as the most significant cause of poor performance in the post-World War II era; that is, institutional change is a potential cause of problems, not simply a cure for them. In the régulation theory, institutional rigidity in times of technologically driven change is the cause of crisis, and institutional change is its remedy. There is no mechanism generating institutional change, and however they arise the new institutions are as rigid as those they replace. This separation of institutions and economic events is replaced in our approach by an interaction in which institutions influence performance, and in the longer term this performance induces institutional change in an evolutionary process.

3.3 The social structure of accumulation theory

The social structure of accumulation (SSA) theory can be regarded as an American parallel to régulation theory, although with some differences (Gordon, 1978, 1980; Bowles and Edwards, 1985). Each displays a Marxian heritage in the emphasis on conflict and power relations between different classes of economic actors, and each stresses the importance of the institutional framework in resolving capitalism's inherent conflicts. In practice this requires a set of institutions, the SSA, that ensures that rates of profit and expected profits are sufficiently high to encourage continued investment and productive activity by firms. As long as this situation prevails, the economy booms; if it is interrupted, crisis follows. SSA theory stresses institutional collapse as a source of crisis, and cites four routes for collapse. First, it may be spontaneous, engendered by contradictions internal to the institutional structure. This is the SSA explanation of the collapse of the US post-war labour–capital accord in the 1960s (Bowles et al., 1990). Second, institutions may be undermined by economic performance, in the form of accumulation of capital; thus the collapse of Bretton Woods is attributed to US capital's loss of international dominance as the European and Japanese economies rebounded in the golden age. Third, a slowdown in capital accumulation can cut off funds needed to support institutions, and crisis intensifies when they collapse. Finally, institutions can become an obstacle to capital accumulation, for example as technical change makes it possible for a few workers to disrupt production.

SSA theory differs from régulation theory in its recognition that crisis is not caused solely by institutional rigidity in the face of technological change, although this can be a cause. Instead, the emphasis is placed on institutional collapse for one or more of the four reasons listed above. To compare these ideas with our own, we first note that institutional collapse is usually the same thing as institutional change. Since institutions determine the way things are done, the collapse of an institution is no more or less than the abandonment of one way of behaving as another replaces it – for example, Bretton Woods was replaced by a different exchange rate system; there cannot be a void unless the activity itself is abandoned. Next, where we have emphasized the process of institutional change, which we classify as being evolutionary or hysteretic, the SSA theorists concentrate on the causes of change. Consequently, of the four causes of institutional change they identify, the second and third could result in induced institutional change, and therefore could be part of an endogenous evolutionary process; however, they might instead be exogenous, caused by events external to the economy under study. In the case of 'spontaneous collapse' we would look for the causes of the internal contradictions, with special attention to any shifts in economic or political power between labour and capital. In our analysis, the example given for the fourth cause would amount to a shift in power to labour, and the focus would be on the institutions that led labour to exercise its power in this way.

Where régulation theory is concerned with a match between the institutional superstructure and a particular technical base such as mass production, SSA theory views institutions rather more broadly, as a general support system for economic activity not linked to any specific technical paradigm. Consequently, and unlike régulation theory, institutions are not simply rendered redundant in the face of changing technology; they collapse for a variety of reasons, including the effects of economic performance. Collapse always leads to crisis, which may be either political or economic, and if economic it may be either a demand-side or a supply-side crisis. For example, the SSA reading of the Great Depression in the United States is that it was a demand-side economic crisis, caused by progressive shifting of income from labour to profits resulting in a shortfall of consumer demand. There is little explanation of why such a shift occurred (and no reliable data to show that it did), and our analysis of the Great Depression in chapter 8 refutes this, locating the initial spending drop in investment, not in consumer spending.

As with régulation theory, SSA theory envisages a period of continuing crisis during which 'institutional restructuring' and political realignments take place. The most important outcome of this process is the new balance of power between capital and labour, for this will determine whether the resulting distribution of income between profits and wages will yield the division of spending between investment and consumption that is needed to support a new epoch of economic growth. There is, however, no clear process of institutional formation that will perform this function, only the declaration that, for example, the post-World War II SSA emerged from 'the interaction of choice and compulsion, conflict and struggle, attack and counterresponse' (Bowles et al., 1990, p. 25). In most readings, both régulation and SSA theories require an entirely new set of institutions before the upswing can proceed, although Kotz (1987, 1990) has proposed that only certain 'core institutions' are needed, as long as they are compatible with old institutions that have survived the collapse.

Finally, both régulation and SSA theories emphasize the effect of institutional change (whether called redundancy or collapse) on economic performance. The idea that economic performance might cause institutions to change is missing from régulation theory; even in SSA theory, which includes the possibility that economic performance might cause institutional collapse, the idea is not developed. Further, it is applied only to collapse and the onset of a period of poor performance; there is no suggestion that economic performance can induce institutional change that would result in an upswing. The period of crisis following institutional collapse is marked by poor economic performance and 'conflict and struggle'. There is no link developed between performance and conflict, and it is the latter that eventually leads to the needed institutional innovation. Neither is there any direct link between poor performance and the new institutions, making it clear that both régulation and SSA theories rely upon exogenous events to bring about the change needed to begin the next upswing. This remains a clear distinction between these theories and our approach, and is the reason neither can be classified as an evolutionary theory.

4 Evolutionary models: 'mature' Schumpeter

Theories of variable institutional structures, rather than assume institutions exogenous, have in effect simply introduced an alternative exogenous force, technology, to 'explain' institutional change and performance. The common assumption of the American institutionalists and of the régulation and SSA theories is that institutional adaptation is needed to ensure that, as technology advances, its benefits can be fully exploited. Although the process of institutional change varies among them, none of the examples cited incorporates evolutionary processes as usually defined. Instead, like mainstream analysis, these explanations break up the historical flow of events. Each describes a process set in motion by an exogenous event, which induces change in economic performance and requires changed institutions, but there is no mechanism by which changed performance induces the needed change; that is, it is not generated within the system.

The key idea of evolutionary theories is that macroeconomic development must be modelled as transformation resulting from endogenously generated change (Witt, 1993). In such models, economic performance induces changes in the economic (and social) structure, and the new structure influences the path of future performance, generating a long-run interaction between them. There are elements of this type of theory in the later work of Schumpeter. In this work, economic development is modelled to a large degree as an evolutionary-hysteretic process arising from the interaction of economic variables and the structure of the economy. However, there remain some essential differences between his approach and ours.

Like Marx, Schumpeter used the term 'evolution' to describe the process of change in a rather loose sense, meaning development as distinct from 'mere growth' (i.e. simple quantitative expansion).[10] Schumpeter held that the motive of the entrepreneur was to achieve growth in the discounted present value of the firm, and that continual innovation was the sole source of that growth. In short, change must arise out of the operation of capitalism itself, and was therefore entirely endogenous, not an adaptation to exogenous forces. He recognized that exogenous forces and 'mere growth' also caused change, as well as interacting with the drive to innovate. However, the historical and irreversible changes caused by innovation, he argues, 'arise out of the behavior of the business communities as such, and would be observable even if the institutional and natural framework of society remained absolutely invariable' (Schumpeter, 1944, p. 3). This is an account of evolutionary *economic* change, endogenously driven by the spontaneous innovational activities of entrepreneurs.

In Schumpeter's business cycle theory (1939, for example), capitalism evolved as innovating entrepreneurs used new technologies and produced new goods. These activities generated long cycles in output and investment. Schumpeter recognized that economic activity could induce change in the institutional structure of the economy, but treated it as a one-way process; the economy induced institutional change, but without feedback from these new institutions to economic performance. This allowed him to ignore institutional change in his earlier works, which modelled capitalism's success. In *Capitalism, Socialism and Democracy* (1942), Schumpeter moves from the purely economic case of evolutionary change to consider the long-run interaction between macroeconomic performance and institutions. The very process of growth and accumulation and rising living stan-

---

[10] He rejected the Darwinian and Lamarckian biological analogues, but admitted that competition was very likely a selection process.

dards sows the seeds of capitalism's downfall by inducing institutional change. More exactly, rising incomes and technological maturity lead to increased worker discontent, to the atrophy of entrepreneurship and eventually to socialism. Schumpeter concluded that in some historical long run a period of successful economic performance of capitalism induces institutional changes which eventually lead to a negative feedback in the form of capitalism's end.

This process of endogenous change is entirely consistent with our approach. However, Schumpeter's heavy reliance on the behaviour of the entrepreneur as the endogenous initiator of change stems from the Marshallian roots of his work and its implied full employment tendencies. It recognizes only changes on the supply side of the economy. We have emphasized demand conditions, which provide the environment, conducive or not, for entrepreneurial activity, and which influence and are influenced by the economic and political power relationships of capital and labour. The inclusion of AD conditions broadens the avenues for institutional and other structural change. Also contrasting with our approach is Schumpeter's view that institutional change would lead to the end of capitalism. Although Schumpeter recognized that economic activity could induce institutional change, this was not included in his economic writings, which provided purely economic explanations of swings in economic activity. It was only in *Capitalism, Socialism and Democracy* that the feedback from institutional change to economic performance was considered, and then its sole effect was to cause the end of capitalism as Schumpeter defined it. This is a clear contrast with our view of institutional change with feedbacks (i.e. the interaction process) as the normal behaviour of capitalism.

5 Concluding remarks

The purpose of this chapter has been to provide context for our approach to analysing capitalist development. We have chosen three types of theory, each of which bears some relationship to this approach, although none includes all its elements. We began with long cycle theory, partly because of its familiarity but also because it provides a fairly straightforward statement of the idea that capitalism experiences prolonged swings between good and poor performance. However, of the three categories of theory discussed here, it is the least like our approach. The main differences lie in the exclusive reliance on technology as the determinant of performance and the absence of an explanation of the causes of a new upswing.

The second group of theories demonstrates ways of treating institutions in macroeconomic analysis. With technological advance viewed as a benign force for progress, the American institutionalists examined how institutions responded (or failed to respond) to changing technology, allowing its benefits to be realized. Commons and Ayres considered ways that institutions might be formed that would serve this function. Also in this group, the régulation and the SSA schools pay close attention to the role of institutions as providers of an environment conducive to good economic performance; poor performance results when institutions are not appropriate to the existing technology, or when institutions collapse. Our approach also stresses the importance of institutions to the ability of the economy to perform well, as well as seeing institutional change as a source of economic decline. But, in spite of the many parallels with the régulation and SSA schools, we still find significant differences, primarily in our view that institutions are not only determinants of performance; they can also be changed by performance, generating endogenous linkages between episodes of good and poor performance.

It is this idea of institutional change induced by economic performance, envisaged in our approach as a longer-run phenomenon, that brings us close to Schumpeter's views expressed in *Capitalism, Socialism and Democracy*. Although Schumpeter saw these induced changes bringing the end of capitalism as he defined it, and deliberately omitted all but technical change from his other works which dealt with periods within capitalism, the process and the outcome of institutional change have characteristics that can be found in our analysis.[11] However, we develop these ideas further, to provide a clear description of economic performance inducing institutional change, and to include change that does not necessarily cause poor economic performance. Together with the view that institutions influence performance, and working within a shorter time frame, this yields the interaction of performance and institutions that we have proposed in chapter 6 as an evolutionary process that allows capitalism to transform itself. Also outlined in chapter 6 is a causal chain mechanism in which exogenous forces induce changes in institutions and, as a result, in performance. These two complementary hysteretic mechanisms constitute the core of our method of modelling capitalist development.

---

[11] One clear difference between our work and Schumpeter's is the stress he places on the entrepreneur. Because our objective is to explore the role of institutions rather than technology, we have not developed our analysis along these lines. The place of the entrepreneur is implied in our analysis of the effect of institutions on aggregate demand, which determines the economic conditions under which entrepreneurial decisions are made.

Part II
Explaining the development record

Modelling the historical record

The task of part II is to explain economic developments in the advanced capitalist economies during the twentieth century to illustrate the explanatory power of the evolutionary-Keynesian framework outlined in part I. This long-run period covers four distinct episodes: developments from the end of the nineteenth century to the 1930s, the 1930s, the golden age of capitalism beginning soon after World War II and lasting until the 1970s, and the period from the 1970s until the present. The end of each episode is defined by a radical change in performance as a new episode begins, tracing out a sequence of alternating episodes of good and poor performance.[1]

Our explanation of capitalist development centres on the structural changes that provide linkages between consecutive historical episodes. When outlining our framework in chapter 6, we stated that changes in institutions provide the key links between episodes in the post-World War II era, whereas technology change served this function prior to World War II. However, to identify a change in one structural feature as the linkage leading to a new episode does not exclude a role for others; whether or not these also change, they can reinforce or prolong the new type of performance. For example, it will be argued in chapter 8 that the structural change linking the episode prior to the 1930s with the Great Depression was technology. But the failure of institutions to adapt to the developments in technology also contributed to the depth and persistence of the depression. In chapter 9 the establishment of the golden age is attributed to institutional change. An important result of this change was to facilitate the adoption and spread of new technologies, which reinforced the successful economic performance of the episode and confirmed the benefits conferred by the new institutions; both effects contributed to the episode's continuation. In describing our framework we temporarily neglect these complications and

---

[1] Unless noted otherwise, the sample includes all the countries listed in table 2.1 of chapter 2.

focus on only one type of structural change as the primary linkage between episodes.

Whatever the linkages, when structural change is induced by the performance of the economy, the observed record of alternating episodes of high and low unemployment and slow and rapid growth is modelled as evolutionary processes with negative feedback. Performance-induced structural changes in one historical episode generate radically altered performance in the next. As further noted in chapter 6, it cannot be expected that significant changes in economic structures are always completely and clearly linked to economic events. Exogenous changes in (collective) tastes, technologies and institutions can cause large shifts in performance, and must also be considered as possible linkages between episodes; these may take the form of shocks such as wars, or exogenous trends such as the extension of the franchise. When performance is altered by structural change that has been directly caused by exogenous forces, hysteretic but not evolutionary processes are at work. Episodes of superior and poor performance have structural explanations whatever the structural change involved, and whether or not the change is endogenous or exogenous. Finally it must be repeated that we do not offer a long cycle explanation of events, because the historical record does not indicate any regularity in the alternating episodes. The duration of the episodes varies (from a period of about one decade to others lasting several decades), as do the causes bringing an episode to an end.

In the next four chapters we provide evidence that over the past century episodes of superior as well as poor performance are endogenous to capitalist development and support our perception that capitalism is not self-regulating. The record does not suggest that in the absence of shocks or market imperfections capitalist systems would have followed a full employment growth path. Episodes of poor performance have been too long and too severe to be explained solely by exogenous shocks. And, as already shown in chapter 5, attributing episodes of poor performance to institutions that cause deviations from the competitive norm does not withstand the test of historical evidence. From our analysis of the record we conclude that the quality of macroeconomic performance is ultimately governed by the structural features of the time. The form of these structures in any episode is largely unpredictable and, as experience shows, often undesirable. In the chapters of part II, changes in performance from one episode to the next will be explained in these terms.

The role of institutions

Institutions were key components of the framework developed in part I, and they continue to be so in part II. Like tastes and technologies, they are structural determinants of economic outcomes. Modelling capitalist development requires the inclusion of institutions as well as tastes and technologies as part of the economic structure because institutions affect performance by acting as constraints. Indeed, as described in chapters 5 and 6, short-run episodes of good or poor unemployment performance reflect the presence or absence of certain institutions. These permit or hinder the simultaneous achievement of multiple macroeconomic goals.

Obviously not all institutions are relevant in influencing performance. In this regard, to determine which institutions matter we benefited by having in our study an episode that was relatively free of exogenous shocks that might obscure the results. In chapter 5 this allowed us to compare our views with other studies of institutional differences during the golden age to determine which institutions had an important influence in restraining inflation under full employment conditions. Even in this period of generally good economic performance there was sufficient variation to show how institutions account for differences in performance among the countries in the sample. These results provide valuable clues about the likely effects of institutional change within an individual country, permitting analysis of the causes of changed performance and helping to establish the linkages between successive episodes.

The choice of techniques

What will be apparent to the reader is our reliance on several techniques to advance our arguments. For example, in explaining how the Great Depression in the United States evolved out of a lengthy period of industrialization beginning in the late nineteenth century, there is no attempt to use standard econometric techniques. Much of the interest of economists and economic historians in the 1930s is in determining the causes that initiated and sustained the downturn. Quarterly data, essential to separate the leads and lags in the process, are not available even for the United States. However, by making use of annual data it is possible to give a plausible explanation of events, when combined with a non-linear model of the business cycle as an organizing device, which we have done in chapter 8. This does not lead to a formal model with mathematical equations, but provides an exposition in which the central ideas of this class of dynamic models are implicit in the narrative.

Somewhat different techniques are used to tie together events of the 1930s and 1940s with the golden age beginning in the 1950s. The difficulty in modelling these linkages arises from variation in the development patterns of these economies in the years leading up to the golden age. The severe depression experienced in the developed economies in the 1930s was widespread, but the response to this event varied considerably. Some responded to the mass unemployment of the 1930s by adopting right-wing totalitarian forms of government with radical economic and political programmes; in others, efforts were made to preserve democracy. In addition, the amount of devastation caused by World War II varied widely among countries, with some sustaining very heavy damage and others, such as the United States, experiencing virtually none. In spite of their divergent inter-war histories, after World War II and a short period of reconversion and recovery, there followed a quarter of a century during which the advanced capitalist economies experienced similar development paths. To determine the links between the 1930s and 1940s and the golden age, chapter 9 has relied on events and data pertaining mainly to the larger economies. The objective is to explain the reasons for the remarkable reversal of fortunes that culminated in the golden age of capitalism.

The similarity in development patterns, together with the development of a macro data set covering a wide number of countries, allowed the use of conventional statistical techniques in chapters 5, 10 and 11 to explain the growth and unemployment records of the developed capitalist economies. These techniques are supplemented in chapter 11 by a less formal analysis to take account of interactions between policy, unemployment and inflation during the episode following the golden age.

Finally, it is important to bear in mind that our study deals with a sizeable group of developed capitalist economies and, to be manageable, many events particular to each individual economy must be ignored. A general approach is adopted consistent with the broad historical features to be explained; it is capable of extension to case studies, allowing the analysis to be enriched by detail specific to the individual economies.

What lies ahead?

Chapter 8 explains the linkages between the period of industrialization in the United States, from the turn of the nineteenth century until the end of the 1920s, and the Great Depression. The linkage was technological. Lack of comparable data has limited the analysis to the United States. However, it is widely accepted that the depression in other economies was primarily the result of the international transmission of events that originated in the United States. Chapters 9, 10 and 11 explain the alternating episodes of good and poor performance from the Great Depression until the end of the twentieth century, linking the episodes to features of the evolving institutional framework. This has two parts:

the linkage between the inter-war episode and the golden age, and the linkage between the golden age and the age of high unemployment. In each case, a shift in the distribution of power between capital and labour is a key feature of the linkage. The advent of the golden age was accompanied by a rise in labour's relative power, and its eventual fall ushered in the current episode.

8   Understanding the Great Depression

1 Introduction

Chapter 6 outlined the framework for analysing historical processes in which institutional changes provided the causal linkages between episodes. Chapters 9 to 11 apply this framework to the historical record, showing it to be the appropriate formulation for modelling the post-World War II era. Historical events also suggest that, in an episode extending from the end of the nineteenth century to the end of the 1920s, performance-induced change in technology was the structural change linking this episode to the Great Depression of the 1930s. In this chapter, a technology version of our framework shows the linkages connecting the two episodes of the pre-World War II era.

The data available to support analysis of this period are more limited than we would like. In contrast to the post-World War II period, comparably defined data describing the macroeconomic records of the developed capitalist economies are scant for the earlier era, making reliance on the American record necessary. However, the severity of this shortcoming is reduced by the existence of transmission mechanisms in the 1930s, so that events in the United States were quickly felt in the rest of the developed capitalist world.[1] Consequently, an explanation of the events of the 1930s in the United States also provides understanding of events in other economies. Table 8.1 records the unemployment and growth performance of the American economy from the turn of the nineteenth century to the end of the 1930s, showing the large decline in growth rates and the rise in unemployment rates in the 1930s compared with the 1920s and the period before World War I.[2] As in most explanations of the Great Depression in the United States, ours gives a central role to economic developments in the 1920s. However, unlike other studies, ours traces these developments to

---

[1] This is a widely held view. For example, in support of her own acceptance of it, Romer (1993, p. 20) quotes Lewis (1949, p. 52): 'It is clear that the centre of the depression was the United States of America, in the sense that most of what happened elsewhere has to be explained in terms of the American contraction, while that contraction is hardly explicable in any but internal terms.'   [2] For related data covering the OECD economies, see table 2.1.

Table 8.1 *Unemployment rates (U), growth rates of real GDP*
(Q̇) and real per capita income growth (ẏ) in the USA:
1900–1939 (%)

	1900–9	1910–19	1920–9	1930–9
U	4.4	5.0	4.7	18.4
Q̇	4.1	2.8	3.5	0.1
ẏ	2.2	1.3	2.0	−0.6

Note:
GDP growth, e.g. for 1900–9, is computed as $[(\text{GDP index}_{1899}/\text{GDP index}_{1909})^{1/10} - 1].100$.
Sources: for unemployment rates, Lebergott (1964), p. 512; for GDP growth, Maddison (1991), pp. 211, 214.

even earlier events; these were changes in technology that began in the last quarter of the nineteenth century as part of the industrialization and eventual modernization of the American economy.

Sections 2 and 3 outline a simple non-linear model of the business cycle, commonly used to analyse 8–10 year cycles in overall activity. It serves as an organizing principle in section 4, which explains how the characteristics of the boom phase of a business cycle determine whether the subsequent downturn will be a mild or a serious depression. Section 5 uses this framework to explain how the Great Depression grew out of events of the 1920s. In section 6 a simple extension of the time horizon from the 1920s back to the end of the nineteenth century allows us to explain how long-term trends in technology forged links between the earlier period, the 1920s and the 1930s. Section 7 describes the severity of the downturn of the 1930s.

Section 8 initiates discussion of an alternative explanation of the Great Depression in the United States, the monetarist explanation of Friedman and Schwartz (1963a), with its emphasis on avoidable policy errors committed within an otherwise self-regulating economic system. This interpretation is rejected in section 9. Section 10 presents a diagram showing the single route of structural change, and section 11 contains the conclusions. An appendix discusses the non-linear dynamics of the golden age period in order to clarify some of the key points of the text.

2 A non-linear dynamic model

Most explanations of the Great Depression in the United States implicitly assume the economy to have strong self-regulating tendencies which are subject to deviations from equilibrium owing to periodic AD shocks. In some versions, negative AD shocks activate mechanisms propagating prolonged deviations from a full employment equilibrium. For example, a stock market crash causes a decline in expenditures on consumer durables, which causes expectations to worsen, which induces additional declines in spending and output, and so on. We find this kind of modelling to have little merit. Unless the mechanism generating expectations is made explicit and consists of something more than previous expectations, such processes merely endow the system with unexplained inertia; they are not causal explanations.

Instead, to give structure to the economic processes at work, we combine a Keynesian income-generating mechanism, for example a generalized accelerator-multiplier model, with sectoral 'ceilings' that constrain particular kinds of spending and output. These form the basic ingredients of a non-linear dynamic model which generates cyclical movements in total output.[3] We alter the usual model to include two sectoral ceilings rather than one. One is a technology ceiling that limits output in the capital goods industry, and the other will be referred to as a 'monetary ceiling' affecting the flow of funds between sectors. Finally, we incorporate technology spillovers and externalities as the third essential ingredient of our model of the Great Depression.

For convenience, the foreign sector is ignored, and the economy is divided into the household, business and government sectors. Households divide their expenditures between non-durable goods and services spending and expenditures on consumer durables and residential housing. The latter we define as household or consumer investment, to be contrasted with investment expenditures by the business and government sectors. The spending category 'family-related expenditures' plays an important role in the model. It includes all those non-consumption expenditures that provide services connected with family formation and the establishment of a place of residence, whether these are undertaken by households, businesses or governments. Specifically, family-related expenditures include consumer investment in household furnishings and equipment, new residential buildings, commercial investment in stores, restaurants, garages and other non-residential buildings, all in the private sector. In the public sector, construction of residential buildings, hospitals, schools and other non-residential buildings, sewer and water systems, and all current non-defence outlays are included. The exclusions are consumer expenditures on non-durables and services, automobiles, government expenditures on defence and much of business investment. A point to note is that booms and slumps in residential housing are, with lags, associated with booms and slumps in other family-related expenditures.[4]

---

[3] One of the pioneers in developing these models is Goodwin (1990).
[4] For further discussion see Cornwall (1972, ch. V).

Although used here to explain the American economy of the late nineteenth and early twentieth century, the model is applicable to any developed capitalist economy in which: (1) discretionary fiscal policy is not a recognized instrument of stabilization policy; (2) monetary policy influences the economy solely by affecting the reserve position of the commercial banks; (3) financial markets are well enough developed to allow easy movement of financial wealth between different kinds of institutions; and (4) the bulk of residential housing construction is carried out by private firms.

3 The ceilings

3.1 The ceiling in the capital goods industry

The operation of ceilings plays a key role in the model and in explaining the Great Depression (Cornwall, 1992 and 1972, chs. VI and X). Consider first the effects of the ceiling in the capital goods industry. It can be reasonably assumed that new capital goods for sale to other businesses (i.e. new business plant and equipment) are usually produced to order rather than for inventory. In contrast, new capital goods for the consumer sector, whether residences or consumer durables, may be produced to order or for inventory. A consequence of producing to order is that in strong booms orders for new business capital exceed the output capacity of the capital goods sector, leading to increasing backlogs. The technology or capacity ceiling in the capital goods industry introduces a non-linearity into the model. As will be shown presently, it and the monetary ceiling have significant stabilizing effects, which are particularly important when fiscal policy intervention is absent or reserved for only the most severe conditions.[5]

We assume that the capacity of the capital goods industry varies in response to AD pressures but not enough to eliminate backlogs of demand during the boom. Equally important, many of the larger construction firms produce both residential construction for the household sector and new plant for the business sector. Which of these is chosen will depend upon relative profitability. It is assumed that the rate of profit is usually higher for business construction projects so that, when the demand is there, the larger construction firms shift resources in order to satisfy this demand.[6] The shift in physical resources over the cycle is another effect of the ceiling in the capital goods industry.

---

[5] These ceilings act as flexible constraints on particular types of spending and must not be confused with the constraint on AD and total spending featured throughout the study.

[6] These assumptions are supported by case studies conducted by the research department of the Boston Federal Reserve Bank in the 1960s. However, even in the absence of a shift in resources within the construction industry, the fact that production of capital goods is to order plays a stabilizing role.

3.2 The monetary ceiling

Instruments of monetary policy affecting only the reserve position of the commercial banks are often called 'neutral' because they ration credit solely on the basis of its cost. However, at least until the period of deregulation in the 1980s, monetary policy in fact has been biased, discriminating against the mortgage and housing markets by rationing credit during expansions in GNP. Consider an expansion that has been under way long enough for the authorities to become concerned about inflation, leading the central bank to tighten credit conditions by slowing the growth of bank reserves. This leads to an increase in interest rates on new debt instruments, including mortgages. However, the observed sluggishness of mortgage interest rates means that they rise less rapidly than rates on more marketable securities, for example corporate and government bonds, leading lenders to back away from the mortgage market.

In addition, 'thrift institutions', for example mutual savings banks and savings and loan associations in the United States (trust and mortgage loan companies in Canada, and building societies in the United Kingdom), which customarily match mortgage lending with deposits, experience a relative decline in their deposits during the middle and late stages of the boom. During periods of rising interest rates on marketable securities, the rates that thrift institutions can pay on their total deposits rise relatively slowly, because they can raise mortgage rates (to finance higher deposit rates) only on new mortgages, and these are a fraction of their total mortgage holdings. The response is 'disintermediation', as potential depositors by-pass financial intermediaries and place their funds directly in the capital market where rates of interest have risen relatively. Since mortgage dealings are largely carried out through financial intermediaries, the housing market suffers. The disintermediation process acts as a ceiling on the supply of funds, restricting the amount available for household investment. The process is symmetrical. During recessions and early stages of the boom a reversal in the flow of funds or an 'intermediation' process occurs, stimulating mortgage lending and residential construction. The presence of the monetary ceiling will also have an impact on other forms of family-related expenditures. The next section describes the stabilizing role of the ceilings.

4 The relationship between cycle phases

Assume that in the absence of ceilings the dynamic income-generating mechanisms lead to cyclical movements. The point to be made is that the strength of business investment largely determines the shape of fluctuations in overall economic activity over the cycle. When business investment booms are large in amplitude and long in duration, a strong boom in GNP develops, and recessions tend to be mild and short. Conversely, weak business investment booms, although generating a milder boom in overall activity, lead to downturns that are sharper and longer, other things being equal.[7]

The strength of the business investment boom determines whether or not the economy will interact with the monetary and capital goods ceilings. The stronger and longer is this boom, the milder will be the subsequent recession, for two reasons. First, the stronger is the boom in business demand for new construction, the more residential housing will be squeezed, the more other types of family-related expenditures will be cut back, and therefore the greater will be the deferred demand for family-related expenditures to be satisfied in the subsequent downturn of business investment. Underlying this 'crowding-out' effect is the shift of resources in the construction industry to the construction of business plant and disintermediation in the financial markets. There is a second stabilizing factor at work. The stronger is the business investment boom, the greater will be the backlog of unfilled orders for new capital goods when the boom in business investment demand comes to an end. Other things being equal, this will lead to a more moderate and slower decline in business investment outlays and GNP during the recession as there will be a greater stock of deferred business demand to work off. The significance of this is that, once the recession sets in, the turn-around in overall economic activity will require a smaller increase in housing and other forms of family-related expenditures to offset the smaller and less rapid downturn in business investment expenditures.

In effect, when the two ceilings operate in the boom, downward movements in aggregate output and expenditures will be bounded from below, a result of the counter-cyclical movements in family-related expenditures. Recessions are mild because the downturn is not widely diffused across spending categories; this can be traced to the lack of diffusion of the same spending categories in the later stages of the previous boom. An idealized picture of these offsetting movements in the critical spending categories is shown in figure 8.1.

The impact of a business investment boom too weak to bring the ceilings into operation is easily sketched. With a weak business investment boom, during the upswing in total output residential housing and related expenditures will be less affected, as the shift in resources by construction firms to non-residential construction will be lessened. Moreover, with the overall boom weak because of the weak business investment boom, monetary

[7] See Cornwall (1992, pp. 138–40) for a more detailed account.

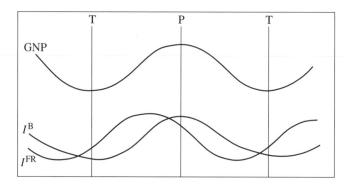

Figure 8.1 Offsetting movements in business investment, I^B, and family-related investment, I^{FR}, over the cycle in GNP
Notes: T = trough; *P* = peak

policy will be less restrictive and disintermediation weaker. Finally, the backlog of unfilled orders from business for new capital goods will be smaller than in the strong business investment led boom. As a result, once the economy turns down, the decline in business investment expenditures will be more rapid as will the decline in overall activity, and a greater offsetting increase in family-related expenditures will be needed to reverse the downturn.

Without the ceilings constraining family-related expenditures, the boom will be widely diffused throughout the economy and, as a result, spending declines will also be widely diffused and the recession will be severe. Aggregate activity will not be bounded from below by pent-up family-related expenditures, as it is with strong business investment booms.[8] The 'floor' to the economy can be a circular flow outcome in which AD and output have fallen to such low levels that for practical purposes all output is consumed.

5 The absence of ceilings in the 1920s

As discussed in the Appendix to this chapter, in each of the post-World War II booms the early stages of a recovery were notable for the rapid growth of non-business investment outlays, especially family-related expenditures,

[8] A diagram corresponding to figure 8.1 for a weak business investment boom (and the Great Depression) and the events leading up to it would show business investment and family-related expenditures moving together over the entire cycle, ending in a more pronounced downturn.

Table 8.2 *Annual expenditures for GNP and selected items in the United States: 1919–1929 (1929 US$ billion)*

Year	GNP	FS	C'	C^D	I^H	$I^{B'}$	I^B
1919	67.8	65.0	44.7	5.0	1.5	10.3	8.3
1920	68.5	64.3	46.4	4.9	1.0	9.7	8.3
1921	65.5	65.5	50.2	4.0	2.1	7.8	6.2
1922	70.4	70.1	51.4	5.1	3.6	9.4	7.7
1923	80.0	77.2	54.6	6.6	4.2	11.3	9.6
1924	81.6	82.5	58.4	6.9	5.0	11.2	9.3
1925	84.3	82.7	56.2	7.8	5.4	12.7	10.6
1926	89.9	88.6	60.3	8.6	5.4	13.9	11.8
1927	90.6	90.2	62.5	8.2	5.1	13.7	11.3
1928	91.9	92.3	64.1	8.4	4.7	14.1	11.6
1929	98.0	96.3	68.1	8.8	3.4	15.3	12.8

Note:
GNP = gross national product, FS = final sales, C' = consumption expenditures on non-durables and services, C^D = expenditures on consumer durables, I^H = residential housing expenditures, $I^{B'}$ = gross fixed business capital formation plus government construction and durable munitions outlays, and $I^B = I^{B'}$ minus government construction.
Sources: Kuznets (1961), Tables R-3 and R-5; and US Department of Commerce, *Construction Volume and Costs, 1915–1954*, Table 1.

whereas the middle and later stages of the boom in GNP were dominated by investment outlays of business. These offsetting movements were attributed to the ceilings causing postponement of family-related expenditures in the latter part of each GNP expansion until the downturn in overall activity made resources available for their realization. Ultimately the strong business investment booms of the golden age generated the offsetting movements. This was not true of the boom of the 1920s. Table 8.2 presents annual data covering household and business spending categories during the 1920s. Business fixed investment outlays were strong in the first few years following World War I and in 1929 but in the intervening years they hardly increased.[9] Kuznets (1961, table R-30) finds business demand for new construction to be weak during the 1920s (not shown in table 8.2), indicating that firms in the construction industry were not overburdened with new orders for plant and would therefore be relatively free to move into the

---

[9] Almost half of the 10 per cent increase in business investment from 1928 to 1929 can be attributed to a spurt in public utility and communication investment related to a need to expand distribution and transmission facilities. See Cornwall (1972, pp. 211–12) and sources cited.

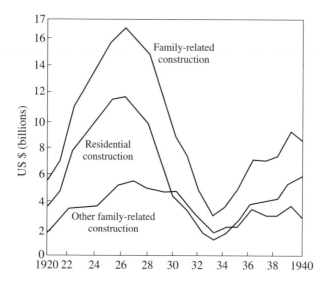

Figure 8.2 Family-related construction expenditures, 1920–1940
Note:
Family-related construction expenditure is the sum of residential construction
and other family-related construction.
Source: US Department of Commerce, *Construction, Volume and Costs*, 1915–54.

residential construction market if the demand was there. As a result, an outstanding feature of the boom of the 1920s was the growth of family-related
construction expenditures, especially residential housing. Figure 8.2 shows
this clearly. This suggests that the ceiling in the capital goods industry did
not operate in the 1920s.

The same can be said of the monetary ceiling. Consider first the behaviour of interest rates in different financial markets. Throughout the 1920s
the spread between interest rates on AAA corporate bonds and rates paid
on deposits at mutual savings banks narrowed steadily and significantly. As
a result, households found deposits at mutual savings banks (and by infer-
ence savings and loan institutions) becoming more attractive compared to
bonds. A process of intermediation would be expected, with households
placing their funds with financial intermediaries rather than directly in the
capital market. The rapid rate of growth of deposits in the thrift institutions
throughout the 1920s confirms this. And since these lenders tend to match
deposits with mortgages, there was also a rapid growth of mortgage holdings, not just at the thrifts but at commercial banks and insurance companies as well. This continued throughout the 1920s (Cornwall, 1972, pp.

213–16), suggesting the absence of any monetary ceiling that would ration mortgage funds to potential home owners, forcing them to postpone the purchases of houses.

Nevertheless, residential construction peaked in 1926 and other family-related construction peaked in 1927, developments suggesting the reverse – that these expenditures were being squeezed out in the mid-stages of the boom in GNP and would therefore have to be postponed until the subsequent recession. However, this would be an erroneous interpretation, given the weakness of the business investment boom. Furthermore, data on household formation and housing starts indicate a large stock of surplus housing that continued to grow from 1923 well into the 1930s. The downturn in housing expenditures after 1926 can be attributed to an oversupply of housing; its continuing oversupply after 1929 would lead to a further cutback in housing and other family-related construction expenditures following the downturn (Gordon and Wilcox, 1981). The failure of these spending categories to help turn the economy around is also shown clearly in figure 8.2.

6 Why were the ceilings absent in the 1920s?

Business investment, although increasing, was relatively weak during the 1920s boom in the United States, so that it failed to sufficiently crowd out household and other investments related to family formation. To explain the weakness of business investment expenditures it is necessary to include the period from the turn of the nineteenth century until the 1920s as part of an extended boom that preceded the Great Depression. With this addition, the weakness in business investment in the 1920s is shown to be the result of technology change that links this extended boom with the depression of the 1930s. This is seen by writing the identity $I^b/Y^b = (I^b/\Delta Y^b) \cdot (\Delta Y^b/Y^b)$, where I^b is business investment, Y^b is the net output of the business sector and Δ indicates a change in the variable. Clearly, the business investment–output ratio can be written as the product of the marginal capital–output ratio (the reciprocal of the marginal productivity of capital) and the rate of growth of business output.

Several studies of capital formation in the United States reveal that, whereas the marginal and average capital–output ratios in manufacturing and mining rose at an early stage of development, eventually a secular decline in these ratios set in. The peaks in this inverted U pattern in manufacturing and mining occurred in the 1920s. Data beginning in the late nineteenth century for public utility investment show a steady decline in both ratios, indicating that the overall marginal and average business capital–output ratios were also falling during the 1920s. For some given rate of growth of business output, $\Delta Y^b / Y^b$, the decline in $I^b / \Delta Y^b$ would lead to a decline in I^b / Y^b explaining the weak business investment behaviour of the 1920s in terms of the 'capital-saving' nature of innovations (Kuznets, 1961; Borenstein, 1954; Ulmer, 1960; Lorant, 1966; Kendrick, 1961, pp. 164–70). Once housing and other family-related expenditures had fallen sufficiently, the investment 'offsets' to the savings generated by the boom were insufficient to sustain the boom levels of overall activity.

In the language of new growth theorists, the inverted U shape of the capital–output ratio reflects the effects of externalities and spillover effects, operating in this case throughout the economy. Lachman's (1947, 1948) point, already noted in chapter 4, was that economists have for too long treated the capital stock as a collection of homogeneous units competing with each other, leading to the textbook assumption of falling marginal and average productivity of capital as the stock increases. However, once it is recognized that economic development is a transformation in which the composition of output constantly changes as income levels rise, the composition of the capital stock must be considered, since it is a collection of qualitatively different units. These differences have made new units of capital complementary to existing units and to units yet to be produced.[10] The conclusion to be drawn from this analysis is clear. The underlying structural developments in technology, arising as a normal part of a long boom covering the building of the economy's infrastructure followed by a phase dominated by growth in manufacturing, caused the severe downturn that was to become the Great Depression.

7 The Great Depression

According to the above analysis, the severity of the Great Depression was due to the business investment boom in the 1920s being too weak to bring the ceilings into operation. This weakness was attributed to technology developments that arose as part of the industrialization and modernization of the American economy. Consider first the duration and amplitude of the decline in GNP in the 1930s' downturn. The depression began late in 1929 and reached bottom in 1933 with GNP falling 29.7 per cent over the period.[11] This can be contrasted with the four post-war recessions of the 1950s and 1960s, which had an average duration of a little less than three

[10] Similar development examples in which spillover effects relate infrastructure investment and the productivity of the manufacturing sector are found in Kennedy and Dowling (1975) and Allen and Stevenson (1974).

[11] Unless otherwise indicated, all annual figures throughout the chapter are in constant dollars and are taken from US Department of Commerce, *Survey of Current Business*, September 1989, table 2. Quarterly data are from the *Survey of Current Business*, January 1976, table 1.2.

quarters and an average decline of approximately 2.0 per cent. A prominent characteristic of the 1930s' downturn was its wide diffusion across spending categories. This would be expected when so many of the non-consumption spending categories were moving together during the previous boom. From the peak year of 1929 to the trough in GNP in 1933, not only were the declines in business fixed investment and consumer durables plus housing expenditures uninterrupted and dramatic (72.2 and 62.5 per cent, respectively), so was the decline in consumption expenditures on non-durable goods and services (17.0 per cent). Using a different measure of final spending components, as seen in figure 8.2, from 1929 to 1933 there was a 76 per cent decline in family-related expenditures less household expenditures on furnishings and equipment (i.e. family-related construction), which fell from approximately US$15 billion to US$3.6 billion. The behaviour of government expenditures shifted sharply over the course of the downturn in GNP. In constant dollars, total government expenditures rose from 1929 to 1931 by 13.4 per cent and then fell from 1931 to 1933 by 7.7 per cent, as governments sharply cut spending in response to rising budget deficits.[12] Taking the 1929–33 period as a whole, government expenditures rose 4.6 per cent. The sum of all final expenditures other than consumer outlays on non-durable goods and services declined 49.5 per cent over the same period. Further analysis of spending during the Great Depression is taken up in section 9.

8 Theories of the Great Depression

The extent of the literature on the Great Depression has encouraged efforts to classify the numerous explanations that have been proposed. Gordon and Wilcox (1981) rank these theories along a spectrum of four views ranging from 'hard-line monetarism' to 'hard-line non-monetarism'.[13] At one extreme, hard-line monetarists see the 1929–33 downturn as both initiated and aggravated by monetary factors, with non-monetary forces, for example 'autonomous' declines in private spending, playing no part. Hard-line monetarists tend to be believers in capitalism's self-regulating tendencies, the most famous and influential statement of hard-line monetarism being the study by Friedman and Schwartz (1963a). At the other extreme, hard-line non-monetarists argue that the causes and severity of the decline can be traced to non-monetary forces, with the decline in the stock of money reflecting a purely 'passive' response to the decline in spending and income.

---

[12] Roosevelt ran on a platform of annually balanced budgets in the 1932 elections.
[13] See Eichengreen (1992) for an alternative classification scheme.

In between these two positions fall 'soft-line monetarism' and 'soft-line non-monetarism'. Each view allows that both monetary and non-monetary factors could have been at work in the first half of the downturn (1929–31). However, they differ in their explanations of the forces aggravating the situation from 1931 to 1933. The soft-line monetarist view finds that monetary factors played the crucial role in turning the recession into a depression. The soft-line non-monetarists, while allowing monetary factors a role in the 1931–3 period, see non-monetary forces such as the collapse of residential construction playing the critical part throughout the whole of the 1929–33 decline.

In terms of this classification system, the view adopted here is best characterized as soft-line non-monetarism, stressing structural change that produced fundamental weaknesses in the US economy. The forces underlying the early stages of the downturn and turning the recession into a depression arose out of the particular nature of the expenditures driving the boom of the 1920s, with the special characteristics of the boom determined by structural changes in technology. However, some allowance is made for monetary factors playing a supporting, but secondary, role. To evaluate the different views and to provide additional support for our 'non-monetary' explanation of the 1930s in the USA, we address the following questions: what initiated the decline; what magnified the downturn; and could stimulative monetary policies after 1929 have been sufficient to bring an end to the downturn in GNP before the lower turning point in 1933?

9 Did monetary or non-monetary forces dominate?

9.1 The forces initiating the downturn

A commonly held view is that the US recession began in mid-1929 and was expected to be short and not serious (Temin, 1993; Romer, 1993).[14] The precipitous slide from recession into depression is then linked to the stock market collapse in September 1929. Just as the stock market surge of 1927–9 had generated large capital gains, which, because of their wealth effects, resulted in large increases of spending by consumers, so the sharp decline in consumer outlays in 1930 was traced to the collapse of the stock market (Gordon and Wilcox, 1981, p. 96). Romer (1993) makes the stronger case that the main effect of the collapse was its impact on expenditures for consumer durables, which fell 21.0 per cent from 1929 to 1930, while consumption expenditures on non-durables and services fell only 5.3 per cent.

---

[14] Some allege the difficulties were initiated earlier by the tightened monetary policy and the rise in interest rates in 1928, primarily to dampen stock market speculation, but in part to stem a feared gold outflow (Temin, 1993, p. 89).

However, a difficulty with either theory of what initiated the decline in overall activity is that the fall in GNP of 9.4 per cent from 1929 to 1930 included declines in other spending categories less closely related to the stock market decline. For example, the decline in residential housing expenditures and business investment from 1929 to 1930 is readily explained in terms of the causal mechanism outlined in sections 5 and 6, and these two spending categories are over three times as large as outlays on consumer durables. Figure 8.2 shows the precipitous decline in family-related construction spending to have begun well before the stock market collapse. It can be argued that this spending drop initiated the decline in GNP.

9.2 Forces magnifying the decline

In answering the questions about the forces magnifying the decline and whether stimulative monetary policies could have brought an early reversal to the downswing, we follow Friedman and Schwartz (1963a) in dividing the period between the initial decline in economic activity and the actual trough in 1933 into subperiods, using dates of successive banking crises to separate the subperiods. Each date was succeeded by a large internal drain from the banking system as depositors converted deposits into currency, leading to serious liquidity problems for the banking system.

Production and expenditure data are available on a quarterly basis and help to illuminate the forces at work in the first half of the downturn. Of particular importance are movements in the real sector between the stock market peak in September 1929 and the first and second banking crises of October 1930 and March 1931, respectively. After a slight increase in the first half of the year, industrial production peaked in August 1929. As seen in table 8.3, from 1929–III to 1930–III, the period of decline preceding the first bank crisis, it then fell 23.3 per cent. GNP fell 12.1 per cent and the money supply fell 2.4 per cent over this same period. Since prices also declined, the declines in GNP in constant prices and the real stock of money were even smaller.[15] Finally, over the same one-year period manufacturing investment, which had peaked in 1929–II, fell over 36 per cent and corporate profits after taxes fell 79 per cent.

The first bank crisis of October 1930 was followed by additional liquidity crises in March 1931, in September 1931 and again in early 1933. Depositors' efforts to convert deposits into cash forced banks to dump securities on the open market on a large scale, setting off widespread bank failures and declines in the money supply. Even so, it is clear from table 8.3

---

[15] According to Gordon and Wilcox (1981, figure 1) there was virtually no change in the stock of real money balances over this period.

Table 8.3 *Quarterly figures for industrial production (IP), GNP, manufacturing investment (I^m), corporate profits after taxes (PR), and the money supply (M_2): 1929–III to 1931–I*

Quarter	IP 1947–9 = 100	GNP US$bn	I^m US$m	PR US$m	M_2 US$bn
1929 -III	60	26.4	682	1,696	46.3
-IV	56	25.8	685	1,406	46.3
1930 -I	53	24.9	600	984	45.6
-II	51	24.4	500	727	45.3
-III	46	23.2	435	357	45.2
-IV	43	20.9	373	132	44.6
1931 -I	42	20.2	312	84	43.8

Notes:
GNP, manufacturing investment and profit figures are quarterly totals in current dollars; M_2 includes currency held by the public plus demand and time deposits at commercial banks. All figures are seasonally adjusted when required.
Sources: Moore (1961), Tables 9.1, 15.0, 16.1 and 22.1; Friedman and Schwartz (1963b), Table A1.

that from 1930–III to 1931–I, approximately the interval between the first and second bank crises, the decline in the nominal supply of money was only 3.1 per cent. This can be compared with declines in industrial production, GNP, manufacturing investment and corporate profits after taxes of 8.7, 12.9, 28 and 76.5 per cent, respectively. Considering the entire 1929–III to 1931–I period, a 5.4 per cent decline of the nominal supply of money must be compared with declines in industrial production, GNP, manufacturing investment and corporate profits after taxes of 30, 23, 54 and 95 per cent, respectively.

To explain continued declines in spending, Romer (1993) cites the banking crises, which reduced the money supply directly and, by increasing depositors' fears of bank failures, led to a large currency drain that reduced the money multiplier as well. To these, she adds increased pessimism and, to account for declines in investment spending in particular, she resorts to expectations about real interest rates, which rose as prices fell. Although recent, this work does not extend far beyond its Friedman and Schwartz roots. Also building upon the Friedman and Schwartz base is the 'new view'. This concentrates on financial market disruptions, rather than upon money per se. The progress of this line of investigation is summarized by Calomiris (1993), and springs from work on imperfect capital markets. Fisher (1933) first emphasized the effect of 'debt deflation' (reallocation of wealth away from the indebted) on spending, and Minsky (1975) expanded on the theme. Mishkin (1978) analysed the effect of debt deflation on consumer demand in the depression, and stressed changes in the distribution of wealth. High consumer indebtedness at the onset of the depression therefore led to the unusually large drop in consumption spending. Bernanke (1983) extended this line of argument to include firms, whose borrowing costs increased owing to asymmetric information as 'insider' sources of funds dried up and external borrowing increased. Debt deflation also caused bank failures, ending relationships between firms and bankers, and dealing with new bankers introduced additional asymmetric information problems and caused further increases in borrowing costs. These higher costs are used to explain the drop in investment spending.

Proponents of the 'new view' accepted the importance of monetary shocks, arguing that they and the financial market disruptions early in the recession had long-run effects because they altered the institutional structure of credit markets. One of the more interesting aspects of the new view explanations is the lack of resort to events in the 'real economy', i.e. to non-monetary factors. We reject these explanations because they overlook the critical role played by the weak business investment boom of the 1920s in accentuating the downturn. As we have argued, the absence of ceilings constraining non-business investment during the boom of the 1920s would reflect the weakness of business investment. As a result, investment by these other sectors of the economy would not be squeezed nor would business sector demand for new capital goods cause large backlogs that could be worked off only when the economy turned down. Once business investment turns down, it and GNP could be expected to fall rapidly. Annual figures in constant dollars show a decline in 'non-residential fixed investment' (roughly equivalent to business investment) from 1929 to 1930 of over 17 per cent and an additional decline from 1930 to 1931 of almost 36 per cent. Even the sharp rise in government outlays of 13.4 per cent from 1929 to 1931 (far exceeding the increase in government outlays over the course of any post-World War II recession) was not enough to keep final spending net of consumer outlays on non-durables and services from declining over 30 per cent from 1929 to 1931.

It is difficult to maintain that monetary forces played any more of a role in the declines in activity prior to either the first or the second bank crises than they did in causing the initial downturn. Even if the possible endogeneity of the decline in M_2 is ignored, the conclusion is straightforward. When endogeneity is allowed for, the decline in the stock of money becomes an effect rather than a cause of the decline in the real sector.[16] In any event, the

---

[16] See Cornwall (1972, pp. 225–7) for a discussion supporting the endogeneity of money supply and lack of loan demand during this period.

reductions in the money supply were simply too small compared with events in the real sector to offer a monetary explanation even prior to 1931. It is difficult to weight the impact of financial market disturbances but, even if we accept that they helped to magnify the decline, we must conclude that non-monetary forces were dominant.

9.3 Could correct monetary policy have saved the day?

Large decreases in the money stock came in March 1931 after the second bank crisis. Certainly a decline in M_2 of 16.5 per cent from 1931 to 1932 and of 11.5 per cent from 1932 to 1933 indicates perverse behaviour on the part of the monetary authorities (Friedman and Schwartz, 1963b, table A-1). Having said this, it must be noted again that government spending also fell sharply during this period (7.7 per cent) and the sum of all final expenditures other than expenditures on non-durables and consumer services fell a further 27.4 per cent. Monetarists argue that the decline in the money supply was the crucial force driving down the economy during the last two years of the Great Depression. We maintain that non-monetary events continued to dominate. The difficulty in supporting either position is that by 1931 events and their impacts had become so interwoven that disentangling cause and effect during the final two years of the downturn is impossible. Rather than take a position on the relative weight of monetary versus non-monetary factors in the 1931–3 period, consider the following question: would the depression have been appreciably milder if monetary policy had been stimulative enough before the lower turning point to prevent the bank failures and to generate a rate of growth of the money supply equal to the long-term trend rate of money incomes? A positive answer to the question will be considered evidence that the forces aggravating the downswing were temporary disturbances – among which errors of policy have loomed the largest in the literature – to an otherwise self-regulating system. A negative answer is treated as evidence that non-monetary forces, including structural change, were responsible for the severity of the downturn.

If monetary policy could have saved the day early in the 1930s, the earlier analysis argues that it must have done so by stimulating family-related expenditures. As already pointed out, the 1920s saw a residential building boom that was adding to the stock of new housing at a rate far in excess of the additions to the stock of families. And, in spite of the sharp decline in the number of dwelling units built beginning in 1925, new homes built still exceeded new families formed after 1925, and did so continuously until 1933, adding to the excess stock of housing (Cornwall, 1972, table 10.2). In these circumstances it could not be expected that a growing money supply (and falling interest rates) would have had much effect on residential housing or on other family-related expenditures throughout the four-year downturn. Nor could much be expected in the way of an increase in business investment, given the speed of decline in total activity and the rapid deterioration in profits once the downturn came. On balance, it appears that there was little monetary policy could have done once the economy turned down. Investment demands by the household and business sectors were simply too interest inelastic and too little affected by real balance increases to turn spending around after the downturn had begun.

Certainly bank failures and bankruptcies led to a reduction of financial wealth and consumption, and some help from a more stimulative monetary policy could have been expected here. As a result, if monetary policy had not been perverse, the depression would not have been as severe, nor would it have lasted as long as it did. However, it would have been only marginally less severe and have proceeded only slightly less rapidly. Strong stimulative fiscal policy could have played a role in reversing the downturn and in moving the economy back toward full employment but, given the attitudes and beliefs of the times, the required fiscal stimulus was politically unacceptable.[17] Only after four years of decline, when consumer expenditures on non-durable goods and services had risen from 70 to 80 per cent of GNP and total government expenditures plus consumption had risen from 80 to 90 per cent of GNP, did the downturn hit bottom. The United States economy could then, for all practical purposes, be described as a circular flow economy in which no further fall in total output would occur because total income earned was automatically returned to those who produced it.

10 Technology as the source of structural change

Figure 8.3 depicts our analysis of the structural change linking the 'industrialization' episode prior to the Great Depression (episode 1) to the Great Depression itself (episode 2). The left-hand box represents the set of structural variables for episode 1. This, together with an endogenous Keynesian mechanism (not shown) describing AD, determines the precise macroeconomic performance of episode 1, represented by the left-most horizontal arrow. However, we focus on the structure of technology because it determined the general characteristics of macroeconomic performance during the industrialization episode. Data for unemployment in the United States begin in 1900, and table 8.1 shows the average unemployment rate from 1900 to 1929 to have been 4.7 per cent, a rate equal to the golden age average shown in table 2.1. Even making some allowance for the quality of these early data, they create a clear impression that there was no constraint on

---

[17] The régulation school would refer to this inability of institutions to adjust to technology as a 'crisis'.

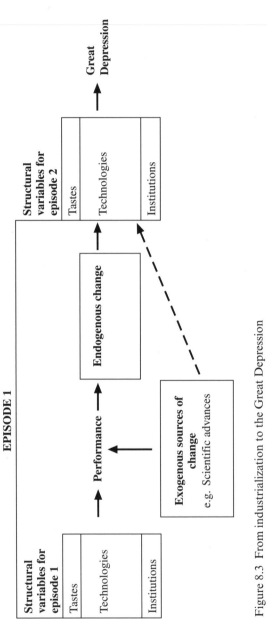

Figure 8.3 From industrialization to the Great Depression

AD in the period. The absence of an inflation constraint is supported by Maddison's data (1991, table E.2), which for the years 1900–14 show only a very modest rise in the consumer price index from 84.2 to 101.3, and a decline between 1921 and 1929. Unacceptable inflation rates did not play a role in bringing episode 1 to an end; altered technologies did. Therefore, figure 8.3 differs from figure 6.1 in having technology rather than institutions as the primary structural determinant of performance – that is, whether unemployment is high or low.

Figure 8.3 shows only one route leading to the reversal in performance that initiated episode 2, and that route is through changes in technology, represented by the series of horizontal arrows from left to right. The interaction between performance of the economy and its technology resulted eventually in the marked change in unemployment in the 1930s. The two middle horizontal arrows moving from left to right in figure 8.3 represent this evolutionary development. Although we have not done this, exogenous changes in technology can be easily added to the account, their influence represented by arrows from the 'exogenous sources' box. The analysis is restricted to changes in technology that, by affecting the state of AD, reverse performance. In explaining the linkage between the episode prior to the Great Depression and the 1930s, we have singled out technological developments as the catalyst generating negative feedback. Therefore all arrows end at the technology panel of the right-hand box and, although positive feedback effects are not precluded, they are not illustrated in the figure.

11 Conclusions

By the turn of the century a coast-to-coast railway system had been installed in the United States and the stock of other infrastructure capital was expanding rapidly. As table 8.1 demonstrates, this was the beginning of an era, extending through the 1930s, covering two episodes of radically different macroeconomic performance. Disregarding the interruption caused by World War I, the first episode was characterized by low unemployment and high growth rates in the United States, the second by high unemployment and low to negative growth rates. The argument of this chapter is that these episodes are causally related by pervasive developments in the economy's technology. In the first episode the boom in business investment was strong until the 1920s, especially non-residential construction and public utility investment in electrical power facilities (Kuznets, 1961, pp. 576–9). This additional infrastructure investment prepared the way for innovational and expansionary activities in such manufacturing industries as chemicals, electrical appliances and automobiles, justified by rising consumer demand induced by rising incomes.

Considering the entire business sector during this period of strong infrastructure investment, trends in technology at first caused rising marginal and average capital–output ratios. This was followed by their decline, which began in the public utility sector just before the end of the nineteenth century and spread to manufacturing and the rest of the industrial sector by the 1920s. We have argued that these technology developments were the underlying cause of the Great Depression. They led to such weak business investment demand in the 1920s that the stabilizing effects of the ceilings did not come into play; the Great Depression was the result.

By linking an episode of superior performance prior to the 1930s with the Great Depression, these events illustrate a process in which change is generated within the system, in this case by an evolutionary process of interaction between technology and performance culminating in negative feedback. During the early part of the first episode, infrastructure investment still dominated business investment, but incomes were also rising as productivity grew. Eventually these rising incomes generated the shifting demands needed to justify the shift in production to manufactured goods with high value added. As incomes rose further, the continued shift in the composition of output and the spillover effects of past investments in infrastructure led to rising economy-wide capital productivity. This eventually weakened investment demand in the business sector and brought on the depression.[18]

Some economists see major events such as the depression of the 1930s as the result of minor causes, such as the stock market collapse or the failure of the monetary authorities to initiate large-scale open market operations early in the downswing. In contrast, we believe that major events have major causes. Events such as the collapse of the stock market should be treated as shocks to an unstable system, a system incapable of righting itself once the cause of the disturbance had been removed. To prevent the downturn turning into a depression, institutional change in the shape of acceptance and implementation of strong stimulative fiscal policy was required. Unfortunately, reigning beliefs and attitudes would not tolerate this institutional adaptation to an altered technology. In 1930 unemployment was rising rapidly, reaching double digit rates by the following year; it remained in the 14–25 per cent range for the balance of the decade (Maddison, 1991, table C.6).

Keynes' *General Theory* had provided a programme for economic recovery through stimulative fiscal policy and a clear warning of the dangers to economic and political stability unless steps were taken to remedy high unemployment. Although the economic impact of rearmament and World

---

[18] For an early study emphasizing the importance of capital-saving innovations as a major cause of the depression, see Hansen (1939).

War II led to a marked reduction in unemployment rates, strong doubts remained that in peacetime governments would be prepared to use stimulative fiscal policy when necessary to keep unemployment down. So strong were these doubts that in the closing years of World War II large numbers of economists foresaw the return of mass unemployment once war was ended and military budgets reduced. Underlying this pessimism was the belief in what can be termed a 'vulgar stagnation doctrine', which declared that mature capitalism is destined to experience weak booms, prolonged recessions and a reserve army of the unemployed.

Chapters 9 and 10 show how very wide of the mark these forecasts proved to be, and examine the reasons capitalism experienced the period of historically low unemployment rates and high growth rates that came to be called the golden age. However, it should be emphasized that the mistaken forecasts of capitalism's future made near the end of the war do not refute any part of our explanation of events in the inter-war period. The boom of the 1920s was weak because of the weakness of business investment, which was not offset by additional strength in other forms of non-consumption expenditures. This led to the severity of the depression of the 1930s. In the United States, events following World War II indicate a resumption of weak business fixed investment well into the golden age. The difference between the golden age and the 1920s lies in the offsetting increases in government expenditures and consumer investment as shares of total output.

Appendix

The post-war recessions

The mildness of the recessions of the 1950s and 1960s was noted in section 7 and contrasted with the severity of the downturn of the 1930s. Given the pronouncements and actions of the authorities, it would be difficult to attribute relative stability to the use of discretionary fiscal policy in the later period. In fact, total government expenditures fell in the first and last of the short recessions and increased slightly in the middle two, with government expenditures at the state and local level increasing in all four recessions. Since the federal government is the only authority likely to pursue discretionary stimulative fiscal policy, its spending behaviour is especially relevant. During the four recessions the change in federal government expenditures in constant dollars was −18.0, 0.3, 2.7 and −4.5 per cent, respectively.[19] The key to the mildness of the recessions can be traced to the

---

[19] All quarterly data in this appendix are taken from US Department of Commerce, *Survey of Current Business*, September 1976, table 1.2.

mildness of the decline in business investment and the relative lack of diffusion of the declines in spending across the different spending categories.

In all four of the recessions of the 1950s and the 1960s, business investment fell but the average decline from peak to trough in GNP was 3.5 per cent, to be compared with the 72 per cent decline from 1929 to 1933. The behaviour of residential housing in the recessions of the 1950s and 1960s was qualitatively as well as quantitatively different from that of the 1930s. When measured from peak to trough in GNP these expenditures either increased or, if they declined, they did so only moderately, reflecting the turn-around of housing expenditures before the trough in GNP. The rise in residential investment indicated both the shift of resources in the construction industry from non-residential to residential construction as well as the shift of financial assets from the capital market to thrift institutions (i.e. intermediation).[20]

Taking into consideration all final expenditures (including government outlays) other than consumption expenditures on non-durables and services, the decline in these expenditures from peak to trough in GNP averaged 5.5 per cent. When contrasted with a decline of 49.5 per cent in the same final expenditures from 1929 to 1933, the mildness of the recessions would be expected.

The relationship between cycle phases

This brings the argument to the point made earlier in sections 4 and 5 of the text; recessions will be mild or severe depending upon whether the previous boom was strong or weak. When it is strong, it will very likely be the result of a strong business investment boom that brings into operation the monetary ceiling and the ceiling in the capital goods industry. As mentioned above, these ceilings operate to stabilize the economy in two ways. They lead to the deferral of some kinds of spending until the recession – that is, they lead to a less widely diffused boom and recession – and they reduce the rate of decline in activity by reducing the rate of decline in business investment once the economy turns down.

First, consider the impact of the ceiling in the capital goods industry in stabilizing business investment expenditures over the cycle. Production of new capital goods for the business sector is overwhelmingly to order, and the best measure of these orders is the US Department of Commerce's 'new orders and contracts, plant and equipment series'. This 'demand' for new business capital series can be compared with the same department's figures for the 'supply' of new business capital, 'gross fixed non-residential invest-

---

[20] See Cornwall (1972), ch. IX, Diagram 9.1.

ment'. During the four post-war booms of the 1950s and 1960s the peak in new orders and contracts typically preceded the peak in fixed non-residential investment by one or two quarters. In addition, the longer new orders remained high during the boom, the longer non-residential investment outlays remained high.

The behaviour of new orders and contracts and non-residential investment in the recession is more revealing. Comparing the peak to trough declines in new orders and contracts with the declines in non-residential fixed investment shows there was an average decline of 17 per cent in the former compared with a 7 per cent average decline in the latter. This reflects the operation of the technology ceiling in the previous boom.

Data are also available illustrating the operation of the monetary ceiling and its impact on the subsequent recession. During the mid to late stages of each boom, residential housing expenditures fell sharply. In part this reflected the shift of resources by firms in the construction industry out of the residential construction market. But mortgage flows and deposits at thrift institutions also fell sharply as the yield on mortgages and deposits at thrift institutions rose by less than interest rates on marketable securities. Considering the four booms, total mortgage flows in the US economy peaked on average four and a half quarters before the peak in GNP, during which time residential housing expenditures fell substantially, as did other forms of family-related expenditures (Cornwall, 1972, tables 8.8 and 9.2). In the period following World War II but before the general breakdown of the early 1970s, these ceilings operated, dampening fluctuations in overall activity. In contrast, the 1920s illustrated a phase in capitalist development in the United States in which ceilings did not operate. As a result, a shock such as the stock market collapse was enough to expose the downward instability of the economy because the ceilings did not operate in the 1920s and ultimately because of longer-term trends in the economy's technology.

9 Foundations of the golden age

1 Introduction

Compared with the pre-industrial era, the long-term success of capitalism in providing rapid growth in output and per capita incomes is undisputed. The share of this growth in the golden age was very large, even when compared with earlier rapid growth periods. For example, between 1901 and 1913 industrial output in Western Europe rose by about 50 per cent; between 1950 and 1962, it doubled (Shonfield, 1965, p. 10). Examination of longer periods reveals that capitalism provides growth in episodes, punctuated by failures such as the Great Depression (see, for example, table 2.1). Were it not for the golden age, more recent events – the inflation of the 1970s, the stagnant productivity growth that followed, and the still continuing high unemployment – would not appear exceptional by historical standards. But the golden age demonstrated the altogether more agreeable possibility that some of capitalism's problems could be avoided, allowing its benefits to be realized on a grand scale and enjoyed by all segments of society.

The wartime destruction of productive capacity presented an opportunity for modernization. The determination of national governments to put their economies back on a normal footing, and the readiness after 1947 of the USA to assist them, ensured that the acquisition of new capital and the spread of modern production methods would go speedily forward. But, as we know from chapter 8, the adoption of these capital-saving technologies in the United States produced the weak investment boom of the 1920s that was a leading cause of the Great Depression. Their post-World War II spread throughout the OECD did not have the same effect. The economic systems that arose were quite distinct from the capitalism that had existed earlier in the century. This was the result of sweeping institutional change. Particularly significant among the characteristics of these new systems were the redistribution of power in favour of labour and governments' acceptance of responsibility for economic performance and for the welfare of

156

their citizens. These changes led to the post-war political decisions at the national and international levels that established the new institutional framework. These institutions fostered the high and growing aggregate demand that would justify investment in new technologies, making possible the rapid growth experienced in the golden age.

The economic success of the golden age depended upon there being no constraint on aggregate demand, which grew without serious interruption over the period. Such economic stability reduces macro risk, with beneficial implications for investment and growth. It also eliminates wide swings in unemployment, which was at historically low rates in this period. But low unemployment was not necessarily accompanied by high inflation; many countries had no inflation constraint preventing the continuation of full employment, as discussed in chapter 5.

The ability to stabilize these economies at high levels of aggregate demand also depended on the absence of constraints other than inflation. These are open economies, raising the possibility that high aggregate demand might lead to balance of payments constraints, inducing governments to introduce restrictive policies, particularly under the fixed exchange rate system of the time. In addition there may be political constraints, such as the fear of 'big government' or of large or rapidly growing budget deficits, that cause government action to restrict spending. Lastly, there is the danger that a long period of high AD will be ended by supply constraints, whether shortages of labour, capital, available innovations or raw materials. But, in this era, neither budget deficits nor expanded government intervention were perceived as problems, and supply and payments constraints were also avoided, permitting continued low unemployment, high AD and rapid growth of both AD and productivity. In the absence of constraints on AD, the events of the golden age can be analysed using the demand-determined growth model of chapter 4.

Chapter 5 introduced the reasons for there being no inflation constraint in most economies, and the analysis is extended here to include the other constraints. The argument is that avoidance of the constraints was the result of institutions established in the immediate post-war years. These institutions defined the new form of capitalism that emerged in the early 1950s. The task of this chapter is to examine the historical events and trends of the 1930s and 1940s that led to the formation of this new institutional framework. Among these sources of institutional change, some were endogenous, induced by pre-war economic performance; the resulting new institutions generated a negative feedback on subsequent economic performance, as proposed in chapter 6. It is this endogenously generated change that provides the evolutionary mechanism linking the pre-World War II episode with the golden age. Other sources of change, particularly those that led to new institutions at the international level, are perhaps best regarded as primarily exogenous. Many of these stem from World War II and the US policy response to the Cold War that followed. Some of them, however, have an endogenous component, whether reflecting a desire to avoid the mistakes that led to poor performance in the past or reinforcing changes already evident prior to the war.

Sections 2 to 6 trace the sources of change in order to examine how these new institutions and the new economic order arose. These sections are necessarily descriptive, as we examine the social and political trends and changing beliefs that led to fundamental shifts in the roles that labour, capital and governments were expected to play in the economy. To deal with the varied experiences of many countries over this turbulent period requires a judicious selection of supporting historical facts. These are to be viewed as illustrations of the changes that were occurring, and are chosen to clarify both similarities and differences among countries. The nature of the changes recounted in these sections defies quantification or expression as a set of equations. Instead, we trace the sources of institutional change, using the framework developed in part I. Section 7 examines how the United States, as the new hegemon of the 'free world', influenced these changes. Section 8 draws together the sources of change, providing a summary of the linkages between the inter-war and World War II years with the golden age. The routes of change are illustrated by a modified version of the figure introduced in chapter 6.

Following this, section 9 discusses the potential constraints on aggregate demand and how the new institutions enabled many economies to avoid them; section 10 contains the conclusions. Chapter 10 then uses analytical methods more familiar to economists to explain how, within an institutional framework conducive to sustained strong aggregate demand growth, the rapid productivity growth of capitalism's golden age came about.

2 Setting the scene

To argue that the golden age arose from the 'right' constellation of institutions leaves open the question of how these institutions were established. The question is all the more to the point when we recall that the golden age was not expected to rise from the ashes of the Great Depression and World War II. Most of the economics profession predicted a repeat of the depression once hostilities were halted. This pessimism can be traced in part to a recurrent preoccupation with what was perceived as an irreconcilable conflict between capitalism and democracy. Social unrest and even revolution were the feared consequence, with the Russian revolution providing an example. The events of the inter-war period gave new urgency to doubts about the compatibility of capitalism and democracy. In chapter 24 of *The General Theory*, Keynes voiced his concerns about the dangers of large disparities in wealth and income, not only to investment, growth and employment but to the continued coexistence of capitalism and democracy. The view that universal suffrage would lead to socialism as wage earners sought 'distributional fairness' was already familiar. But events in Europe had presented the alternative possibility that democracy would be sacrificed to capitalism, as authoritarian governments, supported by capitalists, seized power. Keynes rejected these gloomy predictions. His view was that both of these outcomes could be avoided provided labour was fully employed and capitalists could retain control over the production process. Under these conditions capitalism would gain broad political acceptability, removing the need for conservative forces to oppose democracy and for radical forces to oppose capitalism.

By the early 1950s, most of the OECD economies had entered an era of near full employment; capital was still in control of production, socialism had been avoided and democracy saved. But what had emerged was a new capitalism. The new economic systems embodied fundamental institutional change; this carried dangers that Keynes had not fully explored. Full employment might well be enough to fend off socialism, but it would greatly increase the power of labour in wage bargaining. Not only would full employment increase labour's affluence and with it the willingness to strike, it would also create buoyant demand, increasing the cost to employers of any disruption in production. Acquiescence to wage demands would have inflationary implications that could bring full employment to an end. Resistance would trigger strikes that would likely distort or reduce investment, with detrimental effects on future employment and growth. Yet, in spite of this new threat to capitalism, about 25 years of low unemployment, low inflation and rapid growth occurred. The social consensus that was reached in the early post-war years is at the core of this economic success. To understand how the golden age came about therefore requires an understanding of how this compromise between capital and labour was achieved and of the key role of government in the process.

3 Labour: rising power and changing beliefs

3.1 Trends in relative power: an overview

To provide context for the discussion, consider the conflict between capitalism and democracy that led to fears for the continued survival of both. It derives from the tension between the theoretical equality of political power bestowed by universal enfranchisement and the actual inequality of economic power generated by market capitalism. Discussion of this conflict has centred on the distribution of income between labour and capital and on the control of the workplace. Important in labour's income share are social benefits that prevent destitution in the event of job loss, essential in economic systems prone to periodic failure.[1] The outcomes for both income shares and economic control are in large part determined by the relative power of capital and labour and by the prevailing institutional framework.

These outcomes change over time as economic and political power shift. Early in the twentieth century, political power had begun to shift in favour of labour in the capitalist economies. Literacy rates had increased rapidly in the latter years of the nineteenth century (Flora, 1983, ch. 2). As well, industrialization had brought urbanization and greater mobility as public transportation systems improved, increasing the access of the average citizen to information and ideas (Goldthorpe, 1978). The rise of socialist labour parties and of organized labour movements embodied these ideas, and provided channels for labour to make its demands clear to governments. Early demands concerned the right to form unions and conditions of employment; prominent among the latter was the demand for an eight-hour day. Success was limited. Although union membership was growing, it remained low prior to World War I, and the eight-hour day was to come only in 1918.

Labour's economic power is strengthened by greater levels of unionization, and also by the division of labour typical of advancing technology that makes production vulnerable to work stoppages in key areas, and entire economies vulnerable to strikes in key industries. However, the exercise of this power is very costly unless labour has some protection from the rigours of the market. In its absence, labour was to remain hostage to fluctuations in output and employment until after World War II. The institutions that provide this insulation include legislation ensuring fair labour practices and the provision of social safety nets, and governments actively pursuing policy goals of low unemployment and high income growth. Events in the inter-war period were to lay the groundwork for the establishment of these institutions, which were essential to the success of the golden age.

3.2 The inter-war period

By 1920, democracy had broadened to provide universal male enfranchisement (Flora, 1983, ch. 3), and union membership was growing rapidly (Korpi, 1983, p. 31). Ideas that had earlier been associated with radical left-wing fringe groups began to spread. Increasing numbers came to believe in

---

[1] Japan chose another solution. Rather than a well-developed social safety net, the bulk of the workforce was guaranteed 'employment for life' by large corporations.

a fairer distribution of the benefits of capitalism and in the need for social insurance against the vicissitudes of the market. The vote and the union were to become the means to pursue these goals. Adherence to left-wing political parties – communist, socialist and labour – rose rapidly, as shown by the percentage of left-wing votes cast in elections of the period (Korpi, 1983, p. 38). The hardships of the Great War had given focus to labour's expectations of a better life, and labour was poised to secure its reward.

There were to be serious setbacks. In Europe, the immediate post-war years were a time of both social and economic disruption. Boundaries were redrawn, creating large numbers of displaced persons who, together with demobilized armies, sought work as wartime production ceased. In Russia, the communists had seized power in 1917. Now, worker unrest was evident elsewhere; there were strikes in France, the UK and the USA, factories were occupied in Italy, and existing regimes were replaced in Austria and Germany. These events delayed reconstruction and contributed to the depression of 1920–1 in Europe. Perhaps more significantly, they justified and reinforced governments' fears of increasing social unrest.

In Europe, post-war reconstruction proceeded rapidly in the early 1920s, in spite of very severe inflation problems. Fears of crippling industrial strife or more serious social unrest induced governments to make some concessions to labour, but these fell far short of its goals. In Germany and Austria, labour representatives secured some protection for wages, which rose in line with the rapidly rising price level, although lags resulted in real income losses. These early forms of social bargain ended abruptly when governments undertook financial stabilization plans in the mid-1920s and unemployment rose. In the UK the post-war boom collapsed in 1920 and unemployment rose to 11 per cent; it averaged over 8 per cent for the remainder of the decade. Between 1920 and 1932, British unions lost half their membership.

The economic collapse of the 1930s in the democracies of Western Europe and North America brought further setbacks, with worsening conditions for labour as mass unemployment took hold. Unions in the UK and Germany called for expansionist policies, but neither the British Labour Party nor the German Social Democrats could be persuaded to break with the economic orthodoxy of balanced budgets. In France, the Popular Front government's attempts to meet labour's demands for such policies were quickly reversed.[2] Sweden was an example of government departing from its traditional economic stance, as the Social Democrats used expansionary measures and laid the foundations of the welfare state. These demands for

---

[2] The social division that followed in Germany opened the opportunity for Hitler's rise to power and the subsequent abolition of the free labour movement. In France, similar social stresses contributed to capitulation in 1940 and the establishment of the Vichy government.

government intervention to offset the effects of the slump are a demonstration not simply of the extent of labour's organization and purpose, but of a shift in thinking regarding the ability and duty of governments to manage the economy.

The steep rise in unemployment after 1929 had revived fears of social and political instability, and this resulted in some gains for labour, except in Italy and Germany, where fascist governments abolished the free labour movements. Elsewhere, even in North America where the labour movements were relatively weak, new legislation amounted to a formal recognition of labour as a legitimate player in economic affairs. In some cases this legislation increased the legal power of labour, such as the Wagner Act in the USA, but, given the high unemployment, its symbolic importance outweighed its immediate practical value. Fears of social unrest also led to some improvement of the rudimentary social benefits that existed at the time, and many governments embarked on public works programmes. In effect, governments had begun to accept a part in managing the economy, a role which labour had proposed. This management role was extended as countries prepared for war, was entrenched for the duration of the war, and persisted in various forms as a feature of post-war capitalism.

3.3 The war years and reconstruction

In North America and the UK, the advent of war allowed labour to recover as full employment resumed. Wartime cooperation between labour and government confirmed labour's official status. In the USA and Canada, this cooperation amounted only to union acceptance of a no-strike policy, with wage arbitration. In Britain, unions were involved in wartime planning, including the allocation of labour to individual firms (Armstrong et al., 1984, p. 34). However, everywhere the main impact of war on labour was labour's increased confidence stemming from shared hardships, and its increased determination to achieve its goals. The suffering endured in the depression and the sacrifices of war had given moral power to labour's claims.

In many countries this was transformed into political power at the ballot box. In Western Europe, labour emerged from the war more radical than at any time in its history. Its longstanding concerns with wages and social programmes were now joined with demands for state ownership in key sectors and for state management of the economy. In the UK, where there had been relatively little disruption, union membership had increased and demands for state ownership were added to those for better wages, full employment and social programmes. The election of a Labour government in 1945 gave expression to these demands, and industrial strife was largely avoided.

Disrupted by war, labour was not well organized in Italy and France, but nevertheless its political power was evident. In each country, resistance movements played a decisive role in ending German occupation. They were manned largely by the working class, among whom communists and socialists were the majority (Armstrong et al., 1984, p. 41). In France, the Communists and Socialists received over 50 per cent of the vote in the 1945 election. In addition to social reform, these left-wing parties demanded nationalization of banks and key industries. In this they were initially supported by the right-of-centre Christian Democrats.

Despite being abolished by a fascist government in the 1930s, the German labour movement demonstrated a capacity for rapid reorganization. Before the US army arrived, representatives of the old unions had met in Cologne. Drawing upon past experience of weakness caused by divisions in the union movement, they were insistent upon unity – that is, a single union with industrial branches. Labour's concern with unity and demands for nationalization were repeated at the political level. Calls for nationalization, full employment, state control of foreign trade and a new democratic constitution sprang from a broad base, coming not only from Social Democrats and Communists but also from the Christian Democrats. The occupying powers refused to allow national unions to organize, permitting only local unions in a loose federation. In addition, a large influx of refugees increased supply, further weakening labour's power.

There had never been a strong Japanese labour movement, and post-war events ensured that this would continue. The labour force had increased by about 15 per cent over its pre-war level, largely owing to the return of some 6 million refugees from Japan's Asian empire (Armstrong et al., 1984, p. 26). In 1945 the USA introduced labour laws modelled on its own domestic legislation, and union membership grew rapidly. By 1946, widespread demonstrations, the occupation of factories and strikes had become the norm. Unions were able to achieve wage increases and job security for their members, but at the expense of productivity and profits. These gains were the result as much of employer weakness as of union strength. The US occupation powers took action, banning a proposed general strike in 1947 and removing government employees' right to strike. The policy shift caused by the Cold War led to measures by the USA, with the support of the Japanese government and employers, to replace existing unions with new ones that promised harmonious industrial relations.

Even where labour was weakest, the effects of depression and war had been to strengthen the belief that the benefits of peace and prosperity should be more equitably shared. This belief was not confined to labour, but was held by other segments of society. In many countries, labour was able to elect governments that would pursue its goals, providing direct evidence of its political power. Even where this did not happen, governments gave greater weight to labour's claims than at any time in the past. As always, the economic benefits sought by labour depended upon prosperity, and this was yet to come. Except in Japan and Germany,[3] reconstruction proceeded rapidly until 1947, when the shortage of dollar reserves threatened to stall it for lack of imported food and capital goods. This coincided with the start of the Cold War, which led to abrupt changes in US policy that were to play a key role in the recovery of Europe and the establishment of a durable compromise between labour and capital.

4 Capital's role in the new order

4.1 Capital's special function

The radicalization of labour and its early post-war success in electing governments friendly to its cause appeared to present a democratic challenge to the longstanding influence of business in political and economic affairs. This influence rests on the functions performed by the business community in private enterprise systems. The decisions of business leaders determine the technology to be used, the way in which work is organized, the locations of industry, the allocation of resources and the structure of markets. In exercising control over production, business controls output, prices, employment and growth. Business leaders therefore perform a public function, making decisions upon which economic security and living standards depend. Consequently business is not simply one of many interest groups pursuing its agenda with government. In practical terms it is part of government – not elected, but clearly governing economic performance. The electoral fortunes of governments are tied to economic performance, and this alone would predispose governments to extend to business leaders privileges that would induce them to perform their economic functions successfully.[4]

This symbiosis was clearly evident in the nineteenth century. In the USA and Britain, changes in corporate law limited owners' liability and legislatures granted special benefits to encourage business activity, railway building being a notable example. Governments in continental Europe and Japan went further in fostering business development, with systems of subsidies and loans as well as legal privileges. As the size of business enterprises grew, so did their influence with governments, which recognized the functions of business as indispensable to the welfare of the broader society. In the 1930s, efforts to remedy the depression were

---

[3] At this early stage, US policy was to prevent Germany from regaining industrial power and to offer no assistance to the rebuilding of the Japanese economy.
[4] For a thorough treatment of these ideas, see Lindblom (1977), chs. 13–15.

not confined to public works, agricultural supports and relief for the unemployed, but also included massive financial assistance to private companies.

4.2 *The new order*

The challenge from labour at the end of World War II was aimed directly at the essential control function of business. Calls for nationalization and economic planning would remove decision-making power from business and place it in the hands of governments, at least in those industries identified as candidates for state control. Labour's demands flowed from four main sources: the political ideologies of the left-wing parties they sponsored and supported; the impact of *The General Theory* on labour's support for government intervention; the experience of wartime planning and the high incomes and full employment it delivered; and the widespread public hostility to capitalists depicted (with more or less accuracy) as fascists, fascist collaborators, war criminals or war profiteers. The US occupation of Germany and Japan brought a second threat to business power in those countries. Prior to the dramatic policy change that the Cold War brought, the USA was intent upon a programme of decartelization in both countries.

A wave of nationalization swept across Europe as governments took over key sectors of their economies. Exceptions were the Netherlands, Belgium and Germany. In the UK, the Bank of England as well as coal, gas and electricity were nationalized. In France, many commercial banks and insurance companies were added to the list. In Italy, the government had inherited the Institute for the Reconstruction of Industry from the fascist government, and it was expanded. As a result, the governments of these three countries came to own between 10 and 20 per cent of industrial capacity. Similar programmes of state ownership were enacted in the smaller European economies.

Heavy investment spending was essential to replace worn-out or obsolete capital, or to convert capital to peacetime production, but private enterprise faced a new and distinctly less congenial business environment. Public condemnation for wartime activities and the demonstrated responsiveness of governments to public pressure for state ownership were manifestations of the new power relationships that had emerged. Working-class deference to authority had been replaced by the exercise of political power, and the various combinations of state ownership, control and planning adopted in the European economies, far from being merely retaliatory, were integral components of their policies for economic reconstruction. Reconstruction was not to be exposed to the hazards of free market capitalism, but was to be an orderly process following priorities established by governments. High among these priorities was investment in the private sector, not only to ensure recovery but to promote modernization and future growth. Development would be directed to high priority industries (whether or not nationalized) identified in government recovery plans. Private sector firms had little option but to conform. In some industries the possibility of nationalization remained, and for many others survival depended on the acquisition of capital and raw materials that governments controlled.

The shift in political power to labour that lay behind these government initiatives carried the threat of further restrictions should business fail to cooperate. It also carried the threat that labour would more readily engage in strikes and other behaviour disruptive to production in support of demands for the improved pay and working conditions that were expected and, in many countries, had been promised by the new labour-friendly governments. This additional risk to profit came at a time when large investment outlays were needed. Combined with governments' clear resolve to direct the course of post-war reconstruction, this fear of labour militancy created an environment that in many economies induced business to agree to a compromise with labour.

However uncongenial the business environment may have appeared at the time, these changes were to have little long-run impact on the special relationship between government and business. Although the extent of planning and other interventions varied widely among countries, all depended upon continuous consultation with business leaders to ensure their cooperation and to meet planning objectives. Within the confines dictated by these objectives, in the 80 or 90 per cent of the economy that remained in private ownership, business continued to exercise its right to manage. Nor did nationalization imply democratic control. The newly nationalized industries were often run by managers drawn from private enterprise, exercising similar management power. Not only were the traditional management powers of business intact, but nationalization and planning had forged additional links between business and government. The 'new order' reconfirmed the special position of business.

5 Government: acceptance of interventionism

Where the shift in power to labour had developed, with ups and downs, over a long period, the about-face in governments' beliefs was relatively abrupt. The atmosphere of the inter-war period was coloured by the Russian revolution and by the political and industrial unrest that had followed World War I in the major European countries; the depression of the 1930s crystallized these fears and triggered profound changes in governments' views of their role in the economy.[5] The rapid spread of the slump from country to country and the severity of its impact were enough to distinguish it from earlier recessions. But worse, the economic systems of these countries showed no ability to right themselves, and the slump persisted. The first responses took the form of currency devaluations and tariff increases to encourage exports and limit imports, and of expanded credit to reduce bankruptcies, including government loans to private firms. New agricultural support programmes were established and existing ones expanded. With few exceptions (the USA and Japan among them), unemployment insurance programmes were already in place, although they were limited in coverage. By the mid-1930s, faced with continuing high unemployment, most governments had initiated immense public works programmes to alleviate unemployment; the Tennessee Valley project was established in the USA, in the Netherlands the Zuider Zee was reclaimed, in Italy swamps were drained and roads built, the French built the Maginot Line, and Germany remilitarized. In contrast, the British Treasury persisted in its view that public works projects would merely drain resources from the private sector, so that they would yield no net gain in employment. Instead, there was greater reliance on unemployment insurance, although loans to private firms helped to provide employment in localized areas. These measures went beyond relief for the unemployed; their target was economic performance itself. This represented a sharp change in the traditionally liberal, *laissez-faire* ideology that had dominated economic thought for over a century in Britain and the USA.

Expenditures on such a scale required some degree of economic planning. Planning had been used in some West European economies in order to speed up industrialization after a late start. It was now put to an entirely new use, as governments sought a solution to unemployment and recession, and it was used in a wider group of countries, including the USA. The preparations for war further extended the role of government in the European and US economies, providing evidence of the effectiveness of government spending to create and sustain high levels of employment. This was a demonstration of the ideas that Keynes had propounded in *The General Theory*. Unemployment ceased to be regarded as an unavoidable fact of life; rather it was the responsibility of government to use economic policy to keep the economy at full employment. In the UK this view was accorded official status when all political parties espoused the goals laid out in the second Beveridge report (1944).

[5] In the period since 1918, the UK, Finland, Sweden and Switzerland were the only European states that had survived as democracies without interruption. In the rest, political as well as economic stability were in question.

6 The post-war compromise in outline

6.1 Domestic developments: Western Europe, the UK and Japan

Based on their experience of economic planning immediately before and during the war, governments and civil servants came to see such economic management as the best route to reconstruction and recovery, whether in conjunction with nationalization of basic industries or without it. There was enormous variation in the degree of planning, from the British approach of continuing wartime controls to the far more elaborate French Monnet Plan. But whatever route was chosen, success would depend on the cooperation of labour and on capital resuming its essential function of organizing production, following national priorities. To meet the demands of labour and simultaneously induce business leaders to undertake the large investment that would be required, governments negotiated the compromises that not only would permit recovery, but would prove to be central to the period of rapid growth that ultimately followed.

In the political climate of the time, the competing demands of labour and capital may have appeared irreconcilable. However, these differences coexisted with a common desire for rapid reconstruction and a return to normal peacetime life, providing an environment conducive to compromise. Governments sought political and economic stability and the restoration of national prestige and economic power. Labour wanted employment, decent incomes and security in times of unemployment and other misfortune. Business could see the opportunity for profitable enterprise, but feared labour's strength and radicalism. The compromises that were reached, although differing in detail and emphasis from one country to another, had features in common that would meet the priorities of all parties. First, most governments accepted full employment as a goal.[6] They also took steps to ensure that union rights were clear, that collective bargaining was an orderly process, and that conditions of employment and procedures for lay-offs were fair to labour. Social safety nets were improved, regarding both the numbers covered and the benefits that could be claimed. In return for these benefits, labour agreed to wage restraint, with rises lagging productivity in the early post-war years to generate higher profits for investment. Tax concessions, government loans and subsidies encouraged firms to distrib-

---

[6] This commitment varied widely in its practical aspects. For example, it was an integral part of the British Labour Party's platform, to be achieved by fiscal measures as Keynes had prescribed, and it was enshrined in the French Constitution; in West Germany it was made only in the late 1950s; the public commitment in Italy was sacrificed in private in the name of greater productivity; and in the USA it was reduced to a responsibility of the President, who had no power to achieve it.

ute only a small proportion of profits and to invest the rest. That labour agreed to wage restraint is an indication of the relative preference for security prevailing among workers who remembered the Depression all too clearly. Labour had gained a political presence that yielded many of the economic benefits it had long sought, and more were promised as productivity and incomes rose. Labour's agreement gave capital reason to expect economic stability and orderly industrial relations, reducing the risk for the large investments it was to make. These compromises were the foundation of the social bargains discussed in chapter 5, and they laid the groundwork for recovery and growth.

Recovery proceeded rapidly. Estimates of the stock of productive capital suggest that the totals had not changed appreciably as a result of the war, and in Germany and the USA they appear to have increased (Armstrong et al., 1984). The quick repair of much wartime damage, plus new investment, had increased engineering capacity. Other sectors had fared worse. Transportation systems in France, Germany and Italy were in disarray; bombs had destroyed railways, bridges and much of the rolling stock, and what remained was in poor repair. Transportation became a priority, and rail traffic quickly returned to pre-war levels. Labour was plentiful, supplied by demobilized armies and refugees, and production rebounded rapidly in response to pent-up demand. By 1947, most countries had restored industrial output to its pre-war level.[7] The extent of this rebound depended upon imported food, raw materials and capital goods from the USA. The USA provided food aid channelled through the United Nations Relief and Rehabilitation Administration (UNRRA), but this ended in 1946. Aside from this, imports were financed by dollar reserves and US loans. Consequently, Europe's dollar reserves were being rapidly depleted, having fallen by one-third in the space of only two years as imports ran well ahead of exports. Balance of payments problems threatened to slow the pace of recovery. This would delay the promised prosperity, with serious implications for the new social bargains and perhaps for political stability itself. The intervention of the USA was to solve this problem, with far-reaching effects both internationally and domestically for these economies.

6.2 The USA and the lack of compromise

At the end of the war, the US economy was stronger than it had ever been, producing about 40 per cent of world output and controlling 70 per cent of

---

[7] Primarily because of the policies of the occupying powers, but also resulting from the extent of disruption, West German and Japanese industrial production remained below 40 per cent of its pre-war levels. It was not until 1951 that production overtook pre-war levels (Armstrong et al., 1984, p. 69).

the world's gold and foreign reserves. US capital was in a strong position. The war had seen continuous expansion of the economy, and the USA had escaped the destruction endured elsewhere. The profit rate was high, and after-tax profits would rise further when high wartime tax rates were reduced.

With full employment for the duration of the war, organized labour had gained strength. Union leadership had agreed to a no-strike policy and to limited wage increases. Nevertheless, incomes rose steadily, boosted further by a longer work week and increased participation of married women. With the return to peace, overtime was reduced and weekly wages declined. In 1946, 116 million days were lost as wage demands were backed by a wave of strikes (Armstrong et al., 1984, p. 32). Wages increased by 15 per cent or more (ibid., p. 115), but employers took the opportunity to secure unrestricted rights to hire, fire and discipline workers and to control production. A law giving the government emergency powers to break strikes was abandoned only because the rail strike at which it was aimed ended. In spite of agreement that reduced military spending would create a recession, business vehemently opposed any government commitment to full employment. The proposed Full Employment Bill became the 1946 Employment Act, which committed the government to the promotion of free enterprise as the source of jobs. Business went on to demand legislation that would weaken unions, a campaign that culminated in the Taft–Hartley Act. US business had reasserted its power.

These anti-labour moves were assisted by changes within the labour movement. Anti-communist sentiment fuelled by the Cold War enabled elements in the Congress of Industrial Organizations (CIO) to purge much of the left-wing opposition and to consolidate their own power. These were union leaders prepared to accommodate the requirements of business. The CIO adopted a policy of 'no interference' by political parties. Unlike the experience in Europe, the US labour movement severed links with political parties that might have represented its interests. Perhaps not surprisingly, there were no improvements to the US social safety net in these years.

7 The USA as the new hegemon

7.1 US trade and payments policy

The domestic institutional changes that had already taken place in Western Europe during the first few years following World War II were to play a very large part in subsequent events. But international political developments also played a decisive role. Particularly important was the international policy of the USA. The USA had emerged early in the war as a proponent of a multilateral system of liberalized trade.[8] With the largest economy and a strong trade surplus, and holding the bulk of the world's foreign reserves, American views on the post-war international order dominated the Bretton Woods Conference and subsequent international agreements in the 1940s. There was broad recognition of the need for a system of multilateral trade and payments designed to discourage the competitive devaluations and controls that had blighted trade in the inter-war period. In sharp contrast to the strength of the USA, the countries of Western Europe faced post-war reconstruction with large trade deficits and dwindling foreign reserves. Consequently, the Bretton Woods institutions (the International Monetary Fund and the World Bank) as well as the General Agreement on Tariffs and Trade were the outcome of compromise between the US objective of trade liberalism and the deficit countries' strong preferences for planned trade and protectionism.[9] These agreements embodied the long-term commitment to the trade liberalism sought by the USA, but permitted controls in the shorter term with some US assistance for payments deficits. Although the USA believed that the transition period would be brief, controls persisted and consistent implementation of policies to liberalize trade was delayed until the 1960s.

The machinery provided by the IMF was designed to support the pegged exchange rate system of the Bretton Woods Agreement by financing temporary payments imbalances, thus reducing the temptation for deficit countries to devalue their currencies. The General Agreement on Tariffs and Trade negotiated in 1947 promoted multilateral trade liberalization, beginning with the removal of quotas and controls and proceeding in stages to the removal of tariffs. Although these measures were of immense importance in the longer term, they had little relevance for the immediate problems faced by countries trying to rebuild economies ravaged by war. The IMF was barred from making loans for reconstruction. These were the realm of the International Bank for Reconstruction and Development, established at the same time, but it made no loans until 1947, and even by 1953 its loans totalled only US$1 billion (Armstrong et al., 1984, p. 53). Neither was aid channelled through UNRRA available for reconstruction, since, even before the end of the war, the US Congress had interpreted 'rehabilitation' to be equivalent to relief. Consequently, prior to the introduction of the European Recovery Program (also known as the Marshall Plan) in 1947, the largest source of funds for reconstruction was lending by the USA (on quite stringent terms) to Britain and France.

---

[8] Article VII of the 1941 Lend-Lease Agreement required Britain to eliminate its system of imperial trade preferences.
[9] For a concise account of these compromises, see Brett (1985), ch. 3.

7.2 *The Cold War, the European Recovery Program, and some US concessions*

In the absence of other sources of finance for reconstruction, by early 1947 there was a growing belief that continued recovery depended upon support from the USA. For the European countries, the impending dollar shortage confirmed fears about competitiveness and the trade balance, increasing their resistance to abandoning controls. In the event, they were to receive the assistance they needed without relinquishing protection from international competition. The timing of the European Recovery Program (ERP) was dictated by both economic and political events in the USA as well as in Europe. The emerging dollar shortage raised fears that a loss of exports would cause a serious downturn in the USA. Conditions in Europe and Japan were still less than orderly; labour unrest was aggravated by food shortages and inflation. Increased political instability was the likely result of any slowdown of the recovery. All of this coincided with the emergence of the Cold War. US Cold War policy hinged upon alignment with a strong and stable Europe; political stability was essential, and required economic stability. US policy for Germany was immediately reversed, and the restoration of German industrial power became central to the US vision of a united Europe. There was a similar about-face in Japan, as part of a general policy of strengthening the 'free world'.

The exact part played by the ERP has been a source of debate. There are two views concerned primarily with the impact of the dollar transfers. One claims that Marshall Aid was critical in financing investment and imports of raw materials, food and technology. The other views the dollars transferred as largely superfluous, because recovery was well established. It is true that, large as the Marshall Plan transfers were, they were modest compared with total investment in those economies, amounting to less than 10 per cent of gross fixed capital formation after the first two years (Reichlin, 1995). In light of this, another line of assessment concentrates upon the longer-term impact of the Marshall Plan on domestic institutions and on the commitment to the new international institutions that resulted from the negotiations between the USA and aid recipients (Crafts, 1995a). This view argues that these institutional changes, especially the strengthened social bargains and moves towards European integration, supported rapid and sustained growth.

Although the USA was clearly the dominant economy at the end of the war, it was not able to promote the free market or even quickly to achieve the international objectives agreed upon at Bretton Woods. Instead, the international political-economic system that eventually arose has been termed 'embedded liberalism' by Keohane (1984). It is characterized by governments that pursue interventionist domestic policies and liberal inter-national economic policies. This system did not arise spontaneously, but was engineered by the USA. The ERP provided the necessary leverage. The most urgent goal was stability and rapid recovery in Europe, which was to be the first line of defence in the Cold War. Grants were contingent upon undertakings by recipient governments that were intended to further long-run US objectives while solving the immediate problems. US interest in European integration is clear in the establishment of the Organisation for European Economic Co-operation. Its purpose was to coordinate recovery plans and to encourage specialization among the participating countries. Specialization was also seen as a step toward multilateral trade.

As well as making a long-run commitment to free trade, grant recipients were required to join the European Payments Union (EPU) and to remove quotas on intra-European trade. The EPU required currency convertibility among its members, but permitted inconvertibility vis-à-vis the rest of the world. As a first step, aid recipients were required to agree to realign and stabilize their exchange rates and to balance government budgets as a means to domestic price stability. The policies needed to achieve domestic price stability promised to worsen the already uncomfortable level of labour unrest in the late 1940s. Further measures were needed if political instabil-ity was to be avoided. While the deflation resulted in a shift of income toward profit, import licensing and foreign exchange rationing were per-mitted, thus avoiding devaluations and worsening terms of trade. This helped to maintain the standard of living. It is estimated that without these measures there would have been a fall in the terms of trade sufficient to offset the effect of the ERP (Eichengreen, 1995a, ch. 7).

7.3 The ERP and European domestic policy

In addition to liberalization of international trade and payments, the USA was committed to an ideal vision of a united Europe modelled after the USA, both politically and economically. In particular, it was believed that free enterprise capitalism and a US-style industrial relations system would deliver the productivity growth and rising living standards that would resolve social conflict.[10] In Japan and West Germany, where as the occupy-ing power it was most able to impose its preferences, attempts to decartel-ize industry and to install US-style unions had little lasting effect. Elsewhere, even with the leverage afforded by the ERP, the realities pre-cluded the establishment of this model. In the UK and Europe, the USA faced governments responding to the views of highly politicized labour

---

[10] Maier (1987) refers to this as the 'ideology of productivism'.

movements. Nationalized industries and the welfare state were central to the social bargains. Economic management was viewed as essential to reconstruction and to the full employment most governments had promised. Political stability precluded any backing away from these measures, and the ERP was to strengthen them, confirming the welfare state and mixed capitalism as part of the new order.

There were two areas in particular where the administration of the ERP strengthened European institutions that ran counter to US preferences for the free market. The first stemmed from the concerns for stability and growth. Labour unrest grew from conflict over distributional fairness, and was exacerbated by food and commodity shortages and price stabilization measures required of aid recipients. In the view of its administrators, the role of Marshall Aid in this area was to moderate conflict by increasing the 'size of the pie'. This reduced the cost to labour of agreeing to the wage restraint that would allow profits to fund the investment necessary for economic growth. Marshall Aid therefore strengthened the compromise between labour and capital by reducing the cost of agreeing to this key component. For many European countries, this amounted to endorsing industrial relations systems quite different from the US model.[11]

The second area where US *laissez-faire* preferences were sacrificed arose from the ERP emphasis on intervention in the form of planning. Recipients were required to formulate four-year plans for the use of the aid funds, so that administrators could monitor their use and see that goals were likely to be met and aid ended as scheduled. 'Indicative' planning was used, which entailed some government controls but rested primarily on governments making priorities clear and providing inducements for investment and production consistent with these priorities. This approach modified rather than replaced market signals and required a high level of government intervention. Intervention was therefore in effect endorsed by the requirements of the ERP.

The US vision of a united Europe was reflected in the original requirement that recipients were to coordinate their plans for the use of Marshall Aid to promote specialization of production across international boundaries. This was not acceptable to European governments, and the USA abandoned the requirement, fearing that it would foster international cartels to the detriment of free trade and competition. The US objective of a strong Germany in an integrated Europe met with stiff opposition, especially from France and the UK. French opposition was rooted in history and in remaining unsettled questions about the Saar. In the event, it was a French plan, offered as an alternative to the US proposals, that formed the start-

[11] Chapter 5 discusses these different industrial relations systems.

ing point for European integration. This was the European Steel and Coal Community, which was designed so to entangle the German and French economies that future hostilities could not be contemplated.[12]

7.4 Productivity policy

Important among the many objectives of the Marshall Plan were the restructuring and modernization of European industry. This involved more than merely replacing destroyed or worn-out capital and more than simply increasing productive capacity; it emphasized the increase of productivity. The Technical Assistance component of the ERP accelerated the transfer of technology and stressed adoption of the US model of production as the route to permanent productivity increases. Governments cooperated, using cheap credit, tax concessions and direct loans and subsidies to encourage firms to adopt the best technologies; labour was urged to cooperate to ensure rising living standards. Government-sponsored productivity missions sent experts, industrialists and union officials to the USA as part of a drive to reduce the technology gap. There is disagreement about the direct impact of Technical Assistance.[13] Nevertheless, it reversed pre-war policy by encouraging the export of US technology, which could be adapted to suit local preferences even when the complete 'US production model' was not adopted. It can be argued that the longer-run effects were very substantial, eased technology transfer being essential to the process of 'catching-up' which accelerated industrialization and productivity growth in many of the OECD economies.

7.5 The new capitalism

Thus it was political intervention that ensured recovery, not the *laissez-faire* model favoured by the USA. The new international institutions succeeded in fostering rapid trade growth and delivered orderly international payments. The concessions made by the USA permitted delays in the implementation of the full system envisaged at Bretton Woods, giving the protection that was needed to allow stability during reconstruction and modernization. The USA played the key role in establishing this new international order. At the national level, state intervention reduced instability and expanded welfare programmes protected labour. The newly formed

---

[12] See Hobsbawm (1994), ch. 8. The European Steel and Coal Community was to develop into the European Economic Community in 1957, which eventually became the Common Market.

[13] Silberman and Weiss (1992, p. 18) claim that it had a powerful effect on productivity, but Crafts (1995a, pp. 263–4) finds no empirical support for this claim in the UK case.

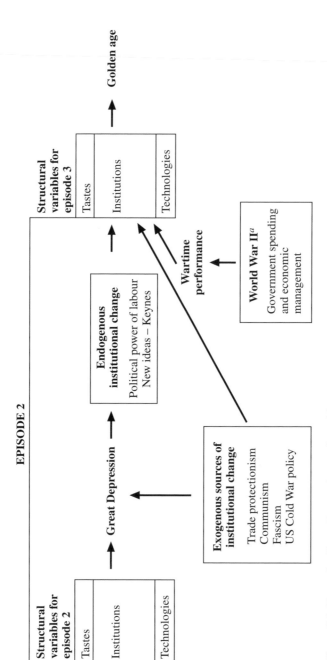

Figure 9.1 From the Great Depression to the golden age

Note:

[a] World War II is treated separately from other exogenous shocks, because the change in economic performance it caused cannot be regarded as part of normal capitalist development. This performance induced institutional change by demonstrating the effectiveness of government intervention. At the same time as convincing other segments of society of the value of intervention, it reinforced labour's previously established beliefs, but this interactive effect cannot be shown on the figure.

social bargains further reduced the risks attendant upon investment. These institutions and the beliefs they embodied produced a new form of capitalism that reconciled growth and change with political and economic stability. Together with the new international regime, this new capitalism made the golden age possible.

The recovery took off in 1950, engineered by state intervention and international economic management. Hobsbawm (1994, p. 273) summarizes the new order that arose:

> For thirty years or so there was a consensus among 'western' thinkers and decision-makers, notably in the USA, which determined what other countries on the non-communist side could do, or rather what they could not do. All wanted a world of rising production, growing foreign trade, full employment, industrialization and modernization, and all were prepared to achieve it, if need be, through systematic government control and the management of mixed economies, and by cooperating with organized labour movements so long as they were not communist. The Golden Age of capitalism would have been impossible without this consensus that the economy of private enterprise . . . needed to be saved from itself to survive.

8 The routes of institutional change

The chapter so far has recounted the changes that occurred in the inter-war period and in the immediate post-World War II years that contributed to the establishment of a new order, with new institutions designed to address problems experienced in earlier times. In this section we summarize these changes in terms of the three routes shown in figure 6.1 (page 104). In figure 9.1, the left-hand box represents the institutions, technology and tastes prevailing during the Great Depression episode, and the right-hand box represents the golden age episode. The figure shows the changes that link the golden age to the depression of the 1930s. However, the golden age did not emerge directly from the 1930s. The events of the 1940s administered exogenous shocks that are also included. Among these, World War II is treated separately, since it provided its own unique route for institutional change. Although there were changes in technology, they are omitted, in order to focus attention on the overwhelming importance of institutions in this period.

The first route is endogenous, induced by economic performance. The most significant institutional changes induced by the economic performance of the 1930s resulted from rejection of the view that unemployment was a temporary and unavoidable phenomenon that would automatically right itself. Labour, which already believed government to be responsible for its welfare in times of adverse economic conditions, now came to believe that government could and should undertake measures to improve those conditions. The changing beliefs of labour and its increased political activity are shown as endogenous routes for institutional change in the figure. Also induced by the economic performance of the time was the revolution in economic thought formalized in *The General Theory*; Keynes and his ideas were to have a pervasive influence in the post-war world. These changing beliefs are represented by the horizontal arrows linking performance in the Great Depression with the endogenous change box in the figure.

In the 1930s, union membership and power declined, forcing labour to seek a solution in the political arena. Political ideas were the most significant exogenous influences of the time, but their rapid spread must be attributed to economic performance. Communist and other left-wing ideologies offered an alternative to the existing economic order, and labour-oriented parties gained membership. Governments (and more generally 'the establishment') had long feared social unrest rooted in leftist ideologies. Now fascism presented another alternative, adding to these fears. Here, too, economic performance played a role, as the lengthening depression induced governments to undertake measures that contained elements of the post-World War II institutions. These included labour legislation, improved social benefits and public works programmes. Although public works programmes were regarded as temporary responses to the current problems, governments had begun to accept a part in managing the economy. The political ideas that were the origin of government fears can be regarded as exogenous to most countries, but the bad economic performance of the time induced governments to take these steps. As in the case of labour's changing beliefs, government responses were the result of the combined effect of exogenous (political ideas) and endogenous (economic performance) factors.

The second route for change is also evolutionary, but was induced by performance resulting from an exogenous shock. The prime example of the 1930s is the beggar-thy-neighbour international trade policy adopted by one government after another. This is shown in the figure by the vertical arrow from the 'exogenous sources' box to performance in the Great Depression. The disastrous effects of these policies induced governments to agree to the multilateral trade and payments system negotiated at Bretton Woods, but its implementation was secured by another exogenous development, the advent of the Cold War.

The public works and other relief measures undertaken by governments in the 1930s are evidence that governments had come to accept responsibility for the welfare of their citizens, but World War II demonstrated their power over economic performance. Viewed in isolation, wartime full employment can be seen as a simple response to national emergency, but at this period it served to reinforce ideas that had developed earlier. It was a practical demonstration of the effectiveness of Keynes' ideas for sound management of a peacetime economy. It contributed to the spread of the belief to all segments of society that unemployment was avoidable; full employment became the target of economic policy and a prime responsibility of government. A second outcome of war was the experience and confidence gained by governments and civil servants as economic managers. Such direct intervention was to become an essential component of post-war reconstruction outside of North America. Expanding acceptance of this wider role for government is shown in the lower right-hand box of the figure as institutional change induced by wartime economic performance. However, in this case performance was the result of an exogenous event as the requirements of war dictated government policy. For this reason, it is treated as a separate route to institutional change in the figure, and is shown by arrows from the lower right-hand box leading to the episode 3 'institutions' box.

Finally, we turn to the effects of the Cold War and the US policy response as exogenous determinants of institutional change, the third of the three routes for change identified in chapter 6 and shown in figure 9.1 by the diagonal arrow from the 'exogenous sources' box directly to the 'institutions' box for episode 3. As discussed earlier, the USA was unable to realize its original plans for the international trade and payments system, but the compromise that arose created a system of relatively stable exchange rates and controlled capital flows that fostered the rapid growth of trade, both within Western Europe and between Europe and the rest of the world. US efforts to promote a united Europe were rejected, but were replaced by European initiatives for cooperation. Neither was the US free market model adopted in Europe. Although the ERP gave the USA some influence, European political and economic stability were the uppermost Cold War priorities. The nationalizations, social safety nets and full employment policies adopted by recipient governments were accepted as essential to this stability. Finally, ERP aid was conditional upon the recipients' producing economic plans for its use, confirming interventionism. In effect, the USA gave its seal of approval to the new capitalism that had arisen in post-war Europe.

9 Avoiding the constraints

9.1 Demand-determined growth

The balance of this chapter examines how the institutions established in the early post-World War II years removed constraints on aggregate demand during the golden age in most economies. In the absence of constraints on aggregate demand, these economies were able to reach and sustain full employment, allowing them to realize the rapid growth rates typical of the period. Chapter 4 presented our extension of Keynesian analysis, emphasizing the dynamic effects of full employment on productivity and income growth rates, the case of demand creating its own supply, although within some limits. The limits are reached when the supplies of labour, raw materials or capital goods cannot keep pace with growing demand. Potential supply constraints therefore require a brief assessment.

9.2 Supply constraints

At the end of World War II, labour was plentiful in Western Europe and Japan as armies were demobilized and refugees further increased their labour forces. The reallocation of labour from agriculture provided labour supply to the expanding industrial sectors; as this source was depleted, immigration and increased female participation continued to increase supply. Raw materials production had increased during the war, a response to demand, and both European and US investment in the Third World were increased in the post-war period to assure continued supply increases. Capital goods production had also increased in the USA, but once the Cold War had made European recovery a priority there were fears that US production could not meet domestic and European demand simultaneously. A change in US policy established West Germany as a major capital exporter. Lastly, it must be noted that an institutional change easing technology transfer from the USA to its Cold War allies removed another potential supply constraint. Marshall Aid encouraged a massive transfer of technology from the USA to Europe and Japan. During the Marshall Plan years, and for a decade thereafter, governments made concerted efforts to close the technology gap (Maddison, 1991, p. 152). The degree of effort varied among countries, but there can be no question that it played a significant part in the 'catch-up' phenomenon. From the second half of the 1950s onwards, technology transfer was increasingly the result of direct investment by US firms expanding in Europe. The purchase of patents and licences performed the same function for Japan. In sum, the golden age can be characterized as having no supply constraints.

9.3 The inflation constraint

The political power of labour at the end of World War II and the changed views of government regarding its economic responsibilities established the extended welfare state and economic management in Western Europe and the UK as the foundations of a social bargain. The US policy response to the Cold War confirmed these measures. The social bargains had in common labour's agreement to wage growth that lagged productivity growth in the initial recovery period, on the understanding that the resulting high profits would be channelled into investment that would yield rising real wages in the future. This arrangement gave added emphasis to 'fairness' in wage settlements, regarding both real wage growth and relative wages. More generally, in the long term labour expected a fair share of a rising national product. Fairness brought to the fore concerns about whether or not employers would live up to their side of the bargain, since the productivity and profit measures on which settlements depended were calculated by employers. Labour's cooperation depends on its being able to trust the information provided by employers. The level of trust rests upon the machinery of wage bargaining, on labour legislation that affords protection from unfair labour practices, and in general upon an institutional framework embodying fairness and cooperation; this gives greater balance to the labour–capital power relationship.

Achievement of the government goals of growth and full employment was essential to the maintenance of these social bargains, but carried a serious hazard in the form of a potential inflationary bias. In combination with the social safety net, full employment strengthens the economic power of labour relative to capital. Rising incomes and industrialization increase the power of individuals and unions to withstand the costs of strikes, again increasing economic power. If labour is not satisfied that it is treated fairly, and decides to exercise its market power, unacceptably high money wage inflation is likely to result whenever firms can pass on cost increases, creating a potentially strong inflationary bias. It is an outstanding feature of the golden age that, in most countries, rising affluence and low rates of unemployment did not lead to high rates of inflation. These were the economies that had adopted social bargain strategies for wage determination, enabling them to contain inflation at full employment. Others were less successful, and unrestricted collective bargaining (market power strategies) led to inflation as firms agreed to high money wage demands then increased prices to cover rising costs. The inflation could be controlled only by restrictive policies.[14] Higher rates of unemployment were the result in these economies. Table 9.1 summarizes the unemployment and inflation data of figure 5.1 by separating the countries into two groups, according to whether or

[14] Market power strategy was a foregone conclusion in the USA, where capital had reasserted its control in the immediate post-war years. In the UK, reliance on the policies of the Labour government was believed to be a sufficient guarantee of full employment, and unions were in favour of retaining unrestricted collective bargaining. This contributed to the stop–go policies and breakdown of the early wage restraint agreements. In Italy, the main problems were fragmented unions and rivalries among leftist elements.

Table 9.1 *Average rates of unemployment (U) and inflation ($\dot{p}$)*
for 18 OECD economies and for two subgroups: 1960–1973 (%)

Total	Social bargain group[a]	Market power group[b]
$U_{18} = 2.3$	$U_{13} = 1.5$	$U_5 = 4.4$
$\dot{p}_{18} = 4.6$	$\dot{p}_{13} = 4.6$	$\dot{p}_5 = 4.4$

Notes:
[a] Japan, West Germany, France, Australia, Austria, Belgium, Denmark,
Finland, the Netherlands, New Zealand, Norway, Sweden and
Switzerland.
[b] The United States, the United Kingdom, Canada, Italy and Ireland.
Source: OECD, Historical Statistics 1960–1997, Table 8.11; Layard et al.
(1991), Table A3.

not they had established a social bargain. The low unemployment in the 13
social bargain economies supports our claim that they were not subject to
an inflation constraint during this period.

9.4 The balance of payments constraint

Even if the potential inflationary bias can be neutralized at full employment, a second difficulty arises. As employment and aggregate demand
increase so does the demand for imports, creating the possibility of deterio-
rating payments balances and loss of international reserves. Continued
high demand stimulates productivity growth, and import demand continues to increase as incomes rise. Payments problems threaten to bring recovery and growth to an end as governments are forced to adopt restrictive
policies. This was not precisely the problem in the late 1940s. Full employment and rising incomes were promised as an essential component of the
social bargain, but had not yet been achieved, which was a major source of
the labour unrest of the time. Although there was a great need for imports
into Western Europe and Japan, the protectionist legacy of the 1930s and
the shortage of international reserves kept trade at low levels. Existing large
trade deficits with the USA further blighted the prospects for European
economic expansion.

The US objective of non-discriminatory multilateral trade and international specialization was almost certainly the most important factor in
breaking this apparent deadlock. The second was the Cold War.
European recovery was the first priority, causing the USA to modify its
international trade goals in the short run but to establish a transition programme that would support them in the longer term. As well as trade defi-

cits and the looming dollar shortage, European countries' fears regarding the competitiveness of their industries reinforced their lack of enthusiasm for any immediate move to implement the currency convertibility agreed to at Bretton Woods or to remove trade controls. In return for commitment to these goals in the longer run, and to liberalized intra-European trade and currency convertibility in the near term, the USA undertook to provide the needed international liquidity. US trade surpluses were recycled via ERP grants and funding of the European Payments Union, and later via increased military spending under the Mutual Security Act.

Once the EPU was established in 1950, the availability of credit lines allowed intra-European trade, which had been largely confined to bilateral arrangements, to expand rapidly. Membership required a pledge to eliminate discrimination for balance of payments reasons against other members, and substantially to reduce trade barriers. Intra-European trade increased from US$10 billion in 1950 to US$23 billion in 1959, an average annual increase of about 10 per cent; trade with the USA expanded at about 4 per cent per year (Eichengreen, 1995b, p. 172). The effect of the EPU was to keep settlements in gold and dollars to about one-quarter of total settlements. This economy in the use of international reserves permitted expansion of trade between Europe and the rest of the world, and Eichengreen (1995b) suggests that the EPU had the effect of 'jump-starting' Europe's multilateral trade. Trade with the rest of the world expanded at 8 per cent per year from 1955 to 1969. Europe's trade deficits increased in the 1950s and 1960s, but a rising surplus on current account resulted from large surpluses in invisibles. The USA was in current account deficit with Western Europe in 1959, but this became a permanent situation only in the late 1960s (United Nations, 1972, p. 35).

Although some European countries ran payments deficits during these years, they amounted to a small percentage of GDP, and for many countries they were transitory. France and Italy were exceptions. In every case, export growth significantly outpaced GDP growth so that, under reasonable assumptions, rising import demand was unlikely to generate fears of permanent large or increasing imbalances. Further, West Germany and Japan preferred to continue as large surplus countries, a policy that forced them to tolerate deficits elsewhere.

McCombie and Thirlwall (1994) examine the effect of a balance of payments constraint on the ability of an economy to achieve its full employment growth rate of output. In its simplest form, their model considers an economy in payments equilibrium, and assumes no capital flows or changes in relative prices. For continued payments balance, the rates of import and export growth must be equal. Since import demand depends on output, this imposes a limit on the rate of output growth.[15] An extension of the model shows that, if the country is in payments deficit, the balance of payments constrained growth rate will be lower, otherwise the deficit would increase. Finally, if there is a positive rate of growth of net capital flows, these will finance rising trade deficits and allow a more rapid rate of output growth. No matter which of these situations obtains, if the balance of payments constrained growth rate is below the economy's full employment growth rate, the latter cannot be achieved for any significant period. Rising payments deficits will force governments to undertake restrictive measures. The continued full employment enjoyed by most OECD economies is therefore a good indicator that they lacked any payments constraint during the golden age.

9.5 Political constraints

Political constraints such as the fear of 'big government', budget deficits and rising debt to GDP ratios were largely absent in the golden age. Big government was viewed as necessary to the new order, in which government intervention was an essential component of economic stability. Governments had not abandoned the goal of balanced budgets but, in the Cold War environment, priorities had shifted and deficits were tolerated. As prosperity increased, in most countries the deficits that occurred tended to be small relative to GDP. Lastly, the huge debts accumulated during war had created very large debt to GDP ratios, but high rates of output growth were causing these to fall rapidly, even in countries with budget deficits.

10 Conclusion

The purpose of this chapter has been to show how the institutions that framed the post-war economic systems of the OECD can be traced to events in the inter-war period, to provide links between that episode of depression and the prosperous episode that was to follow. Of particular interest are endogenously driven changes, as the poor economic performance of the 1930s led to the widespread adoption of new beliefs centred on governments' responsibility for the welfare of their citizens, not simply as providers of social safety nets but more sweepingly as managers of their economies. These views were expressed by labour-friendly political parties and, following the demonstration of the power of economic policy during

---

[15] The output growth rate (y_B) consistent with continued balance of payments equilibrium is written as $y_B = x/\pi$, where x is the rate of growth of exports and π is the elasticity of demand for imports. For this and the extended versions of the model, see McCombie and Thirlwall (1994), ch. 3.

World War II, by governments formed or heavily influenced by those parties. Labour had achieved political ascendancy, but its economic power was to rise only with the affluence delivered by the golden age.

The success of the social welfare capitalism that was established to meet labour's demands depended ultimately upon there being full employment. A necessary condition for full employment is the absence of constraints on aggregate demand. In most countries, the new labour market institutions were designed to avoid inflation, to maintain international competitiveness, and to minimize industrial strife, all of which encouraged the investment needed for modernization and growth. Investment was further encouraged by events at the international level, as the USA assisted post-war recovery, played a leadership role in the establishment of a stable international economic environment, and encouraged technology transfer. Rapid trade growth relieved potential payments constraints and contributed to high and growing aggregate demand. By the early 1950s, the groundwork was laid for the golden age.

We have argued that the absence of constraints was the outcome of institutional changes, many induced by economic performance in the 1930s, in a process of negative feedback. These changes, and others at the international level, created a new form of capitalism that allowed rapid growth of incomes and full employment in most of the advanced OECD economies. The tools forged by the new institutions were state intervention and international economic management. It was not the invisible hand but these favourable institutions established at the national and international levels that led to the golden age.

10　The golden age

1 Introduction

The previous chapter traced the origins of the new institutions that were
established in the immediate post-World War II period, and which
defined a new form of capitalism. Their origins were to be found in the
poor economic performance of the 1930s, which either caused or accelerated the formation of new institutions at the national level. The war
itself had demonstrated the ability of governments to manage their economies, confirming the view that such management was needed to provide
economic stability and to meet national economic objectives. These
emergent economic systems were at odds with the aim of the USA, as
economic hegemon, to support the reconstruction of the West European
economies in its own image. US ambitions in this direction were eclipsed
by the advent of the Cold War. Instead, the USA accepted these new
forms of capitalism as necessary to the European economic and political stability that had become an absolute requirement of its Cold War
policy.

The Cold War policy imperatives also led to a new international regime
designed to encourage trade and European economic cooperation. The
experience of protectionism in the 1930s had led to general agreement that
multilateral trade and payments should be resumed, but the European
governments prevailed over US preferences, and the system put in place
reflected their fears for the competitiveness of their industries by postpon-
ing full implementation of the agreements reached at Bretton Woods.
Outside of the USA, *laissez-faire* seemed to have been forgotten, or pushed
into a future distant enough to be ignored, even by its most fervent adher-
ents. Economic management at the national level was matched in the international arena by managed trade and payments. At the international level,
as domestically, the requirement of stability was the prime determinant of
the institutions that defined the 'new order'.

Compared with other periods, the stability of the OECD economies

186

during the golden age was truly remarkable. Chapters 2 and 5 have discussed the exceptional unemployment records in the OECD in the same period. The absence of deep or prolonged recessions provided uninterrupted aggregate demand growth, reducing macro risk and fostering the continued business confidence that encourages high levels of investment.[1] This was particularly important for economies in the process of modernization, which entails large expenditures to acquire the latest capital-intensive technologies. Together with stability, the rapid expansion of trade contributed to the growth of aggregate demand, further justifying investment. It was in this environment that many OECD economies achieved the outstanding rates of output and productivity growth that were seen during the golden age.

To consolidate ideas as we developed our analytical framework, chapter 5 included an econometric test that demonstrated the strong influence of both power and institutions on unemployment performance, with emphasis on unemployment during the golden age. In this chapter, we shift the emphasis to a second crucial measure of economic well-being, as we turn to productivity growth and its links to the institutions established in the aftermath of war. These new institutions set the scene for this exceptional performance and fostered its continuance for almost 25 years.

In section 2 we document the high growth rates of output and productivity during the golden age compared with other periods, illustrating the success of economies in which constraints on aggregate demand were indeed absent. Section 3 discusses the sources of rapid growth in productivity, emphasizing the effects of the various components of aggregate demand on overall growth rates. In section 4 we move from the golden age to a longer-run perspective in order to introduce a model relating productivity growth to the transformation of output and employment structures observed as economies develop. This model permits the contribution of demand factors to growth to be disaggregated from the productivity effects of longer-run changes in output structure. The technical content of this section requires the reader's patience, but is kept within bounds by using a diagrammatic presentation; the formal model is relegated to an appendix. Section 5 relates the growth model to the underlying institutional determinants of economic performance. In section 6 an equation based on this model is estimated to assess the sources of growth for a sample of 16 OECD economies. The availability of data limits the time period covered by this exercise to the two post-war episodes. The results of the estimation are reported in section 7. Section 8 restores the focus to

---

[1] See the discussion in the appendix to chapter 8 for the stability of output in the American economy during the golden age.

Table 10.1 *Rates of growth of real GDP ($\dot{Q}$) and labour productivity ($\dot{q}$) for 16 OECD countries: 1870–1998 (%)*

Country	1870–1890		1890–1913		1913–1929		1890–1929		1929–1938		1950–1973		1973–1998	
	$\dot{Q}$	$\dot{q}$	$\dot{Q}$	$\dot{q}$	$\dot{Q}$	$\dot{q}$	$\dot{Q}$	$\dot{q}$	$\dot{Q}$	$\dot{q}$	$\dot{Q}$	$\dot{q}$	$\dot{Q}$	$\dot{q}$
Australia	4.5	−0.1	2.6	1.6	1.3	0.1	2.0	0.9	2.1	1.0	4.7	2.4	3.1	1.5
Austria	2.3	1.5	2.5	1.4	0.3	0.0	1.6	0.8	−0.3	0.3	5.3	5.4	2.4	1.7
Belgium	2.1	1.3	1.9	0.6	1.4	0.9	1.7	0.8	0.0	1.0	4.1	3.5	2.0	2.0
Canada	3.1	1.3	5.0	2.7	2.8	1.1	4.1	2.1	0.0	−0.6	5.1	2.6	2.7	0.7
Denmark	2.2	1.6	3.1	1.8	2.7	1.8	2.9	1.8	2.2	0.4	3.8	2.9	2.1	1.6
Finland	2.5	1.1	3.0	2.0	2.4	1.0	2.7	1.5	3.9	2.2	4.9	4.4	2.5	2.4
France	1.3	1.1	1.7	1.5	1.9	1.7	1.7	1.5	−0.4	0.4	5.0	4.6	2.1	1.8
Germany[a]	2.4	1.6	3.2	1.6	1.2	0.6	2.4	1.2	3.8	2.6	5.9	4.8	2.0	1.7
Italy	1.2	0.6	2.6	2.0	1.7	1.2	2.2	1.7	1.6	1.4	5.6	4.8	2.2	2.0
Japan	2.1	1.7	2.5	1.5	3.7	2.9	3.0	2.1	3.6	2.5	9.3	7.6	3.0	2.1
Netherlands	2.3	1.3	2.3	0.9	3.6	2.0	2.8	1.3	0.3	−0.2	4.7	3.7	2.4	0.6
Norway	1.8	1.3	2.4	1.4	2.9	2.0	2.6	1.7	3.1	1.8	4.1	3.4	3.5	2.2
Sweden	1.8	1.2	2.5	1.7	1.9	0.7	2.2	1.2	2.6	2.6	4.0	3.5	1.6	1.5
Switzerland	1.7	1.2	2.4	1.1	2.8	2.5	2.5	1.6	0.6	0.7	4.5	2.8	1.0	0.4
United Kingdom	2.0	1.1	1.8	0.8	0.7	0.6	1.3	0.7	1.9	0.8	3.0	2.5	1.9	1.6
United States	4.0	1.3	3.9	2.0	3.1	1.8	3.6	1.9	−0.7	0.0	3.6	2.1	2.6	0.9
Unweighted av.	2.3	1.2	2.7	1.5	2.2	1.3	2.5	1.4	1.5	1.1	4.9	3.8	2.3	1.5

Note:

[a] There is a break in 1991 when German reunification occurred.

Sources: For 1870–1989, Maddison (1991), Tables A.6, A.7 and C.8; for 1990–8, OECD, *Historical Statistics 1960–1997*, and OECD, *Economic Outlook, 66*, December 1999, Annex Tables 1 and 20.

the golden age, and utilizes growth accounting based on the estimates to draw out some of the implications of our model. The conclusions are in section 9.

2 Growth in the golden age: some comparative data

Arguments in section 12 of chapter 5 and section 9 of chapter 9 support the view that the effect of the new institutional structure was to relieve most of the OECD economies of constraints on aggregate demand. These were the economies that were able to maintain full employment. Even in countries where capital and labour failed to reach a durable compromise, unemployment was lower than it has been since the golden age,[2] and, like the full employment economies, they benefited from the general prosperity as trade expanded rapidly. The benefit was rapid growth of productivity, which in many economies allowed per capita incomes to increase at a pace hitherto unimagined. The next step is to show what demand-driven economies generate in the way of growth rates compared with other periods. Table 10.1 gives average annual rates of growth of GDP and labour productivity for 16 OECD economies, for selected periods covering over a century.[3] The table shows that, in most of the countries included, both output and output per worker grew faster during the golden age than at any period before or since. The clearest exceptions are the United States and Canada, where similar growth rates had been experienced earlier, from 1890 to 1929 in the United States, and between 1890 and 1913 in Canada. In this chapter we focus on productivity growth performance for two reasons. First, everything else being equal, economies with rapid population growth are likely to have rapid output growth, so that high output growth rates do not necessarily imply improving living standards; in contrast, growth of output per worker is a clear measure of economic dynamism. Second, productivity growth is the source of per capita income growth, and therefore a better measure of increasing economic welfare as economies develop.

3 The sources of growth

In tracing the sources of productivity growth, we turn first to the implications of the demand-determined growth model of chapter 4. Table 4.1 shows two components of aggregate demand – investment and exports – to have exceptionally high growth rates in the golden age. This suggests that

---

[2] See table 2.1.
[3] End points for the early periods are determined by the data available. Data for the early years are not available on an annual basis. As with early data from any source, they should be regarded with some caution. Nevertheless, the general trends are clear.

they were of particular importance in driving the growth of GDP and productivity over the period. In addition to growing AD, the model stressed the part played by high levels of AD, implying that high unemployment may be detrimental to growth. Following a discussion of these demand variables, we turn to two additional characteristics that influence growth rates. The first of these considers the phenomenon of 'catching up'. When it is possible to borrow technology from a more advanced economy, the advantage of a late start in development is the growth bonus conferred by accelerated industrialization. Here, economies differ according to how far they lag behind the technology leader; the greater the lag, the greater the possible growth bonus. The other influence follows from the discussion in chapter 4 of the transformation of output and employment structures, a process integral to development. Here, the growth implications stem from differences in sectoral productivity levels and growth rates; for example, an economy with output concentrated in a high productivity growth sector will, *ceteris paribus*, have a higher average productivity growth rate than one with the bulk of its output produced in a sector with low productivity growth. By considering the impact of these last two variables on growth, we can better isolate the effects of the demand variables. The following discussion of these determinants of growth is the first step in developing a model of growth in labour productivity that distinguishes not only between the impact of different components of AD but also between the latter and longer-run changes in the structure of output.

3.1 Investment

Investment increases productivity both by increasing the capital–labour ratio and by introducing improved technologies. In addition, continued high demand for investment goods induces the capital goods industry to incorporate the latest technologies in its product and may also induce further inventions and innovations, actually speeding up technological progress (Cornwall, 1977, ch. 7). The growth rate of investment is a prime candidate in our list of determinants of productivity growth. To a large extent, rapid growth rates of investment are the result of the interactions between AD, output and investment. High rates of AD and output growth induce high rates of investment growth by reducing macro risk, and high rates of investment growth generate high growth rates of AD and output through the multiplier process.

The high rates of investment growth in most OECD economies during the golden age can be traced to high AD delivered by near full employment. But this is traceable to the new institutions of the post-war period, when full employment became a keystone of many of the social bargains that were established. Besides allowing full employment, the cooperative industrial relations that typified social bargains reduced the risks associated with investment and eased the adoption of new technologies, which, because they changed the working environment, could have been resisted by labour. In the early post-war period, wage restraint had generated higher profits to finance investment, and national governments in Western Europe and the UK were using a variety of policies to promote investment. The second major institutional contribution to high investment growth came from the US Cold War policy, which encouraged technology transfer and modernization to generate the productivity growth and rising incomes that were to secure political and economic stability in Europe and Japan. Partially financed by Marshall Aid in the early years, technology transfer continued as US private firms expanded in Europe. In summary, a virtuous circle of growth was operating in the golden age, as high investment and growing productivity and per capita incomes ensured continued growth in AD, encouraging further investment, and so on.

3.2 Export growth

Export growth was a strong component of the AD growth that took place in the golden age. Its importance to productivity growth is twofold. First, and of particular moment in small economies, the expansion of export markets allows the larger-scale production methods that improve productivity in general. In addition, the need to remain competitive in foreign markets encourages and justifies adopting the best available technologies, further boosting productivity. The protectionist trade policies of the 1930s had reduced trade to low levels, leaving ample opportunity for expansion. This rapid growth of trade was not merely a return to the *status quo ante*. Instead, the composition of traded goods shifted, with over 70 per cent of OECD exports being manufactured goods. Intra-industry trade grew most rapidly of all, accounting for over 80 per cent of the increase in trade between 1959 and 1967 (Grubel and Lloyd, 1975). These trends permitted the exploitation of economies of scale, and expanding intra-industry trade especially encouraged the adoption of both product and process innovations as non-price competition became more important. The implications for productivity growth are clear, and suggest that the growth rate of exports, particularly of manufactured goods, plays a key role in determining productivity growth rates.

Models of export-led growth trace causation from the high AD caused by rapid export expansion to accelerated growth of GDP, and from this to productivity growth. However, the mere existence of an opportunity for trade expansion does not ensure that it will occur and allow these benefits to be realized. In the late 1940s, large payments deficits with the USA and European fears that their industries could not compete internationally threatened to lead to protectionist measures that would slow the expansion of trade. Offsetting this was the continuing need for imports, especially of capital goods, for post-war reconstruction, which could be financed only by expanding exports. That exports did in fact expand in the post-war years, and continued to do so throughout the golden age, must be attributed in large part to the institutions that were developed in the late 1940s and 1950s. As discussed in chapter 9, it was US intervention, and the establishment of trade and payments systems that allayed the main fears of the Europeans, that solved the problem. The USA also provided international liquidity, by recycling its trade surpluses in the early years; by the early 1950s US trade deficits were performing this task. With these new institutions in place, trade was progressively liberalized. Outside the USA, extended periods of an overpriced US dollar further encouraged rapid export growth, which exceeded GDP growth by a large margin.

A second institutional determinant of export growth is found in the social bargains, many of which established wages and prices to meet national goals of international competitiveness. The UK stands out as an example where the tenuous social bargain of the early 1950s failed to perform this task, contributing to recurrent payments problems. These were met by the 'stop–go' policies that have impaired growth and employment in that economy (McCombie and Thirlwall, 1994, pp. 118–19).

3.3 Unemployment

No simple measure of investment or investment growth can reveal the type of investment that takes place. Chapter 4 made the case that the investment strategy chosen by firms is sensitive to the state of AD. When AD is high as well as growing, macro risks are reduced, so that firms tend to choose 'enterprise investment' that increases capacity. This type of investment exploits scale economies and introduces innovations, both of which increase productivity growth. However, it carries the problem of indivisibilities, and consequently the possibility of excess capacity. When unemployment is high for long periods and demand growth sluggish, excess capacity is more likely, and firms tend to adopt a defensive investment strategy. This often amounts to replacing worn-out components of existing equipment. The risk of excess capacity is reduced at the expense of productivity gains.

A second source of risk that attends investment in new technologies comes from the greater adjustments it requires of both labour and management, and from the likelihood that local conditions will require modifications of the technology itself. Because the innovating firm is venturing into new territory, the costs of these adjustments cannot be known, presenting a risk that may be avoided in lean times by shifting to the defensive investment strategy. As with the risk of excess capacity, this keeps productivity growth below the rate that would occur in times of strong demand growth. Its effects on investment lead us to expect unemployment to have a negative impact on productivity growth.

One determinant of the unemployment rate is the nature of labour market institutions, which determine whether or not there is an inflation constraint. There is a second way in which these same institutions can influence the type of investment. In the case of cooperative industrial relations systems, labour is less likely to oppose the introduction of new technologies. This not only encourages firms to invest in new technologies, but reduces the likely costs of the adjustments and modifications associated with such change. Cooperative industrial relations are typical of the low unemployment economies. This characteristic strengthens the likelihood that an unemployment variable will be able to capture the effect on productivity growth of this qualitative dimension of investment.

3.4 Catching up, convergence and the technology gap

The magnitude of investment cannot show the quality of new capital, i.e. the extent of modernization that occurred in many economies. This is of particular relevance to the idea of 'catching up', which entails high rates not only of investment but of investment that embodies the most advanced technologies. In the large literature on catching up, the consistent premise is that the prime determinant of growth is the size of the technology gap, with the most backward economies growing faster, leading to convergence. Backwardness is commonly proxied by the level of per capita income. This relationship can be seen in table 2.2, which shows annual average rates of growth of productivity for 1960–73 and levels of per capita income in 1960 for 18 OECD economies. Although by 1950 (later in West Germany and Japan) recovery had restored pre-war output levels, many of these economies were left with ten or so years of 'lost' economic growth compared with the USA. This created an opportunity for catch-up even in the most advanced of the 'followers'. However, the existence of a technology gap between the USA as technology leader and the more backward OECD economies is not sufficient to ensure catch-up. Institutional barriers could easily prevent it from going ahead, even when the investment funds were available. Among these, the levels of skills and education are of importance, as also is organizational capability, since adaptation to local conditions is the first requirement of absorption of the new production methods.[4] As well, the leader could prevent export of the new technologies. Neither of these barriers was present in the OECD during the period. Under the European Recovery Program, the USA was actively promoting modernization and, after the mid-1950s, US private firms expanded rapidly in Western Europe (but not in the UK). The skills and educational levels were certainly present, and governments were pursuing productivity improvement as essential to the rising living standards upon which, along with full employment, the social bargains rested. In many cases, the social bargains included measures to ease the transition of workers to the new technologies, a decided advantage for those economies. In others, such as the UK, workers resisted such change, fearful that it would endanger jobs.

For economies that exploit technology gaps, the phenomenon of convergence, shown by the inverse relationship between per capita income levels and average productivity growth rates, is the inevitable outcome of the simple mathematics of modernization. The size of the catch-up growth bonus depends, *ceteris paribus*, on the number of capital vintages skipped, so that productivity grows fastest in the most backward economies. It depends also on the rate at which modernization takes place, i.e. on investment in the new technologies. However, if we consider two economies with equal investment to GDP ratios, the more backward of the two (that is, the one with the lower productivity level) will have faster productivity growth, because it skips more capital vintages. Consequently, the output of every worker provided with the new technology rises by a larger proportion than in the less backward economy. Since modernization takes place over a number of years, this growth bonus continues until the technology gap is closed. This shows the productivity advantage of a larger technology gap. In particular it shows that a given 'effort' (for example, amount of investment) yields different results when the technology gap is different. This must be accounted for to assess more accurately the effects of other variables such as exports and investment. We note here that we are not explaining convergence in this model; we are simply taking account of the fact that some countries had a greater potential growth bonus than others from this source.

3.5 Output and employment structure

The average level of productivity and its growth rate in any economy clearly depend on the production techniques in use and on the rate at which tech-

---

[4] Cornwall (1977, ch. 6) discusses the determinants of the catch-up bonus. In addition to opportunity and effort, the ability to absorb new technology plays a vital part. Abramovitz (1986) reiterates these points.

nology advances. But, equally clearly, both levels and growth of productivity vary among different activities, so that the structure of output and employment also play a decisive role. This observation is central to the idea of phases of development. Familiar in the literature is the notion that, as industrialization proceeds, the agricultural sector, with its low productivity and slow productivity growth, cedes its dominance to the industrial (or manufacturing) sector, with its high productivity and rapid productivity growth. The result is a rapid increase in economy-wide productivity and its growth rate. This changing structure of demand results from changes in income elasticities of demand brought about by rising per capita incomes. Demand structure is therefore related to the level of per capita income. Output responds as resources are diverted to production of the goods in high demand. Everything else being equal, two economies with different per capita incomes will have different demand structures, and the one with the largest share of its output in the highest productivity growth sector will have the highest average productivity growth rate. The productivity growth effects of changing output and employment structure are explored in more detail in the next section. The point to be made here is that, via output structure, productivity growth is related to per capita income levels, in addition to the catch-up and demand variables discussed above. This variation in the 'stage of development' therefore creates another source of differences among countries that must be considered if the effects of the other determinants are to be assessed.

The next section introduces a model that provides a theoretical basis for this aspect of productivity growth analysis and for an econometric estimation of the separate contributions to productivity growth of the economy's stage of development, the catch-up growth bonus and the demand variables. The results of this estimation also allow us to establish the sources of differences in productivity growth rates among countries.

4 A model of structural change and growth

4.1 The basic model

Proposed by R.M. Sundrum (1990), this three-sector model of structural change and growth generates a three-phase growth path. The earlier two phases give rise to the notion of a logistic growth path. In the first, agriculture dominates both output and employment, with slow growth and low incomes being the norm. The second is industrialization, during which the output and employment shares of the industrial sector increase; in this phase, growth proceeds rapidly at first but more slowly as high incomes are attained. Clark (1957) proposed the inclusion of a tertiary (or services) sector, an addition that provides an explanation of why growth ceases to accelerate, and predicts eventually slowing growth.[5]

Here, we introduce the model in its original form to emphasize the contribution of this structural transformation process to economy-wide productivity growth, uncomplicated by trade and technology transfer. The formal model is presented in the appendix to this chapter. It is couched in per capita terms, with three sectors: agriculture, manufacturing (or industry) and services. The trend sectoral productivity growth rates ($\dot{q}_i$) are assumed to be constant, with manufacturing highest among them. The economy is closed, so that the sectoral output shares are determined by domestic income elasticities of demand.[6] The income elasticities of demand exhibit a hierarchical pattern. The income elasticity for agricultural output falls as incomes rise; the elasticity for manufactures also falls, but more slowly relative to rising incomes; and for services, income elasticity begins to rise once incomes reach the middle range. These assumptions are consistent with the changing output structure shown in table 10.2.[7]

A final simplifying assumption of the model is that there is a constant proportion of the population employed (not necessarily full employment), so that the growth rates of average productivity for the economy ($\dot{q}$) and per capita income are the same. The growth rate of demand for any sector's output is $\epsilon_i \dot{q}$, where ϵ_i is its income elasticity. Also, for any given sectoral distribution of labour, the per capita growth of each sector's output is the same as its productivity growth rate, denoted $\dot{q}_i$. If this is lower than the growth of demand for its output, labour will be reallocated to that sector. Labour is therefore reallocated from sectors with lower ratios of income elasticity to productivity growth ($\epsilon_i/\dot{q}_i$) to sectors with higher ratios (see equation A10.1 in the appendix). With constant sectoral productivity

[5] Similar patterns are demonstrated by non-capitalist economies and by the later-developing countries of the Third World. The exceptions appear to be very small economies that skip the industrial phase and move on from agriculture directly to services (usually tourism).

[6] It might be argued that price elasticities also play a role. However, while it is true that some opportunities exist for substitution, e.g. purchase a washing machine or send clothes to the laundry, a large part of service sector activities are not substitutes for manufactures, but complementary, e.g. freight transportation and retail services. Consequently, at this level of aggregation, income elasticities are expected to be decisive.

[7] Using cross-section data, Summers (1985) claims that the service sector's output share is constant, its rise with per capita income being illusory, caused by the rising relative price of services, although his data show a rising real share for lower-income countries from 1970 to 1975. Baumol et al. (1989) support the unit elasticity view, using post-war US data. Leaving aside problems inherent to the data, we note that in open economies the service sector share does not depend on income alone, but is also sensitive to export demand, which can maintain high manufacturing and agricultural sector shares. Thus countries with the same income can have different service sector shares and, if the growth rate of exports is greater than that of income, as in the USA, the service sector share may be kept constant or even decline. See section 4.3 in this chapter for further discussion of the effect of exports on sector output shares.

Table 10.2 *Per capita income, output and employment structure, 1960*

Sector	Per capita income (1980 US$)		
	4,000[a]	4,000–5,000[b]	5,000[c]
Output shares (%)			
Agriculture	14.8	9.6	4.2
Industry	38.1	40.1	38.0
Services	47.1	49.4	56.8
Employment shares (%)			
Agriculture	29.3	17.2	10.6
Industry	33.5	39.5	39.0
Services	37.2	43.3	50.4

Notes:
[a] Japan, Italy, Austria, Belgium, Finland, Ireland and Spain.
[b] W. Germany, France, Denmark, the Netherlands and Norway.
[c] The United States, the United Kingdom, Canada, Australia and Sweden.
Source: OECD, *Historical Statistics*, various issues.

growth rates and rising incomes, the more rapid decline of income elasticity for agricultural output results in labour shifting to the other sectors. Table 10.2 shows this pattern of changing employment structure.

Even without any reallocation of labour, the average productivity growth rate will rise as the output share of the sector with the fastest productivity growth increases. When labour is moving into that sector, its output share grows more rapidly, and so does the economy's average productivity growth rate, which converges to the growth rate of the high productivity growth sector. However, labour reallocation has a second effect whenever productivity *levels* differ among sectors (see equation A10.1). For example, if the highest productivity growth sector is absorbing labour and also has a higher productivity level than the others, average productivity will grow even faster. This is easily seen if we assume the productivity level in manufacturing to be twice that in agriculture. Then the productivity of every agricultural worker reallocated to manufacturing is instantaneously doubled, even before the effect of the higher productivity growth in that sector makes its contribution to the average. Since labour reallocation is a continuous process as transformation proceeds, the effect of differing productivity levels has a continuing effect on average productivity growth.[8]

---

[8] McCombie (1991) has shown labour shifting to services to have had a large negative effect on productivity growth in the OECD.

Table 10.3 *Sectoral productivity growth rates and levels for selected countries*

Country	Productivity growth rates, 1950–87 (annual averages, %)			Productivity levels, 1987 (% of economy average)		
	Agriculture	Industry	Services	Agriculture	Industry	Services
United States	4.3	1.8	0.9	92	121	93
Japan	5.2	7.3	3.3	34	125	95
West Germany	5.3	4.2	2.5	42	100	105
France	5.5	4.7	2.2	68	122	93
United Kingdom	4.2	2.9	1.7	86	131	87
Netherlands	5.4	4.0	1.3	97	121	95

Source: Maddison (1991), tables 5.13 and 5.14.

Table 10.3 shows sectoral productivity growth rates for several large OECD economies. Although agricultural productivity growth was low in the early part of the twentieth century, for most of these economies since World War II it has been highest among the sectors. Nevertheless, labour reallocation to other sectors still yielded a growth bonus, stemming from agriculture having the lowest productivity level. Table 10.3 also shows that, in spite of rapid productivity growth, the level of productivity in agriculture failed to catch up with productivity elsewhere in the economy.[9]

To complete the process of transformation, we note that at high incomes the service sector comes to dominate both output and employment shares, as seen in table 10.2. Productivity growth and levels are lower in this sector than in manufacturing (except for Germany), as table 10.3 shows, leading to a decline in average productivity growth for the economy, which begins to converge to the productivity growth rate of the services sector.[10] The three phases of development are shown in figure 10.1(a), where average pro-

---

[9] The rapid agricultural productivity growth since World War II has enabled rapid transfer of labour to industry. This, together with the high demand for labour in industry, may have induced the rapid technological change needed to raise agricultural productivity growth. However, part of the increase in the earlier post-war years may be attributed to the shedding of underemployed agricultural labour in some countries.

[10] This 'negative effect' of de-industrialization is also to be found in Rowthorn and Wells (1987) and Baumol et al. (1989), who make similar arguments regarding unbalanced growth. Another view is that not only does the expanding service sector permit efficiency gains from specialization, which increase productivity in some service industries, but the development of markets for specialized services improves productivity in other sectors where these are intermediate inputs (Curtis and Murthy, 1999). This effect would be seen in our model as increased sectoral productivity growth rates, but does not imply that service sector productivity growth overtakes other sectors.

(a)

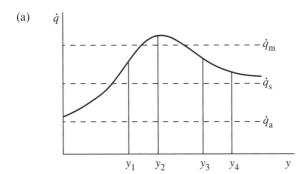

(b)

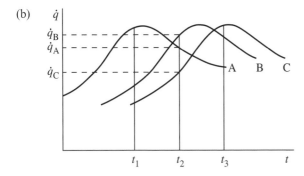

Figure 10.1 Productivity growth and the stage of development

ductivity growth ($\dot{q}$) is plotted against per capita income (y). The productivity growth rates for agriculture, manufacturing and services are denoted by $\dot{q}_a$, $\dot{q}_m$ and $\dot{q}_s$, respectively. In line with the stylized facts reported in the tables, average productivity growth can be seen to accelerate at the beginning of industrialization and to continue its convergence toward the manufacturing sector productivity growth rate, but at a slowing rate, until the service sector begins to expand. After this it declines, converging to the lower productivity growth rate of the service sector ($\dot{q}_s$).

4.2 The stage of development and productivity growth

The hypothesis here is that the currently advanced capitalist economies follow the development path shown in figure 10.1, and that each can be usefully categorized as being at a particular stage of development, measured for example by per capita income or by output structure. This view of development ultimately rests on the assumption that the institutions of capitalism and the preferences of the populations are sufficiently similar among these countries to generate a common development pattern. Such a pattern is consistent with the data, providing support for this assumption. An implication of this analysis is that two closed economies with the same per capita income level and same trend growth rates of sectoral productivity will have the same output and employment structures and hence are predicted to have the same average productivity growth rate. This is the benchmark growth rate against which actual performance can be judged.

The importance of the stage of development in determining productivity growth can be seen in figure 10.1(b). This plots productivity growth ($\dot{q}$) against time (t), and shows three economies, identical except that they develop at different times. That is, these economies have identical sectoral income elasticity functions and identical sectoral productivity growth rates. At time t_2 economy A experiences the slow growth predicted when the service sector share rises, B is in the rapid growth industrialization phase, while C has barely left the agricultural stage. However, these differences in productivity growth are entirely explained by the stage of development.

Figure 10.1(b) also shows that at time t_3 the three countries are exhibiting the characteristics addressed by the 'convergence' or catch-up hypotheses. That is, the later the economy develops, the higher is its productivity growth rate, so that per capita incomes are converging. However, the explanation here relies not on technology borrowing but on the stage of development only.[11] This is to say not that technology borrowing is unimportant, but that its impact may be less than the estimates usually suggest. We use this model to decompose the productivity growth rate according to whether it is a straightforward result of the stage of development or whether it must be explained by other variables. In the open economy, output structure is influenced by export demand, so that it is not an accurate measure of the stage of development. Instead, we use per capita income, which determines (via the sectoral income elasticities) the structure of domestic demand.

4.3 The open economy model and deviations from the common growth path

Here we consider several economic variables that are widely accepted as determinants of productivity growth, as discussed in section 3. These are export success, technology transfer (or catching up), investment and high unemployment (or economic slack). However, they are used here to explain differences in productivity growth that cannot be attributed to the stage of development. They cause divergence from the benchmark growth rate by acting on either sectoral productivity growth rates or sectoral output shares.

---

[11] Note also that at time t_1 quite the reverse is happening, as the earlier an economy has developed, the faster it grows, and incomes are diverging.

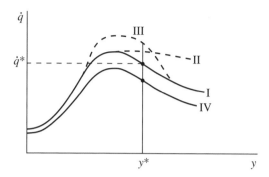

Figure 10.2 Deviations from the common growth path

Figure 10.2 shows the benchmark or common path of development (I) as well as three examples of deviations from it. Path II shows the effect of export success in manufactures, which prolongs the rapid growth phase by keeping the manufacturing sector's share of output high. This delays or reduces the decline in productivity growth caused by the shift to services. For an open economy, the relevant sectoral elasticity is a weighted average of domestic income elasticity and export demand elasticity (see equation A10.5 in the appendix). As long as this weighted average is greater than the domestic income elasticity, the exporting sector's output share will be increased. If the exporting sector is the rapid productivity growth sector (i.e. manufacturing), average productivity growth will be higher than in the closed economy case (Cornwall and Cornwall, 1992).[12] In general, anything that increases the output share of the high productivity growth sector will increase economy-wide productivity growth.

Path III in figure 10.2 shows a productivity growth bonus arising from technology transfer or 'catch-up' in the manufacturing sector, which causes an increase in the sector's productivity growth rate (W. Cornwall, 1991). In the figure, as in the model, it is assumed that the trend sectoral productivity growth rates are common to all economies. Then, catching up amounts to skipping several vintages of capital, the number skipped being greater the more backward is an economy relative to the leader. The source of the growth bonus is the adoption of new technology in a progressively larger proportion of the sector. The effect is much the same as that obtained when labour is shifted from a low to a high productivity

[12] Cornwall and Cornwall (1992) also show how export success provides a mechanism for leapfrogging, permitting later developing economies' per capita income levels to overtake those of the technological leader. It is interesting to note that 'export success' in a low productivity growth sector will lower average productivity growth.

level sector; in this case, output per worker in the sector increases because of the new technology. This growth bonus is exhausted once the entire sector is modernized, and productivity growth falls to its trend rate. Although this explanation has assumed modernization to take place in the manufacturing sector, it could occur in any sector; an increase in any of the sectoral productivity growth rates will result in higher average productivity growth.

The lower growth of path IV results from the adverse impact of extended high unemployment on productivity growth (see Lindbeck, 1983). An increase in unemployment has a once-over depressing effect on per capita income, which could be shown as a leftward shift of the growth curve. However, the dynamic effects of unemployment are of greater moment because of their lasting adverse impact. Dynamic effects are more likely to take hold when there are extended periods of economic slack, so that economies plagued by high unemployment rates are expected to have slower average productivity growth than those that maintain full employment. The dynamic effects of unemployment stem largely from its impact on the investment behaviour of firms. Firms delay or cancel new investment when there is economic slack, partly because of existing unused capacity and also because of increased risk. Planned investment in new technology is particularly susceptible because of the greater risks that it entails. In addition, when unemployment is high, labour appears to be plentiful, reducing the impetus to adopt the more capital-intensive new technologies. The effect is to slow down the adoption and diffusion of new technologies, causing sectoral productivity growth rates to fall.

Figure 10.2 shows the separate effects of these deviations from the common growth path. At income level y^* the benchmark growth rate is $\dot{q}^*$, determined by the sectoral productivity growth rates and the output structure at that income level, and assuming the economy to be closed with no economic slack. If there is economic slack, productivity growth at the same income level will be slower because of depressed sectoral productivity growth rates, shown on path IV. For the economy borrowing technology, sectoral productivity growth rates are higher, and at income level y^* it will be on path III. Lastly, for an economy with exports concentrated in high productivity growth manufactures, higher average productivity growth results from the greater share of output and employment in that sector, shown on path II. Thus, if we regard the stage of development of an economy as a historical given (measured here by its per capita income level), its actual average productivity growth rate may be above or below the benchmark rate for any combination of these reasons, each of them measuring some aspect of its economic performance.

5 The sources of growth: the formal model

Based on the model outlined in the previous section, we can write a productivity growth equation as:

$$\dot{q} = f(SD; B, XG, I, U), \tag{10.1}$$

where $\dot{q}$ is average productivity growth of the economy, SD is a measure of its stage of development (e.g. per capita income), B is the growth bonus conferred by catching up, XG and I are export growth and investment, respectively, and U is the unemployment rate, included to pick up the effect of economic slack. The purpose of the stage of development variable is to decompose productivity growth into the part predicted as the outcome of the common pattern of development and the part that must be explained by differences in economic behaviour, which are encapsulated by the remaining variables. For example, if two economies were at the same stage of development, a difference in their productivity growth rates could be explained by different export behaviour.

Equation (10.1) is consistent with the growth model described in the previous section, and is also connected to the institutional analysis of chapter 9. This connection is found by examining the determinants of the variables included in equation (10.1):

$$U = U(\mathbf{V}_1, \mathbf{V}_2), \tag{10.2}$$

where U is the unemployment rate, $\mathbf{V}_1$ is a vector containing variables that quantify labour market institutions, and $\mathbf{V}_2$ includes measures of the demand for full employment, such as voting patterns and political preferences. This is the equation estimated in chapter 5.

$$B = B(TGAP, ED, I), \tag{10.3}$$

where B is the growth bonus resulting from catch-up, $TGAP$ is the opportunity for catch-up or the technology gap between each economy and the technology leader, ED is a measure of the capacity to absorb new technology, e.g. level of labour skill or education; an investment variable (I) is used to quantify the effort made to exploit the opportunity for catch-up. The main impact of the catch-up bonus is expected to occur in the manufacturing sector. Because we expect feedbacks between investment and the technology gap, investment behaviour needs further explanation. For example, we can write

$$I = I(TGAP_{-1}, XG_{-1}, \mathbf{Z}_1), \tag{10.4}$$

where the first two right-hand side variables are lagged $TGAP$ and export growth, and $\mathbf{Z}_1$ is a vector of institutional variables that influence investment activity. Unemployment is not included because it is postulated to affect the type rather than the quantity of investment. Lastly, the determinants of export growth can be written as

$$XG = X(Q_f, C, Z_2),$$ (10.5)

where Q_f is the growth rate of the trading partners' incomes, C is a measure of competitiveness with both price and quality dimensions, and Z_2 is a vector of institutional variables that capture export strategy.

Conceptually, we can view this model as having two analytical levels. The first is represented by equations (10.2) to (10.5), which include the institutional variables and trace the interactions in the system. The second level is equation (10.1), which summarizes the effects of the first level, and expresses productivity growth in terms of the more familiar economic variables. With the exception of the labour market, reliable and consistent data measuring institutional characteristics are not available. Consequently, among the 'first-level' equations, only the unemployment equation has been estimated; the results were reported in chapter 5. Since there is no possibility of measuring the catch-up growth bonus (B), equation (10.3) cannot be estimated and its key explanatory variables are included in equation (10.1) for estimation.

6 The estimation model and the data

The model is written as

$$\dot{q} = \alpha D + \beta V + u,$$

where $\dot{q}$ is the economy-wide average productivity growth rate, D is a vector of variables chosen to identify the stage of development, V is a vector of economic variables, α and β are coefficient vectors, and u is a random variable. The theoretical model of section 5 takes a long-term view of economic transformation. For the group of OECD countries included in our estimation, data that are both reliable and consistently defined are available from 1960. We use four subperiods: 1960–7, 1968–73, 1974–9 and 1980–9.[13] These coincide approximately with the business cycles of the period, and we use the average for each period to remove short-run variations from this source. Consequently, we have a pooled data set, with four observations for each of the countries included in the sample – two for the golden age episode and two for the high unemployment episode. The inclusion of both episodes for estimation serves two purposes. First, it allows us

[13] This is the last complete business cycle, and avoids data problems created by the unification of Germany.

to test the ability of the model to track the change from the golden age to the subsequent episode, that is to explain the sharp drop in productivity growth since about 1973. Second, some variables are expected to have medium- to long-term effects that would not be apparent from a simple cross-section study, such as the effects of catching up or of persistently high unemployment.

The stage of development variable is included to capture the effect of the structure of demand. We use per capita income for this purpose, because of its strong links to demand structure. This choice avoids problems arising from the effect of exports on output shares.[14] In view of the relatively short period covered by the data, and the fact that we consider only developed economies, we expect the observations to lie on a rather short downward-sloping segment of the logistic growth path.[15] But, given the shape of the growth path, and since we cannot be quite certain which segment this is, our first step is to test polynomial functions of per capita income (y). Figure 10.1(a) illustrates the possibilities. If our sample spans incomes y_1 to y_4, a cubic function would approximate the relevant segment. A quadratic would be appropriate for the y_1 to y_3 range, or the y_3 to y_4 range. Finally, if all the data points are on the downward-sloping segment beginning at y_2, a linear approximation may be reasonable.

In keeping with the ideas represented by the alternative growth paths shown in figure 10.2, the remaining variables used are chosen to isolate the effects of export success, technology transfer, investment behaviour and economic slack. First, the growth rate of the volume of goods exports is used as a measure of export success. The decline of trade during two world wars and the protectionist inter-war period presented an opportunity for rapid trade growth, encouraged by the European Payments Union and the General Agreement on Tariffs and Trade, as discussed in chapter 9. In the pre-1973 period, these benefits were still permitting high export growth rates and rapidly rising exports to GDP ratios as export growth outpaced GDP growth. Since manufactures made up the bulk of exports, the growth rate of exports is expected to explain a substantial part of the rapid productivity growth in the golden age.

Second, to capture the catch-up growth bonus, we use the gap between US and domestic per capita income as a proportion of domestic per capita

---

[14] Fagerberg (1996) uses the agriculture output share, but in a study of European regions. Our sample includes Australia, Canada and the United States, so that quite large differences in this share are expected for reasons other than the stage of development.

[15] For the less developed countries, Sundrum (1990, table 3.9) suggests that the declining portion of the curve is attained when per capita income is about US$2,000 (1981 constant dollars). This supports our expectation, since this is below the income levels for all the economies in our sample.

income for each country.[16] This ratio is a proxy for the technology gap, which represents the opportunity for technological borrowing. *Ceteris paribus*, the larger the gap, the greater the effect of a given amount of investment. There was considerable variation among countries in the opportunity for catch-up in the pre-1973 period and in some it was very great. Over the period 1960–73, technology gaps narrowed rapidly in many countries, demonstrating that efforts were made to exploit this opportunity.[17]

Effort in the catch-up process depends in part upon investment behaviour. In addition, as discussed above, investment has an effect on sectoral productivity growth rates, speeding up transformation even in the absence of a technology gap. Investment is also related to export performance; expanding foreign demand justifies increased investment, which in turn improves competitiveness as productivity gains are realized. Hence the contribution of investment to growth flows through several channels, and must be included. Several investment variables were tested. These were the ratio of business investment to GDP, the ratio of machinery and equipment investment to GDP, the ratio of machinery and equipment expenditures to value added in manufacturing, the growth rate of the capital–labour ratio, and, finally, the growth rate of investment in machinery and equipment. Of these, none except the last added any explanatory power to the model. In addition, several variables were tested for interactive effects between the technology gap, investment and export growth. None provided any evidence of such effects. To pick up the effect of economic slack, we use standardized unemployment rates. The variables used in the regressions are defined in table 10.4.

7 Empirical results

Chow tests indicated that we are justified in pooling the data for the four periods. As well, dummy variables were used to test for intercept and slope differences between the pre- and post-1973 periods which had very different performance records. No significant differences were found, indicating that there were no changes in the coefficients between these two periods. This allows us to conclude that the effects of structural changes between the golden age and the subsequent period were captured by changes in the

---

[16] The notion of catch-up or convergence is the subject of a large body of literature. Much of it concerns which economies are converging and some investigates how long this trend has existed; perhaps most interesting is the work that investigates the investment and other behaviour that determines the rate of growth when the opportunity for catching up exists. For a useful review of this literature, see Fagerberg (1994).

[17] This is the experience in the OECD, but not in the underdeveloped world, where divergence from the United States was more general (Baumol et al., 1989; Barro, 1997).

Table 10.4 *Definitions of the variables used in the productivity growth equation*

Variable	Definition
$\dot{q}$	Growth rate of real GDP per person employed; average for each period.
y	Per capita GNP in real 1980 international dollars ('000); value at the beginning of each period.
$TGAP$	$(y_{us} - y_i)/y_i$, where y_{us} is US per capita income and y_i is the per capita income for each of the other countries in the sample; value at the beginning of each period.
XG	Growth rate of the volume of goods exports; average for each period.
IG	Growth rate of investment in machinery and equipment; average for each period.
U	Standardized unemployment rate; average for each period.

Notes:
All data are from OECD sources. Precise sources are available on request. We wish to thank John Helliwell and Alan Chung for providing per capita income data. Four observations for each of the 16 countries listed in table 10.6 were used, for the periods 1960–7, 1968–73, 1974–9 and 1980–9.

values of the explanatory variables used for estimation.[18] The Hausman (1978) exogeneity test showed no evidence of simultaneity in the model. Among several tests for heteroscedasticity, two showed some evidence of its presence. We therefore computed the White (1980) heteroscedasticity consistent t-statistics.

Several specifications of the model were estimated, in order to establish the usefulness of including the stage of development variable. There is no evidence that cubic or quadratic functions of per capita income are correct. This was not unexpected, since the number of low-income countries in the sample is small, and confined to the first period. This does not prove that the true relationship is linear; it proves only that, given the sample, this is the best estimate.

Table 10.5 shows the regression results and test statistics for three variants of the productivity equation. Equation 1 includes the stage of development variable (per capita income) and the technology gap variable ($TGAP$). Because other empirical studies of growth rate differences and convergence include only one of these variables (usually per capita income), equation 2 omits $TGAP$ and per capita income is omitted from equation 3,

---

[18] These structural changes are the topic of chapter 11.

Table 10.5 *Regression results for the productivity growth equation*

	Equation					
	(1)		(2)		(3)	
Intercept	2.499		4.043		0.607	
	(3.14)	[3.61]	(6.58)	[6.42]	(2.13)	[2.06]
Per capita income (y)	−0.207		−0.389		–	
	(2.53)	[3.13]	(7.18)	[6.91]		
Catch-up ($TGAP$)	0.981		–		1.666	
	(2.83)	[3.06]			(7.37)	[6.61]
Export growth (XG)	0.158		0.167		0.182	
	(4.47)	[3.71]	(4.50)	[4.05]	(5.13)	[4.03]
Investment growth (IG)	0.095		0.118		0.088	
	(3.37)	[3.40]	(4.15)	[4.07]	(3.00)	[3.00]
Economic slack (U)	−0.111		−0.080		−0.132	
	(3.79)	[4.93]	(2.76)	[3.33]	(4.50)	[5.28]
Standard error	0.694		0.734		0.724	
Adjusted R^2	0.845		0.827		0.831	

	Test statistic	Critical value	Test statistic	Critical value	Test statistic	Critical value
Test results						
Heteroscedasticity						
(a) chi-square (1)	7.369	3.84	6.831	3.84	8.413	3.84
(b) chi-square (4)			9.578	9.49	11.028	9.49
Stability: Hocking Sp						
Break at 1973–4	0.728	2.137				
Specification: omit TGAP	–		8.005	2.035		
Specification: omit per capita income	–				6.378	2.035

Notes:
The absolute values of the *t*-statistics are in parentheses; the square brackets contain White's heteroscedasticity consistent t-statistics. For the two tests reported, the squared OLS residuals are regressed on (a) the predicted dependent variable and (b) the independent variables.

allowing us to test our specification. In all three equations the estimated slope coefficients have the expected signs and are statistically significant at the 5 per cent level. The positive coefficients of the technology gap, export growth and investment growth show that all increase the average productivity growth rate, while the presence of economic slack reduces it. The negative coefficient for per capita income reflects the expected lower productivity growth rate brought by the increasing service sectors in these high-income economies.

When either *TGAP* or per capita income is omitted from the model, the hypothesis of no misspecification is rejected by several tests; table 10.5 reports the Hocking (1976) test statistics for specification. In the case of each omission there are shifts in the values of the coefficients for the 'demand' variables (export and investment growth and unemployment). When *TGAP* is omitted, the greatest changes occur in the intercept and in the coefficient of per capita income. When per capita income is omitted, as expected the most marked change occurs to the coefficient of the catch-up variable, which nearly doubles. These results support our view that failure to consider both the stage of development and the technology gap leads to distortions of the impact of the other variables.

8 Accounting for growth in the golden age

The estimation spanned two episodes and, besides providing an overview of the period for which data are available, the results allow us to examine each of these episodes separately. Here, we return to the golden age for a closer examination of productivity growth. Using the coefficients of equation 1, the initial values of per capita income and the technology gap, and the averages of the other variables over the period 1960–73, table 10.6 shows the estimated contribution of each of them to productivity growth during the golden age. First, the per capita income variable allows us to place each country at some stage of development at the beginning of our estimation period (i.e. 1960). This is depicted in figure 10.1(a) for example, where the United States and Switzerland would be somewhere near y_4, Spain, Ireland and Japan closer to y_2, and the remaining countries in between. The higher the level of per capita income, the lower is the benchmark growth rate because of the changed output structure. Second, the technology gap shows the importance of the growth bonus to the lowest-income countries as they modernize. For example, Finland and the United States have the same export growth effects, and differences in their unemployment and investment variables account for only one-tenth of a percentage point of productivity growth; the actual difference of 2.7 percentage points is almost entirely accounted for by the technology gap and the output structure implied by the level of per capita income. With a productivity growth rate over four times that of the United States, Japan demonstrates the powerful convergence effects of 'backwardness' (or the stage of development) and a large technology gap, which account for over half of the productivity growth difference. Both Japan and Finland are examples of the very strong convergence tendencies of these economies in the golden age.

Table 10.6 *Sources of growth in the golden age*

Country	y	TGAP	XG	IG	U	$\dot{q}$ estimate	$\dot{q}$ actual	Error
United States	−1.62	0.00	1.09	0.63	−0.53	2.07	2.0	0.07
Japan	−0.48	2.34	2.37	1.28	−0.14	7.86	8.2	−0.34
West Germany	−1.01	0.59	1.58	0.46	−0.09	4.03	4.1	−0.07
Italy	−0.69	1.32	1.85	0.64	−0.58	5.04	5.8	−0.76
United Kingdom	−1.11	0.45	0.87	0.45	−0.33	2.82	2.8	0.02
Canada	−1.19	0.36	1.47	0.70	−0.57	3.27	2.6	0.67
Australia	−1.10	0.47	1.09	0.57	−0.23	3.29	2.5	0.79
Austria	−0.77	1.08	1.58	0.52	−0.20	4.70	5.0	−0.30
Denmark	−1.03	0.56	1.09	0.59	−0.14	3.57	3.0	0.57
Finland	−0.79	1.03	1.09	0.45	−0.22	4.05	4.7	−0.65
Ireland	−0.53	2.01	1.20	1.18	−0.58	5.78	4.3	1.48
Netherlands	−1.03	0.56	1.64	0.55	−0.13	4.09	4.0	0.09
Norway	−0.93	0.73	1.36	0.49	−0.21	3.94	3.1	0.84
Spain	−0.50	2.20	1.92	0.99	−0.29	6.83	6.4	0.43
Sweden	−1.11	0.45	1.26	0.53	−0.21	3.43	3.5	−0.07
Switzerland	−1.53	0.05	1.34	0.52	0.00	2.88	2.9	−0.02

Note:
[a] The variables are defined as in table 10.4.

Next we turn to the effect of the demand variables. Spain, Ireland and Japan had similar income levels in 1960, giving them the same potential advantages from output structure and the growth bonus offered by a large technology gap. They all had high productivity growth rates – 4.3, 6.4 and 8.2 per cent for Ireland, Spain and Japan, respectively. The very considerable spread between these rates is almost entirely dependent on the demand variables. Table 10.6 shows that most of the difference is accounted for by different export performance; casual examination reveals the close relationship between these economies' productivity growth rates and their rates of export growth. The remainder of the difference is largely explained by Japan's investment growth rate, which was about 30 per cent higher than that in Spain or Ireland. This supports our claim that demand is an important determinant of economic performance.

The inclusion of the unemployment rate in the productivity equation is to capture the impact of economic slack that is not already measured by the investment variable. In short, this is a partial effect only, targeted at qualitative aspects of investment rather than its quantity. The effect of economic slack is of comparable magnitude to the effect of investment growth, and must therefore be accorded comparable importance as a determinant of productivity growth rates. If investment growth increases by 1 percentage point or unemployment drops by 1 percentage point, the effect is to raise productivity growth by approximately one-tenth of a percentage point. For example, this suggests that productivity growth in Canada would have been 3 rather than 2.6 per cent if unemployment there had been as low as in Japan, Denmark or the Netherlands.

Although significant for the high unemployment countries, for most there was too little economic slack in the golden age to impair productivity growth. This changed after about 1973, when unemployment began to rise everywhere, contributing noticeably to the decline in productivity growth rates. Earlier chapters have supported the view that such a shift from a period of low unemployment to one of high unemployment is caused by institutional change, and that differences in unemployment rates among countries can be attributed to differences in their institutions.

9 Conclusion

The estimates of productivity growth reported in this chapter show the contribution of various components of aggregate demand, including the positive role of low unemployment. The estimates of their separate contributions are clarified by estimating an equation based on a model of growth and transformation. This allowed us to isolate the effect of 'backwardness', which exerts its own influence on productivity growth independently of opportunities for export growth and catching up. In order to use this model most effectively, the equation was estimated using the longest period for which consistent data are available. Not only does this put the golden age in context as an episode in the development of these economies, but the results are useful in chapter 11 to assess the sources of productivity decline after the golden age.

The part of institutional differences in explaining variation in productivity growth cannot be quantified, owing to lack of data, except for the unemployment variable. In this case, estimates reported in chapter 5 suggest that institutions have a powerful effect. Even in the absence of quantitative verification, we argue that the intervention of governments, not only to secure labour market stability but also to promote investment, exports and the modernization of their industrial sectors, was integral to the success of the golden age. Further, the social bargains that were developed and sustained in most countries typically had export competitiveness as one of the key goals. In addition, many included measures that induced labour to accept technological change, furthering the goal of export growth as well as accelerating catch-up.

What established and sustained the golden age? The primary moving force was the political will, at the grass roots and also at the national and international levels. Chapter 9 traced the institutional shifts that underpinned this determination. These changes stemmed from the events of the 1930s, from the need for post-war reconstruction and from the US concern with the Cold War. The last provided two essential ingredients. The first was the US acceptance of its role of hegemon in the 'free world'. To secure and strengthen its allies, the USA proposed and vigorously supported a series of international institutional innovations that would stabilize international relations. In particular it moved to foster international trade both by promoting the GATT and by the currency and payments system established in the Bretton Woods Agreement. But a series of compromises at the insistence of the Europeans and the requirements of its own Cold War policies resulted in a system that delivered stability and growth for international trade. The second contribution of the USA resulted from the Marshall Plan. The mere existence of modern technologies, even for populations that have the institutions and skills to absorb them, is insufficient for growth, especially in countries impoverished by war. The Marshall Plan accelerated reconstruction and led the way for future private transfers of technology from the USA to Europe and Japan.

The third factor was the establishment of domestic stability in the OECD economies. The new technologies demanded a disciplined labour force; they required large capital outlays and production methods that were vulnerable to disruption, even by a relatively small fraction of key workers. Continued growth required continued investment, and could be expected to provide high levels of employment. The establishment of social bargains in most OECD economies allowed them to achieve industrial harmony, removing potential constraints on aggregate demand so that the opportunities for rapid growth could be safely exploited.

The view in the late 1960s (and even into the early 1970s) was that the old economic problems associated with recurrent recessions had been solved; capitalism had been tamed and given a human face. Events were to show, however, that the institutions that had nurtured the golden age were undergoing change. The changes were fatal, undermining the stability of the system. As argued in chapters 8 and 9, the institutions prevailing in the 1920s and 1930s ruled out the policies needed to prevent the 1929 downturn from becoming the Great Depression. But the severity of the depression played a crucial part in generating the institutional changes that made the golden age possible. We shall argue in chapter 11 that capitalism's most successful episode induced institutional changes that led to the decline in the closing decades of the twentieth century. Each case is an example of an evolutionary process linking historical episodes via negative feedback.

Appendix: a model of growth and transformation

The basic model[19]

$\dot{q}$	average productivity growth rate
y	real per capita income
λ_i	share of the labour force employed in the i'th sector; $\Sigma\lambda_i = 1$
q_i	average labour productivity, i'th sector
$\dot{q}_i$	sectoral productivity growth, i'th sector
$q = \Sigma\lambda_i q_i$	average productivity of the economy
$k_i = \lambda_i q_i/q$	sectoral output share
$\epsilon_i = (\lambda_i'q_i' - \lambda_i q_i)/\lambda_i q_i\dot{q}$	output elasticity of the i'th good (the prime indicates the end of period values)
$\epsilon_i = f_i(y)$	income elasticity of demand for the i'th good

Both population and the labour force are assumed to be constant, as are the sectoral productivity growth rates. First, write

$$\dot{q} = (q' - q)/q = \Sigma(\lambda_i'q_i' - \lambda_i q_i)/q.$$

Using the definitions of λ_i and k_i, this yields

$$q = \Sigma k_i\dot{q}_i + \Sigma(\lambda_i' - \lambda_i)q_i'/q. \tag{A10.1}$$

Equation A10.1 shows the average productivity growth rate to depend on sectoral productivity growth rates and output shares, and on labour reallocation between sectors having different productivity levels.

A second relationship is found using the definition of output elasticity:

$$\lambda_i' - \lambda_i = \lambda_i(\epsilon_i\dot{q} - \dot{q}_i)/(1 + \dot{q}_i). \tag{A10.2}$$

Equation A10.2 shows the changing labour share of the i'th sector as a function of both its income (or output) elasticity and its productivity growth rate. We know that $\Sigma(\lambda_i' - \lambda_i) = 0$, so that the right-hand side of A10.2 yields an expression for the average productivity growth rate in terms of the initial parameters only:

$$\dot{q} = \frac{\Sigma\dfrac{\lambda_i\dot{q}_i}{1+\dot{q}_i}}{\Sigma\dfrac{\lambda_i\epsilon_i}{1+\dot{q}_i}}. \tag{A10.3}$$

Substituting A10.3 into A10.2 provides an expression for the change in each sector's labour share in terms of the same parameters. Using a

[19] This presentation of the basic model draws heavily on Sundrum (1990).

three-sector model, where a, m and s represent agriculture, manufacturing and services, for sector a we have

$$
\lambda'_a - \lambda_a = \frac{\dfrac{\lambda_a \dot{q}_a}{1+\dot{q}_a}\left[\dfrac{\lambda_m \dot{q}_m}{1+\dot{q}_m}\left[\dfrac{\epsilon_a}{\dot{q}_a} - \dfrac{\epsilon_m}{\dot{q}_m}\right] + \dfrac{\lambda_s \dot{q}_s}{1+\dot{q}_s}\left[\dfrac{\epsilon_a}{\dot{q}_a} - \dfrac{\epsilon_s}{\dot{q}_s}\right]\right]}{\dfrac{\lambda_a \epsilon_a}{1+\dot{q}_a} + \dfrac{\lambda_m \epsilon_m}{1+\dot{q}_m} + \dfrac{\lambda_s \epsilon_s}{1+\dot{q}_s}}.
\tag{A10.4}
$$

Clearly, labour shifts into sector a if $\epsilon_a/\dot{q}_a > \epsilon_i/\dot{q}_i$. In general, labour moves from sectors with lower elasticity to productivity growth ratios into those with higher ones.

The open economy model

The changes to the basic model concern only the elasticities; the remaining definitions are unchanged.

$\epsilon_i^* = (\lambda'_i q'_i - \lambda_i q_i)/\lambda_i q_i \dot{q}$ output elasticity for the i'th sector

$\epsilon_i = f(y)$ domestic income elasticity of demand for the sector's output

Given the assumptions of constant population and employment, in the closed economy model $\epsilon_i^* = \epsilon_i$. For the open economy write:

$$
\lambda_i q_i = \lambda_i (q_{id} + q_{ix}),
$$

where $\lambda_i q_{id}$ is domestic demand for the output of the i'th sector, and $\lambda_i q_{ix}$ is net exports of the sector. Next define

$\beta_i = q_{ix}/q_i$ net exports as a share of sectoral output,

$\epsilon_i = (\lambda'_i q'_{id} - \lambda_i q_{id})/\lambda_i q_{id} \dot{q}$ domestic output elasticity, sector i, and

$\epsilon_{ix} = (\lambda'_i q'_{ix} - \lambda_i q_{ix})/\lambda_i q_{ix} \dot{q}$ output elasticity for sector i exports.

Assuming no supply constraints, the growth rate of the i'th sector's net exports is equal to the growth rate of foreign demand. We can now write:

$$
\epsilon_i^* = (1 - \beta_i)\epsilon_i + \beta_i \epsilon_{ix}.
\tag{A10.5}
$$

Export success requires the growth rate of foreign demand to exceed the growth rate of domestic demand in the highest productivity growth sector (for example manufacturing). This is equivalent to requiring $\epsilon_{mx} > \epsilon_m$.

11 Unemployment

1 Introduction

Capitalism's golden age can be characterized in several ways. Unemployment rates were at historical lows and growth rates of labour productivity and per capita incomes in most economies were at historical highs. In the first instance this was attributed to strong and growing aggregate demand pressures. These buoyant conditions were attributed in turn to the absence of constraints on aggregate demand. During this period there were institutions in most OECD countries that relieved the authorities of any real or perceived need to hold AD below full employment levels. These institutions permitted the simultaneous achievement of other goals, e.g. low inflation, external balance. To a large extent the formation of golden age institutions was causally linked to the performance of the economies in the 1930s and 1940s, demonstrating evolutionary and hysteretic processes with negative feedback.

The main task of this chapter is to explain the poor unemployment performance in the episode since the golden age also as the outcome of evolutionary and hysteretic processes with negative feedback. This includes both the impact of institutions on performance and the impact of performance on institutions, to establish a causal linkage between the golden age and the present episode. We argue that high and rising unemployment in the current episode can be traced ultimately to a marked change in institutions, which was to a very large degree induced by the performance of the economy in the golden age. The institutions that had permitted simultaneous low unemployment, rapid growth and low inflation were now replaced by a collection of institutions that no longer did so. The result was the sacrifice of the full employment goal, as political leaders chose to pursue competing goals. The emergence of these new institutions brought the golden age to an end; their continued existence locks the OECD economies into poor performance.

Our focus is on constraints on AD in most OECD economies arising from the unacceptably high inflation rates associated with full employment in the episode following the golden age. This inflation constraint was widespread, and depressed AD in a country's trading partners made it difficult for any country unilaterally to implement a stimulative policy without importing inflation. Hence we concentrate on the emergence of this inflation constraint as sufficient to end the golden age. In chapter 12 we discuss other institutional changes that occurred later in this episode, reinforcing the need to limit AD. Neglecting this second group of constraints in this chapter does not alter its conclusions. Before proceeding to the main task of the chapter, section 2 utilizes the econometric results of chapters 5 and 10 to explain the deterioration of performance in the current episode. The unemployment equation provides estimates of the contribution of power and institutions to the rise in unemployment rates following the golden age. The estimated productivity equation measures the impact of unemployment on the slowdown in productivity growth. This exercise shows how power and institutions are linked, via their effect on AD policy, to unemployment and productivity growth.

To show longer-run changes as the current episode replaced the golden age, the econometric tests used data averaged over each of four business cycles. Consequently, they cannot be used to explore the inflation–unemployment-policy dynamics within the cycles. These are summarized in section 3. Section 4 describes two well-known mainstream explanations of the 'Great Inflation' and the response (or lack of response) of inflation to restrictive policies. Sections 5 and 6 begin our explanation of the current episode by relating the causes of the Great Inflation to developments in the golden age. Having established a linkage to the golden age, sections 7 to 9 provide an explanation of the subsequent worsened unemployment and inflation performance. These sections return to the dynamics, summarized in section 3, generated by the response of policy makers to inflation and the response of inflation and unemployment to policy, an interaction that explains much of the inflation–unemployment record since the golden age. Quantitative methods require simplifying assumptions that make them unsuited to this part of the analysis; instead, the complex interactions between policy, unemployment and inflation are analysed with the help of a diagram. Section 7 considers the possibility that policies used to combat the inflation were counter-productive in the short to intermediate term, and temporarily accentuated the inflationary problem by shifting the Phillips curve further to the right. Section 8 offers an explanation of why restrictive policies and high and rising unemployment rates took so long to bring down inflation, and section 9 considers the impact of a prolonged period of high unemployment on the current position of the Phillips curve. Section 10 presents a diagram summarizing the chain of causation that links the golden age to the current episode, and section 11 contains the conclusions. The reader is forewarned of the novelty of some of the ideas in this chapter, but we believe the main ideas are no more speculative than those of the mainstream interpretations outlined in section 4.

Here we reiterate a central point first raised in chapter 5: the record of poor economic performance in the present episode cannot be attributed to the emergence of greater deviations from competitive conditions any more than the superior performance of the golden age can be traced to there having been fewer of these market imperfections. Contrary to the mainstream view, the economies that performed best had institutions that moved them further from the competitive model, not closer to it.

2 Evidence of decline

By the 1990s, the deterioration of unemployment and growth had spread to all OECD economies. As shown in table 2.1, after 1973 the unweighted average unemployment rate for the 16 economies more than tripled, and average per capita income growth rate fell by more than 50 per cent, as did GDP growth. The rates of growth of labour productivity shown in table 10.1 tell a similar story. The regression results reported in table 10.5 are used here to examine causes of its decline.

Table 11.1 uses these regression results to measure the contribution of changes in the average values of the independent variables for each country to changes in its productivity growth from 1960–73 to 1974–89. The stage of development variable is included to account for the impact of changing output structure on productivity growth; it proved to be the greatest source of productivity decline for five countries, and the second greatest for seven others. However, changing output structure is an unavoidable accompaniment to capitalist development, and it is the remaining variables that are of greater interest as measures of changing AD. For Japan and Spain, catching up played the largest role in productivity growth decline, as vigorous exploitation of the large technology gaps they had at the start of the golden age substantially reduced the opportunity for further catching up. Ireland, also relatively 'backward' at the beginning of the period, was later to start catching up than Japan and Spain, and in fact suffered only a very modest decline in productivity growth, with the greatest contributors to the decline being a drop in investment growth and a rise in economic slack (unemployment). These effects are partially offset by the rising export demand typical in the earlier phases of catching up. Declining export growth was the primary cause of lowered productivity growth for six countries, and came second for four others. Averaged over the 16 countries, it accounted for

Table 11.1 *Estimated sources of productivity growth decline: 1960–73 to 1974–89*

Country	Stage of development	Catch-up	Export growth	Investment growth	Economic slack	Productivity growth changes		
						Actual	Estimated	Error
United States	-0.63		-0.60	-0.17	-0.24	-1.21	-1.64	0.43
Japan	-0.86	-1.66	-1.29	-0.64	-0.11	-5.14	-4.55	-0.59
West Germany	-0.57	-0.17	-0.91	-0.17	-0.46	-2.19	-2.28	0.09
Italy	-0.58	-0.56	-1.00	-0.28	-0.36	-3.43	-2.77	-0.66
United Kingdom	-0.43	0.00	-0.27	-0.14	-0.56	-1.44	-1.40	-0.04
Canada	-0.76	-0.21	-0.68	0.01	-0.38	-1.38	-2.02	0.64
Australia	-0.59	-0.14	-0.38	-0.19	-0.50	-1.45	-1.80	0.35
Austria	-0.60	-0.45	-0.70	-0.26	-0.11	-3.33	-2.13	-1.20
Denmark	-0.57	-0.16	-0.33	-0.30	-0.67	-2.08	-2.03	-0.05
Finland	-0.64	-0.46	-0.62	-0.18	-0.28	-2.58	-2.18	-0.40
Ireland	-0.36	-0.50	0.20	-0.95	-0.75	-0.69	-2.36	1.67
Netherlands	-0.64	-0.22	-1.11	-0.22	-0.74	-2.99	-2.93	-0.06
Norway	-0.58	-0.25	-0.33	-0.57	-0.08	-0.85	-1.81	0.96
Spain	-0.64	-1.25	-0.67	-0.64	-1.17	-3.59	-4.37	0.78
Sweden	-0.66	-0.19	-0.84	-0.16	-0.04	-2.49	-1.88	-0.61
Switzerland	-0.77	-0.08	-0.82	-0.21	-0.05	-1.64	-1.93	0.29
Average	-0.62	-0.39	-0.65	-0.32	-0.41	-2.28	-2.38	1.60
% of decline	26.05	16.55	27.31	13.45	17.23		100.00	

Note:
These computations use the estimated coefficients reported for equation 1 in table 10.5, and the averages for 1960–73 and 1974–89 of the variables defined in table 10.4.

27 per cent of the decline. One may speculate that this reflects the competition from the newly industrializing countries, whose export shares were growing rapidly in the second half of the period covered by these estimates.

Of particular interest to our study is the effect of increasing economic slack, measured here by the unemployment rate. For the United Kingdom and Denmark, increased economic slack was the main cause of declining productivity growth. In these countries, as well as in Australia, the Netherlands and Spain, rising unemployment accounted for about one-third of the total fall in productivity growth. Averaged over all the countries in the sample, it caused about 17 per cent of the drop in productivity growth rates. The combined impact of the rise in unemployment rates and the declines in the rates of growth of goods exports and machinery and equipment investment indicates the decisive role of falling AD in reducing productivity growth in the post-golden age episode.

The inclusion of unemployment as a measure of economic slack in our empirical study shows it to be a significant determinant of productivity growth rates. Unemployment was the subject of a second empirical study that examined the institutional basis for unemployment outcomes. The estimated coefficients of an equation linking unemployment to a demand variable and several institutional variables were reported in table 5.2. The estimated coefficients are used in table 11.2 to assess the extent to which changes in these variables can explain the increase in unemployment rates after 1973.

Membership in the European Monetary System (EMS) exacted a high price, accounting for the largest share of the increase in unemployment (at about 3 percentage points) in the member economies. The need to hold their exchange rates at levels required by the rules of membership appears to have entailed sacrifice of unemployment targets. Because membership was voluntary, it reflects political preferences and can be interpreted as indicating inflation aversion. It has been shown that the coordination of exchange rate policies required by membership affected monetary policy, and that inflation rates fell (Cukierman, 1992; Jenkins, 1996). The international demand variable (WU) is the second-largest contributor to the increase in unemployment in six of the seven members of the EMS, and the largest contributor in five of the non-member countries. It captures the result of high unemployment spreading among countries that trade a large proportion of their GDP. This is a highly significant cause of the rise in unemployment in all of the small European economies in the sample, reflecting their great exposure to international demand fluctuations. International demand is also (after EMS membership) very important for West Germany and France. Equally important for France is lagged inflation, also the prime contributor to higher unemployment in seven other

Table 11.2 *Estimated sources of increased unemployment: 1960–73 to 1974–89*

Country	Proportion of left-wing votes	Strikes	Central bank independence	EMS membership	WU	Lagged inflation	Changes in unemployment Actual	Changes in unemployment Estimated	Changes in unemployment Error
United States	0.00	-0.12	–	–	0.38	1.06	2.24	1.32	0.92
Japan	0.13	-0.44	–	–	0.57	1.13	0.96	1.38	-0.42
West Germany	-0.01	0.27	–	3.02	1.15	0.48	4.12	4.92	-0.80
France	-0.46	0.01	-0.37	3.02	0.88	0.89	5.28	3.98	1.30
Italy	-0.12	0.96	–	3.02	0.90	1.91	3.23	6.66	-3.44
United Kingdom	0.28	1.28	-0.49	–	1.01	1.84	5.17	3.93	1.24
Canada	-0.13	0.91	–	–	1.01	1.08	3.46	2.88	0.58
Australia	0.33	0.90	–	–	0.54	1.36	4.45	3.13	1.32
Austria	-0.04	-1.73	-0.12	–	1.46	0.64	0.96	0.19	0.76
Belgium	0.22	-0.16	0.06	3.02	2.72	0.99	6.90	6.84	0.05
Denmark	0.03	0.47	–	3.02	1.18	0.97	5.91	5.66	0.25
Finland	0.33	-0.09	–	–	1.11	0.98	2.68	2.34	0.35
Ireland	0.02	0.84	–	3.02	2.05	1.83	6.59	7.76	-1.17
Netherlands	-0.01	-0.42	–	3.02	1.89	0.78	6.69	5.26	1.43
New Zealand	0.06	0.63	–	–	1.07	1.65	2.93	3.41	-0.48
Norway	0.23	-0.91	0.06	–	1.47	0.97	0.55	1.83	-1.28
Sweden	0.14	0.06	–	–	1.28	0.91	0.36	2.39	-2.03
Switzerland	0.15	-0.94	0.21	–	1.35	0.48	0.48	1.25	-0.77

Note:
These computations use the estimated coefficients reported for equation 1 in table 5.2, and the averages for 1960–73 and 1974–89 of the variables defined in table 5.1.

countries in the sample. Because of the length of the lags, this variable cannot be regarded as an expectations proxy; instead, it has elsewhere been interpreted as a measure of the cumulative effect of past inflation on the position of the Phillips curve (W. Cornwall, 1999).

On average, EMS membership, international demand conditions and lagged inflation have the greatest impact on unemployment rates, accounting for the bulk of the increase. Nevertheless, changes in strike activity had a significant effect in many economies. In Italy, the United Kingdom, Canada, Australia and Ireland, increased labour militancy explains approximately a 1 percentage point increase in the unemployment rate. In contrast, it is interesting to note that, of five countries that were able to maintain their social bargains throughout the 1980s, Japan, Austria, Norway and Switzerland had reduced strike activity, which contributed to their continued low unemployment. In the fifth, Sweden, there was virtually no change in the already low strike activity. Changes in the proportion of left-wing votes and central bank independence were small and contributed proportionately less to the rise in unemployment.

The ultimate objective of these empirical exercises was to demonstrate the detrimental effect of slack AD on labour productivity growth rates, in support of our extended Keynesian analysis. Particular attention has been devoted to the unemployment rate, used here as a measure of economic slack but more generally as evidence of serious economic malfunction. Chapter 5 reported estimates that related unemployment rates to AD, including the direct effect of international economic conditions and the effect of domestic demand traced to its institutional origins. These institutions influence the position of an economy's Phillips curve and its political preferences respecting unemployment and inflation choices. Observed unemployment is the result of the optimization of preferences, subject to the constraints imposed by the Phillips curve. This optimization process generates the policies that act directly on economic variables and that are modified to respond to changes in those variables. However, the link between institutions and the unemployment rate made in the econometric study is not designed to explore the dynamics of the interactions between inflation, policy and unemployment, a topic introduced in the next section and analysed in section 7.

3 Inflation and the policy response: the record

In concluding chapter 5, we stated that the ability to control inflation over time would be reflected in the unemployment record, because the monetary and fiscal authorities will use restrictive policy as required to reduce inflation. Figure 11.1 provides an overview of this interaction for the G7

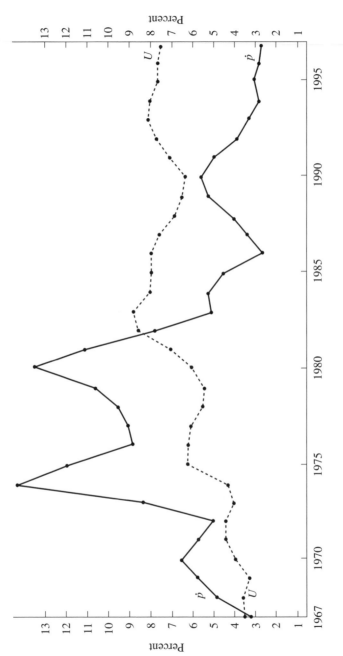

Figure 11.1 Average annual growth rates of inflation ($\dot{p}$) and standardized unemployment (U) for the G7 countries, 1967–1997

Note: Data include West Germany prior to 1993, after which data for the unified Germany are used.

Sources: OECD, *Historical Statistics*, various issues; OECD, *Economic Outlook*, 44, December 1988, Table R11; OECD, *Economic Outlook*, 65, June 1999, Annex Tables 16 and 22.

economies from the mid-1960s until the end of the 1990s. It is clear that by the mid-1970s the transition from an episode of high growth and full employment to another of slow growth and high unemployment was well under way. Early signs of this shift can be identified in the accelerating inflation of the late 1960s to early 1970s and the breakdown of Bretton Woods in the early 1970s. Continued strong inflation in the first half of the 1970s, coupled with payments problems in many economies in 1973–4, was met by the implementation of restrictive policies. These policies achieved a reduction in inflation rates beginning in 1975, although they remained at over double their golden age rates into the 1980s. The main impact was on unemployment, which rose throughout the second half of the 1970s, reaching rates twice those of the 1960s.

As shown in figure 11.1, in the G7 a pattern of spurts of unacceptable rates of inflation followed by restrictive and then looser AD policies had been established which was to recur throughout the 1980s and into the 1990s. In 1979–80, the second oil price shock further compounded the problems faced by governments, as inflation rates began to accelerate once more. The AD policies introduced in the early 1980s were even more restrictive than those of the mid-1970s, with unemployment rates rising sharply and inflation falling to golden age rates by the mid-1980s when policies were eased. Once more the reduction in inflation proved to be only temporary. Even though unemployment rates averaged approximately three times their golden age rates, inflation accelerated during the boom of the second half of the 1980s. Restrictive policies were introduced at the end of the 1980s, causing unemployment to return to the high rates experienced in the early 1980s. In the recession of the 1990s, inflation fell at last to rates comparable with those of the early 1960s, and has remained there. As figure 11.1 shows, the achievement and maintenance of these low inflation rates were purchased at the high cost of prolonged high unemployment. A similar pattern emerges for most of the other OECD economies. The exceptions were Austria, Japan, Norway, Sweden and Switzerland, where social bargains and full employment persisted until the early 1990s.[1]

4 Mainstream views

From a mainstream neoclassical perspective, in the absence of shocks and market imperfections capitalist economies are self-regulating. Market forces automatically generate a growing full employment economy with acceptable rates of inflation, provided the monetary authorities keep the

---

[1] See Cornwall (1994, ch. 7) for an explanation of the different unemployment and inflation patterns in these five economies after the mid-1970s and before the mid-1990s.

growth rate of the money supply reasonably steady, because 'inflation is always and everywhere a monetary phenomenon'. The mainstream explanation of the inability of capitalist economies to live up to expectations since the golden age comes in two versions. One was influential in the period immediately following the end of the golden age; the other gained acceptance somewhat later. The first version is well illustrated by the McCracken Report (OECD, 1978). In the immediate aftermath of the decline in GDP growth and rise in unemployment that began in 1974, this interpretation of events emphasized shocks, including policy errors, as the culprits. These were responsible for the accelerating rates of inflation beginning in the second half of the 1960s, which necessitated the initiation of restrictive policies and rising unemployment rates. The difficulties were attributed to 'an unusual bunching of unfortunate events unlikely to be repeated on the same scale, the impact of which was compounded by some avoidable errors in economic policy' (OECD, 1978, p. 98). The Report also noted that institutional changes in the form of rising expectations and aspirations with respect to living standards and employment were an additional factor in the acceleration of inflation, but these influences were virtually ignored in the Report's policy recommendations. Recovery required 'a sustained expansion, initially less rapid than would otherwise be desirable during which memories of recent inflation should fade, and confidence in rising sales and employment be restored' (ibid., p. 274). It was claimed that conditions similar to those of the golden age would be recreated by 1980 if the Report's recovery programme were followed ('short-term pain for long-term gain'). Clearly the optimism of the McCracken Report was unfounded.

Partly in response to the failure of policies to achieve their objectives, attention turned to market imperfections as the explanation of malfunction, with the term 'Eurosclerosis' widely used to denote this view. This more pessimistic version, benefiting from hindsight, saw the now prolonged difficulties as evidence of structural problems; recovery had ceased to be comparable to a trip to the dentist. This analysis acknowledges that shocks had adversely affected economic performance, especially in accounting for the Great Inflation, but for the longer period it stressed and continues to stress the negative impact of a wide range of institutional developments inherited from the golden age. These had caused real economies to deviate from the competitive textbook model, interfering with their self-regulating tendencies. For example, under more competitive conditions, restrictive policies not only lead to a swift reduction in inflation, but set in motion automatic mechanisms, such as Pigou and Keynes effects, so that, after only a slight delay, the economy resumes its natural equilibrium unemployment and output position.

The failure of unemployment to decline rapidly to golden age levels was traced to outward shifts in the long-run vertical Phillips curve, i.e. increases in the NAIRU. The rising NAIRU was alleged to be an indicator of the growth of market imperfections, especially in the labour market (for example over regulated work conditions, overly generous unemployment benefits and increased union power), creating labour market conditions in which the real wage was too high to employ anything but a diminishing percentage of the labour force. In the words of a representative view of the time:

In this light, the more widespread and intensive influence of unions in Europe than in the United States may help explain the drastically different product wage trajectories in these two parts of the world and Europe's comparative lack of success in reducing unemployment after the recession of the early 1980s. (Lindbeck and Snower, 1987, p. 165)

This made it impossible for unemployment rates to fall to anywhere near their golden age levels without generating ever-accelerating rates of inflation. Inflation also failed to fall to its golden age rates until the 1990s because of relatively weak AD policy in the face of a rising equilibrium unemployment rate. Among the factors held responsible for the inadequate adjustments were monetary policy errors, for example the 'credibility problem', and 'political cowardice'; these interfered with the normally rapid automatic convergence of the economy to a NAIRU equilibrium. Today, with inflation under control and measures to increase labour market flexibility in place, accelerated growth of output is to be anticipated, although something might have to be done about the high unemployment. Both of these versions of the mainstream view show a continued implicit affirmation of capitalism as a self-regulating system, in spite of the persistence of high unemployment since the mid-1970s.

5 An institutional explanation

Our explanation of the end of the golden age and the emergence of a high unemployment episode has two things in common with the Eurosclerosis view of the malfunction: both were rooted in institutional causes and both anticipate a continuation of the malfunction until policy-induced institutional changes occur. We differ fundamentally in our view of which institutions were ultimately responsible for the Great Inflation and for its longer-run effects, especially the upward trend in unemployment rates. Whereas Eurosclerosis views institutional failure to change as the source of the problems, we point to changes in labour market institutions. These changes intensified conflict over the distribution of income, increasing the inflationary bias, and caused the Great Inflation. These events, together with the restrictive policy responses to inflation and the consequent rising unemployment, we identify as part of an evolutionary chain linking the golden age to the current episode of high unemployment. More exactly, for the majority of the OECD economies the link connecting the golden age with the Great Inflation and the deterioration in the employment record after 1973 was the cumulative effect of *induced* changes in institutions, especially in the labour market. Although shocks played a part in the Great Inflation, it must be emphasized that the 'wage explosion' preceded the shocks of the early 1970s. We stress the role of longer-run influences, which were similar across economies because of their similar golden age histories.

To understand the effects of these induced institutional changes requires a brief reprise of some characteristics of the golden age (these have been the subject of detailed accounts in chapters 5 and 9). First, in considering the century-long period covered in this study, an outstanding feature of the golden age was that it established a high point in labour's economic and political power relative to capital; in contrast, the episode since the mid-1970s represents a reversal of this trend. The golden age was an episode of rising affluence, accompanied almost everywhere by expansion of the welfare state and rapid consolidation of union power, increasing labour's power. In addition, greater centralization and integration of production increased the opportunity for small groups of workers to disrupt production. All of these contributed to the shift of power that enabled labour to insist on 'fairness' in wage settlements. In some economies a fair distribution of the growing real income was secured by unrestricted collective bargaining to maximize the money wage, i.e. a market power strategy. This strategy, adopted in Canada, Ireland, Italy, the United Kingdom and the United States throughout the golden age, led to unacceptably high inflation at full employment. Restrictive AD policies lowered inflation but kept unemployment above the full employment rate even before the mid-1970s in these economies.

Elsewhere, labour adopted a social bargain strategy: money wage demands were restrained and wage settlements coordinated with national macroeconomic goals such as wage and price stability and international competitiveness. These economies were able to avoid unacceptable inflation at full employment, even those with very strong trade union movements and left-of-centre, pro-labour governments such as Austria and Sweden. In spite of money wage restraint, real wages grew steadily in line with productivity growth, and these economies enjoyed full employment throughout most of the golden age. In the late 1960s and early 1970s social bargains began to unravel. Rates of wage and price inflation accelerated, leading to strong restrictive polices and a ratcheting upward of unemployment rates in all but five of the original social bargain economies. Austria, Japan, Norway, Sweden and Switzerland managed to contain inflation after a short period of accelerating rates and kept their social bargains and low rates of unemployment until the late 1980s or early 1990s (OECD, *Historical Statistics 1960–1995*, 1997, tables 2.16 and 2.20). In economies that had never adopted social bargains, instead using high unemployment to contain inflation, labour intensified efforts to achieve the benefits of a market power strategy. By the second half of the 1960s and into the early 1970s, labour in all but the five economies cited above voiced its dissatisfaction with recent trends in real wages and other aspects of employment. Efforts to remedy these problems were backed by higher strike activity, often unauthorized by union leaders, and pushing for higher rates of growth of money wages, i.e. the wage explosions of the late 1960s (Flanagan et al., 1983; Perry, 1975; Phelps Brown, 1971, 1975; Salvati, 1984; Soskice, 1978). In these economies restrictive policies were to become an institutional feature.

6 Success and the perception of unfairness as linkages

The question is how to explain labour's rising dissatisfaction with market outcomes. This was manifested in some economies by a shift from labour market strategies based on cooperation and trust, with market power strategies adopted in their place. In others it appeared as an intensification of labour's use of market power to achieve a more acceptable distribution of income and social benefits. Although the mainstream attributed the Great Inflation to a collection of temporary disturbances (e.g. OECD, 1978), other economists, and especially social scientists in other fields, saw events of the period as merely symptomatic of a developing trend in underlying attitudes. Their explanation centres on cumulative change in labour market institutions and in public perceptions, induced by the success of capitalism in the golden age. These institutional change explanations of the Great Inflation reflect the view that the prolonged full employment and growing affluence of the golden age generated changes leading to its own end (Brittan, 1975; Cornwall, 1994; Phelps Brown, 1971, 1975; Goldthorpe, 1978; Salvati, 1984; Scitovsky, 1978). Persistent low unemployment and rising living standards not only had increased labour's power, but had generated the belief that low unemployment and rising living standards were the norm. Anticipating continued growth and employment, people's aspirations rose, and their demands grew faster than the economy's ability to satisfy them.

Viewing matters from a longer-run perspective, consider the basis of fairness claims in wage determination, using the terms of sociologists such as Goldthorpe (1978). In a modern market economy the distribution of national income requires ethical as well as political and legal legitimacy if distributional conflict is to be minimized. This is particularly true the more unequal is the distribution of incomes after taxes and transfers. Economic advantages conferred by the market require status or 'prestige entitlements' if they are to be generally accepted and devoid of divisive implications. In the early stages of capitalist development, religion, immobility, differences in education and inherited status provided this legitimation. However, as capitalism developed, rising geographic mobility, the decline of organized religion, the spread of education and the suffrage and the increasing commercialization of life in general undermined acceptance of market-determined inequalities, calling into question the legitimacy of market capitalism. The growth of the welfare system temporarily slowed this trend, but deference and loyalty in society, in industrial relations and at the factory declined with the growing belief that greater economic rewards were justly deserved and should be claimed.

The expectation that living standards would continue to rise in the period leading up to the Great Inflation was propelled by over 20 years of steady growth in real incomes during the golden age. A growing proportion of the labour force was composed of workers who had never experienced unemployment conditions such as the 1930s, and whose experience told them that full employment was guaranteed by government no matter how exorbitant wage demands might be (Phelps Brown, 1975). These expectations, together with the insistence that distributional outcomes must be fair, led to growing aspirations and increasing demands upon the economic system (Duesenberry, 1991; Skott, 1999). With this and the causal linkage between the golden age and the age of high unemployment firmly in mind, we turn next to a stylized explanation of the interaction between inflation, policy and unemployment.

7 Inflation before the 1990s – a visual summary

The interactions taking place from the end of the golden age until the end of the 1990s are explained in this and the next two sections with the aid of Phillips curve analysis. To simplify without compromising the argument, this period is subdivided into three parts: the Great Inflation itself; the period immediately following the Great Inflation (approximately the mid-1970s to the late 1980s); and roughly the decade of the 1990s. This allows an account of events that emphasizes the essentials.

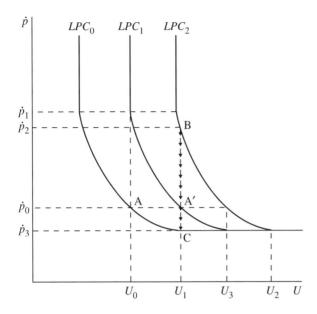

Figure 11.2 Shifts in the long-run Phillips curve

7.1 The emergence of an inflationary bias

We begin with the closing stages of the golden age and the events that brought it to an end. We discuss the social bargain economies first, followed by economies using market power strategy. Assume that point A on the long-run Phillips curve LPC_0 in figure 11.2 corresponds with the full employment rate of unemployment, U_0, and a politically acceptable rate of inflation, $\dot{p}_0$.[2] In other words, the Phillips curve LPC_0 depicts the unemployment–inflation trade-off for economies that had adopted social bargain strategies during the golden age, enabling them to avoid the inflationary bias and any inflation constraint on AD. The impact of replacing a social bargain with a market power strategy, the wage explosions and the emergence of an inflationary bias, are captured by the Phillips curve shifting from LPC_0 to LPC_1.[3] The full employment rate of unemployment, U_0, is

---

[2] As discussed in chapter 3, with long-run Phillips curves all wage–price dynamics have worked themselves out and therefore any point on the (negatively sloped) long-run curve represents a constant rate of inflation at the corresponding rate of unemployment.

[3] The emergence of an inflationary bias should not be confused with the mainstream notion of an increased NAIRU, even though both imply a greater constraint on AD policies. Each is embedded in a different theoretical framework and has a different explanation for movements in the unemployment rate, with different policy implications. Mainstream analysis

now no longer attainable at the politically acceptable rate of inflation, $\dot{p}_0$. In the eyes of the authorities, the choice is to maintain full employment and accept the higher inflation rate $\dot{p}_1$ or to pursue restrictive policies and move down the Phillips curve LPC_1, trading off higher unemployment for lower inflation. In the absence of social bargains, restrictive policies were chosen.

The announced goal of the restrictive AD policies introduced in the mid-1970s was to eliminate the 'inflationary psychology' that had built up during the late 1960s and early 1970s; this would permit the eventual restimulation of the economy. The restrictive policies were to make the fear of unemployment so strong that workers and management would internalize the costs of their wage and price setting during the subsequent expansion. They would avoid high wage demands and high price mark-ups, fearing the resumption of restrictive policies if they did not. As described in section 4, the conventional wisdom was that the restrictive policy responses immediately following the Great Inflation would quickly get rid of the inflation, and a shift to stimulative policies would be in order. Following a slow but steady recovery in AD and employment, a return to something like golden age conditions by the end of the 1970s could be expected (OECD, 1978, ch. 6). Events turned out quite differently.

7.2 Hysteresis in the unemployment rate

In fact, once the inflationary bias emerged, it was prone to policy-induced increase in the short run. Since the mid-1970s, restrictive policies have been used throughout most of the OECD to reduce inflation (as well as to correct payments positions). Although there was some temporary easing of policy in the second halves of the 1970s and the 1980s, from about the mid-1970s until the 1990s unemployment rates exhibited a strong upward trend, shown for the G7 in figure 11.1. In the more immediate period following the golden age episode of full employment, it is reasonable to assume that

footnote 3 (cont.)
    assumes that there is an automatic adjustment of AD, bringing it into line with the exogenous level of output corresponding to the NAIRU. Changes in the actual rate of unemployment reflect the extent to which the self-adjustment mechanisms have moved the economy towards the new NAIRU. In contrast, when a long-run trade-off between inflation and unemployment exists, movements in the unemployment rate reflect autonomous changes in AD, e.g. the impact of policy.
    Second, decreasing the equilibrium unemployment rate in a NAIRU world requires microeconomic measures to shift the NAIRU inward, not Keynesian policy. In a Keynesian world of involuntary unemployment and negatively sloped long-run Phillips curves, stimulative policies are a necessary condition for permanently reducing unemployment. Third, changes in the NAIRU are attributed to exogenous forces, e.g. changes in unemployment benefits, the degree of unionization, labour market mismatches. As we have just argued, the emergence of the inflationary bias, and by implication its worsening or abatement, can be explained by endogenous forces.

the attitude of labour was that, *when labour market conditions improved,* money wage demands must be sufficient to generate a 'catch-up' in real wages. Real wages had not increased at anything like the rates in the 1950s and 1960s, which it had come to expect. In addition, it is also reasonable to assume that the prevailing view of labour was that it was bearing the main cost of fighting inflation; accelerated money wage demands would be the means of redressing the balance if and when labour markets tightened. In these circumstances, and bearing in mind the prevailing high aspirations induced by golden age conditions, the unintended impact of policy-induced increases in unemployment was a further outward shift of the Phillips curve.

Following the breakdown of a social bargain and the shift of the Phillips curve from LPC_0 to LPC_1, the rate of inflation at $U = U_0$ was $\dot{p}_1$, greater than the acceptable rate of inflation, $\dot{p}_0$. The authorities, anticipating a drop in the inflation rate back to $\dot{p}_0$, initiate restrictive AD policy, increasing the unemployment rate from U_0 to U_1. However, labour's response to this 'unfair' policy-induced increase in unemployment causes a second shift in the Phillips curve, from LPC_1 to LPC_2. Labour's aspirations, induced by golden age conditions, are carried over to the new regime, at least in the short run, and its demands are intensified by increasing perceptions of unfairness. Instead of the higher rate of unemployment, U_1, bringing down inflation to the acceptable rate, $\dot{p}_0$, the economy moves to point B and the rate of inflation falls only to $\dot{p}_2$. If the authorities are reluctant to increase unemployment rates further than U_1, this relatively high rate of inflation persists in spite of restrictive policies. The result is that efforts to reduce inflation through policy-induced increases in unemployment are relatively ineffective but have high unemployment costs in the 'short run'.

A similar sequence of events is easily formulated for economies such as Canada and the United States which had never adopted a social bargain. Assume LPC_1 rather than LPC_0 is the appropriate long-run Phillips curve facing such economies before the beginning of the Great Inflation. Prior to the escalation of AD in the late 1960s they are at point A', experiencing an unemployment rate of $U_1 > U_0$, the full employment rate of unemployment, and an inflation rate of $\dot{p}_0$. Following the increase in AD in the late 1960s, let the unemployment rate fall to U_0 and the inflation rate rise to $\dot{p}_1$. If in response the authorities introduce a restrictive policy to combat inflation, there is an induced shift in the long-run Phillips curve to LPC_2, and for the same reasons that the Phillips curve shifted to LPC_2 in the previously social bargain economies. Assume these economies also move to point B.

Note that the Phillips curve LPC_2 is drawn so that the extent of any outward displacement decreases as unemployment rates increase and ceases entirely at all unemployment rates greater than U_2. This is to indicate that increased labour resentment and the desire to recoup real income losses generated by policy-induced high unemployment rates operate with greater force at low unemployment rates and have a declining effect on inflation as labour's market power decreases, eventually becoming zero. It also indicates that increasing unemployment rates above U_2 will not change inflation rates.[4]

8 Why was the inflation fight so long and costly?

Studies of the macroeconomic difficulties before the 1990s focused on the persistent high unemployment, which was attributed to increases in the NAIRU (Blanchard and Summers, 1987; Pissarides, 1988; Alogoskoufis and Manning, 1988). We have rejected this supply-side explanation, arguing instead that deficient AD caused the problems. The concern of this section is why inflation rates were so slow to fall even as unemployment rates trended upward. We trace this to the restrictive policies induced by the increased prevalence and intensification of market power strategies in labour markets. Throughout this period, the authorities responded to the greater inflationary bias by allowing unemployment rates to trend upwards, yet rates of inflation gave no indication of stabilizing at golden age levels until well into the 1990s (OECD, *Economic Outlook*, December 1999, Annex tables 16 and 22). This weak response of inflation to restrictive policies is captured in figure 11.2 by assuming that until the beginning of the 1990s the net effect of AD policies was to shift the Phillips curve to LPC_2, with policy makers choosing point B where $U = U_1$ and $\dot{p} = \dot{p}_2$. Under these conditions, the politically acceptable inflation rate $\dot{p}_0$ could have been achieved only if unemployment rates had been increased above U_1 to U_3. Since the overriding concern of policy makers was to reduce inflation, this raises the question of why they did not take sufficiently strong measures earlier. One explanation relied on the authorities' fear that overly restrictive monetary policies would have intensified a growing liquidity crisis; another postulated political limits to how far unemployment rates could be increased. The explanation we support is that high inflation persisted even as unemployment increased because policy makers underestimated the strength of the inflationary bias and overestimated the speed at which aspirations would adjust to economic conditions.

The behaviour of wage and price inflation in the second half of the 1970s prior to the second oil shock in 1979 is evidence of the persistent effect of the breakdown of social bargains and the greater inflationary bias. Both rates fell in response to the restrictive policies of the mid-1970s, but to rates previously

---

[4] Restrictive AD policies can also lead to outward shifts of the LPC when the labour market is viewed in terms of a number of segments (Cornwall, 1994, ch. 8).

Table 11.3 *Unemployment (U) and inflation rates (ṗ) for the G7, the United States and the United Kingdom: 1979–1992*

		1979	1980–3[a]	1984	1985	1986	1987	1988	1989	1990	1991	1992
G7	U	4.9	6.9	7.3	7.2	7.1	6.7	6.1	5.7	5.6	6.3	6.9
	ṗ	9.8	8.5	4.7	4.0	2.1	2.9	3.4	4.5	5.0	4.3	3.0
USA	U	5.8	8.4	7.4	7.1	6.9	6.1	5.4	5.2	5.4	6.6	7.3
	ṗ	11.3	8.3	4.3	3.5	1.9	3.7	4.1	4.8	5.4	4.2	3.0
UK	U	5.0	10.0	11.7	11.2	11.2	10.3	8.6	7.1	6.8	8.9	9.9
	ṗ	13.4	10.8	5.0	6.1	3.4	4.1	4.9	7.8	9.5	5.9	3.7

Note:
[a] Annual average.
Sources: OECD, *Historical Statistics 1960–1990*, Table 8.11; OECD, *Economic Outlook*, June 1992, Tables 50 and R18, and December 1993, Tables A15 and A19.

associated with lower unemployment rates. Events of the 1980s provided further evidence of the increased bias and the slow adjustment of aspiration levels. As shown in table 11.3, restrictive policies reduced inflation in the first half of the 1980s in the G7 (and elsewhere) to a low in 1986, but these golden age inflation rates were achieved at a very high unemployment cost. Beginning in 1987 there was a moderate reduction in unemployment but, although unemployment rates were still high by post-war standards, rates of both wage and price inflation accelerated. Even though average unemployment rates in the OECD fell only a little over 1 per cent further by 1990, inflation rates continued to rise between 1987 and the recession beginning in 1990.

The weak impact of restrictive policies on inflation and the institutional sources of the inflationary bias are closely related. The breakdown of social bargains in the late 1960s and early 1970s occurred because of labour's belief that distributional outcomes had become increasingly unfair. The restrictive policies that followed confirmed this belief and intensified labour's determination to accelerate wage demands if and when labour markets tightened. By the mid-1980s, attempts to reflate the economies, following what were incorrectly appraised as 'successful' anti-inflation policies, led to unacceptable rates of inflation in the second half of the 1980s, even while unemployment was triple its golden age rate.

9 Unemployment and inflation in the 1990s

It was not until the recession of the early 1990s, after a decade and a half of unemployment rates averaging approximately three times their golden age rates, that inflation fell to golden age rates or less, and remained there throughout the 1990s. The impact of prolonged high unemployment on workers' aspirations plays the key role in explaining these low inflation rates. In our view, the long period of policy-induced high unemployment generated hysteresis in the unemployment rate in a manner analogous to the effects of prolonged full employment in the golden age episode; it caused a shift in the long-run Phillips curve, but to the left.

In section 6 it was argued that the cumulative impact of the extended period of rapid growth in incomes and low unemployment was to increase aspirations with respect to living standards and employment. The eventual result was the wage explosion of the late 1960s and the unravelling of social bargains. The high cost of reducing inflation rates in the pre-1990s period was also attributed to aspirations that had formed in the golden age and continued to influence wage demands in the earlier phases of the high unemployment episode. This was shown in figure 11.2 by an outward shift of the Phillips curve, first from LPC_0 to LPC_1 for economies that had adopted a social bargain, and then from LPC_1 to LPC_2 for all economies. However, as the high unemployment continued, these golden age effects weakened. Following the mid-1970s, with a new generation of workers entering the labour market, the percentage of the labour force experiencing bouts of unemployment and shifts from full-time to involuntary part-time employment status grew steadily.[5] Along with reduced expectations of steady full-time employment, the stagnation of real earnings caused growing numbers of workers to lower their aspirations regarding rising living standards. Further, union density declined, as did the coverage of welfare safety nets provided by government. Labour's ability to enforce fairness in wage bargaining decreased along with its political power during this episode. Wage settlements made on a 'take it or leave it' basis multiplied, greatly dampening the force of any wage–price spiral. By the 1990s labour had lost much of its staying power, i.e. its ability to engage in industrial warfare.

Whereas the breakdown in social bargains and the initial response of labour to restrictive policies following the golden age led to resentment and outward shifts of the Phillips curve, prolonged poor economic conditions eventually shifted the Phillips curve back towards the origin, as aspirations of growing living standards and employment were scaled down (Skott, 1999). A stylized picture of these induced institutional changes that dominated events in the 1990s is shown in figure 11.2. Assume that the authorities maintain a restrictive AD stance so that, following a decade and a half of restrictive policies, there is downward adjustment of aspirations and the

[5] See chapter 2, section 5.

Phillips curve shifts inward so that it now lies to the left of LPC_1, say at LPC_0. Developments leading into the new millennium can then be shown as a movement down the vertical line with arrows from point B on LPC_2 to point C on LPC_0 corresponding to $U = U_1$. At point C, inflation rates are slightly lower than golden age rates and unemployment remains high, with the economies at the beginning of the horizontal segment of their Phillips curves. This is consistent with empirical studies showing both the USA and Canada to be on the horizontal part of their Phillips curves in the 1990s (Akerlof et al., 1996: Fortin, 1996).

10 The routes of institutional change

The economic developments discussed throughout the chapter linking the golden age to the current episode are shown in figure 11.3. The golden age is designated episode 3 and its structural variables are represented by the left-hand box. Although a specific Keynesian AD mechanism (not shown in the diagram) determines the detail, the general macroeconomic performance of the golden age episode is determined by the initial set of institutions. These determine whether or not full employment is consistent with other macroeconomic goals. The set of institutions in the golden age provided this consistency, so that AD was not constrained to be less than the full employment level. This was not the case in the episode since the mid-1970s.

Recall from chapters 6 and 9 that there are three ways in which institutional change may initiate a new episode. The first is the case of pure evolutionary change, the second is an exogenously caused change in performance that induces institutional change leading to a new episode, and the third is through exogenous changes occurring in episode 3 that generate a new set of institutions defining episode 4. As before, we focus solely on negative feedback. Also, we do not consider structural variables other than institutions, because their contribution to change has been very small relative to that of institutions. Institutions, not technology, provide the linkages between the golden age and the age of high unemployment.

The process of pure evolutionary change in the present context was illustrated by performance-induced shifts in labour market strategy in approximately half of the economies, generating unacceptable rates of inflation, restrictive policy responses and rising unemployment. As noted, these policies have persisted for over two decades. At least in the minds of the authorities, keeping AD below full employment levels has been the only way to ensure that inflation stays at politically acceptable rates. Moving across the figure from left to right, these evolutionary developments from the golden age to the current episode are portrayed by the two middle horizontal

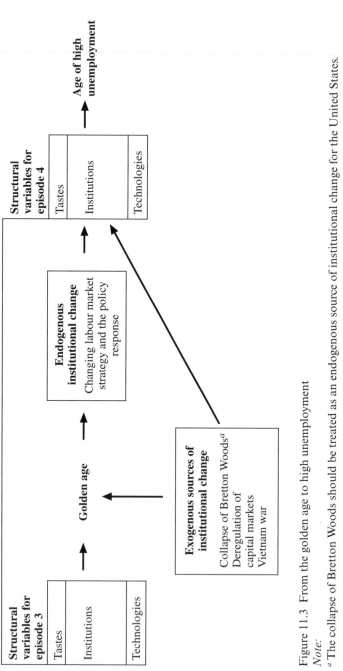

Figure 11.3 From the golden age to high unemployment

Note:

[a] The collapse of Bretton Woods should be treated as an endogenous source of institutional change for the United States.

arrows. The left-most of the two represents the induced changes in the labour market and the series of restrictive policies, which together ended the golden age.

The vertical arrow running from the 'exogenous sources' box to performance in the golden age represents the indirect impact of exogenous events on institutions. It illustrates a sequence for those economies that faced an inflationary bias and relatively high unemployment throughout the golden age. In particular, the escalation of the war in Vietnam, through its inflationary effects and resulting restrictive policy response, further worsened the existing inflationary bias. This increased the perceived need for restrictive policies in the North American economies. Even though initiated by an exogenous event, this dynamic process is also evolutionary since its effect on inflation performance in episode 3 induced institutional change that affected performance in episode 4, i.e. policies restrictive enough to increase unemployment rates substantially since the mid-1970s. Like the 'pure evolutionary' case of changing labour market institutions, it is also hysteretic because the resulting performance in episode 4 depends upon the system's history, i.e. events in episode 3. These two evolutionary processes describe the dynamics of the endogenous linkages between the golden age and the age of high unemployment that developed in approximately three-quarters of the OECD economies by the mid-1970s. The arrow ending at the right-hand box distinguishes the evolutionary processes from institutional changes directly attributable to exogenous sources. The right-hand box depicts the new structural variables for the period of poor unemployment performance that continues today.

The third source of institutional change is the direct impact of exogenous forces on institutions, shown by the diagonal arrow from the 'exogenous sources' box to the institutions segment of the right-hand box. More exactly, exogenous events in episode 3 directly affected institutions in ways that radically altered unemployment performance; that is, they moved the system to a new episode. This illustrates institutional hysteresis but not evolutionary change. The collapse of the Bretton Woods Agreement in the early 1970s, an exogenous institutional change everywhere except the United States, and the deregulation of international capital movements, which gained momentum by the 1980s, are the most significant of these events. This source of institutional change contributed to developments in the majority of the OECD economies, where an inflationary bias and high unemployment had developed by the mid-1970s. For these economies, it reinforced an already existing high unemployment equilibrium trap. But it was the chief cause of the end of the golden age for the five economies that kept their social bargains and low unemployment until the early 1990s. Restrictive AD policies and a rise in unemployment rates for this group can be traced directly to the altered international monetary regime with flexible exchange rates and unrestricted capital flows.

11 Concluding remarks

Section 2 provided econometric evidence of the links between institutions, AD and productivity growth. The main institutional changes that ended the golden age were the breakdown of social bargains and the intensification of the inflationary bias everywhere. The ensuing policies restricted AD and increased unemployment. Although other changes, such as the exhaustion of opportunities for catch-up and the shift of output toward services, played a part, reduced AD and high unemployment contributed significantly to the decline in productivity growth.

Figure 11.2 illustrated our account of the impact of the Great Inflation, its role in ending the golden age and the extended period of rising unemployment and declining rates of inflation in the episode following the golden age. Underlying the shifting Phillips curves were induced institutional changes, occurring over almost half a century, that reflected first rising and then declining aspirations regarding future employment and incomes. Specifically, the cumulative effect of an extended period of low unemployment and rapid income growth in the golden age led to rising aspirations. During the golden age, their impact on inflation was contained by social bargains and by steady growth in productivity. The breakdown in social bargains and the induced decline in productivity growth led to an outward shift of the Phillips curve. As a result, full employment was no longer compatible with low inflation; in other words, an inflationary bias had developed. The policy response to this incompatibility of goals was a curtailment of AD, leading to a rising trend in unemployment rates and an end to the golden age.

Following a period of rising unemployment and declining income growth even longer than the golden age, aspirations eventually adapted to the new reality, leading to leftward shifts of the Phillips curve, first to LPC_1 and eventually to LPC_0. The cumulative shift was big enough to reduce inflation to rates even lower than in the golden age, although the cost in terms of unemployment was and remains high.[6] As a final illustrative point, in section 9, a vertical arrow pointing downward was drawn from point B to

---

[6] The fact that aspirations rose in the golden age and fell in the succeeding episode, leading the LPC to return to LPC_0 in our example, is not to be confused with the unit root case of unemployment persistence (Gordon, 1989; Wyplosz, 1987). Our explanation attributes shifts of the Phillips curve to profound institutional (i.e. structural) change during the episode of high unemployment. The usual unit root example of unemployment persistence assumes the economic structure to be unchanged while the Phillips curve is shifting.

C at $U = U_1$. This described the AD policy position of the mid-1990s, targeted to bring inflation rates below even those acceptable in the golden age. Figure 11.2 also suggests that unemployment rates could be reduced to below U_1 with only a modest rise in the inflation rate. Nevertheless, at point C the unemployment rate remains high.[7] If the inflation cost is small, why not move to point A?

The answer to this question concerns the nature of LPC_0. This is the golden age Phillips curve of the social bargain countries. During the golden age, it was out of reach to countries without social bargains. Now that aspirations are lowered it is applicable to all economies, those that once had social bargains as well as those that did not. However, events following the collapse of social bargains strongly suggest that LPC_0 is unstable at unemployment rates below U_1 unless there are social bargains or similar institutions in place that stabilize it. Any move from C toward A in figure 11.2 will begin the process of restoring labour's aspirations. Then, without social bargains, continued commitment to maintaining unemployment at U_0 will eventually result in a repetition of the rightward movements of the Phillips curve in the late 1960s and 1970s. The most crucial function of the missing institutions is to maintain inflation at tolerable rates at full employment, the function performed by social bargains in the golden age. Realizing that these institutions are lacking, governments and central banks either believe or strongly suspect that their economies are on a Phillips curve that is unstable below current unemployment rates, and so allow high unemployment to continue.

Chapter 11 has concentrated on the constraint on AD arising from an inflationary bias, and our analysis has brought us to the question of why governments are not seeking to establish institutions that will remove this constraint and allow an end to the continuing high unemployment. This is the topic of chapter 12, which considers some additional institutional constraints on AD. These are new constraints that owe their existence primarily to shifts in the distribution of power. These power shifts have nurtured the advent of neoliberalism, a non-interventionist market-oriented version of capitalism that reflects and strengthens the dominance of capital.

---

[7] Many would claim that the USA is already at golden age unemployment rates, but here we remind the reader of the measurement problems discussed in chapter 2, which lead to serious understatement of the actual unemployment rate.

Part III
Political control of the economy

In part II, alternating episodes of poor and superior performance were traced to structural change endogenous to the performance of the economy, forming a causal chain linking successive episodes via negative feedback effects. The structural changes linking the episodes differed, with technology developments providing the link between the period of industrialization and the 1930s, and institutional developments constituting the links between the 1930s and the golden age and subsequently between the golden age and the existing age of high unemployment. Having made a point of the differences in linkages, we have no hesitation in stating that the failure to recover quickly once an adverse structural change has occurred is a failure of institutions to adapt to changing circumstances. As discussed in chapter 8, the depressed economic conditions extending over most of the 1930s could have been ended earlier with a Keynesian deficit spending programme, had there been the political will to introduce it. Although the cause of the Great Depression was technology, recovery was prevented by an institutional constraint on stimulative AD policy. In chapter 11 we argued that the golden age was brought to an end by the eventual incompatibility of full employment and acceptable rates of inflation. The institutional requirements for a full employment recovery today are more demanding than in the 1930s.

Our programme for recovery is implicit in the commentary running throughout our explanation of the structural influences responsible for alternating episodes of poor and superior performance. In part III we will limit discussion of the required policy-induced institutional changes to a brief argument supporting the restoration of the golden age institutional environment, for example a second generation of social bargains, an overhaul of the international monetary regime and the elimination of legal institutions that more directly constrain the level of AD. This is not to advocate trying to duplicate golden age institutions, but rather to find new ones that can perform the same or similar functions in twenty-first century conditions.[1]

However, the neoliberal system that has arisen since the mid-1970s has entrenched a set of institutions that function quite differently from those of the golden age. Under this regime, the role of government in domestic and international economic affairs has been greatly reduced, social bargains no longer dominate labour market outcomes and price stability has become an overriding macroeconomic goal. This institutional shift has been accompanied by a shift in economic and political power from labour to capital. The relevant question is: given the radical nature of these shifts, can we anticipate a radical improvement in performance or, more specifically, can we expect a return to conditions of simultaneous full employment, rapid growth and low rates of inflation? Certainly neoliberalism has delivered low inflation but, as the record clearly shows, this has required a quarter of a century of high rates of unemployment. Nevertheless, supporters of neoliberalism are unyielding in their insistence that their institutional reforms will eventually deliver all of these goals. Indeed, they envisage their programme as an induced, wholly appropriate response to what they see as the excesses and inevitable failure of golden age institutions.

In the concluding part of this study, we argue that neoliberalism will not lead to an episode of full employment growth with acceptable rates of inflation. The institutions of neoliberalism have made a return to full employment difficult if not impossible in most of the economies. As well as failing to deal with an inflationary bias – that is, unacceptable inflation under sustained full employment conditions – the new institutions impose additional constraints on AD. For the most part these institutional changes have been 'politically driven', attributable to the shift of economic and political power from labour to capital. Capital's increased power and the consequent rise of institutional barriers to full employment are outstanding features of the episode of high unemployment that has prevailed since the golden age. Those in power are intent on extending policies that are quite the opposite of what is required. A radical change in institutions is necessary and this is very unlikely until the current programme of neoliberalism has very obviously failed and failed very badly. These topics are considered in chapter 12.

This raises the issue of the political and economic stability of the system. Will the institutions essential to the preservation of democracy and capitalism remain intact under conditions of high unemployment, widespread poverty and exaggerated inequalities in the distribution of income? This is

---

[1] Detailed programmes for recovery can be found in other studies by the authors (Cornwall, 1994; Cornwall and Maclean, 1984).

the issue that troubled Keynes in the inter-war period: the possible incompatibility of capitalism and democracy under conditions of prolonged high unemployment. As Keynes saw it, in these circumstances the economic consequence of universal suffrage could result in the replacement of capitalism with socialism in order to introduce distributional fairness. An equally disturbing possibility was that the political consequences of capitalism could result in an authoritarian state run by capitalists who had put an end to democracy before universal suffrage succeeded in putting an end to capitalism. Is Keynes' concern relevant today? This is discussed briefly in chapter 13.

12   Unemployment and the distribution of power

1 Introduction

Chapter 11 brought our evolutionary-Keynesian account of macroeconomic developments to the present. By the mid-1990s it was widely assumed that the battle against inflation was won, supposedly an omen of good things to come. Governments and the monetary authorities continue to warn of the dangers of reigniting inflation, but these cautions are drowned out by a growing belief in market capitalism's imminent renewal. The performance of the American economy since the mid-1990s is proof enough for the optimists; low inflation, low official unemployment and rising output growth are outshone only by the phenomenal rise of the stock market. Using the American experience as evidence of the efficiency of the market system, a 'neoliberal' model is cited as the universal cure for economic woes. But the market did not deliver low inflation, restrictive policy did; and, even with the aid of policy, it took a very long time to get inflation back to golden age rates, and then only at the cost of high unemployment that has lasted longer than the golden age. During the period from 1970 to 1994, when inflation exceeded its golden age rates, average unemployment in the OECD economies studied increased by 155 per cent, rising from 2.9 per cent to 7.4 per cent. Until 1998, average unemployment continued at rates only slightly less than two and a half times those in 1970 (see table I.1 for sources).

Low inflation has been achieved, but it is still unclear whether it is the sign of recovery it is claimed to be, heralding a new episode of golden age unemployment rates.[1] We have suggested that governments and central bankers still fear inflation, so that strong expansionary policies are unlikely. It was also suggested that this fear is justified in the absence of the social

---

[1] Friedman (1977) in his Nobel Prize address stated that only by reducing inflation rates could unemployment rates be reduced in the long run; that is, the long-run Phillips curve is positively sloped! This view has long been echoed by central bankers. Our contrary view was given at the end of chapter 11.

bargains that were essential to maintaining full employment in the golden age. This leads to the question of why there has been no effort to avoid inflation at full employment by re-establishing social bargains. In this chapter we consider other changes that virtually remove any likelihood of 'reversing history' by means of policy-induced changes in institutions. These changes stem from and increase the dramatic shift in economic and political power from labour to capital that has been taking place since the golden age. This chapter analyses this power shift and its implications for institutions and performance.

Chapter 11 confined its discussion of developments since the golden age to institutions responsible for unacceptable inflation costs of full employment, resulting in constraints on AD. But during the same period other constraints have been established, most of them 'political'. These embody the views held by corporate business and financial interests, who have persuaded governments that prolonged periods of full employment interfere with essential business control of the economy. If full employment also causes high rates of inflation, there is a supporting reason for these constraints on AD. The response to these claims has been the adoption of laws, treaties and other formal institutions that have strengthened capital's power, often by intentionally imposing further constraints on AD, keeping it below its full employment level. It is this additional category of constraints, absent in the golden age, that is the focus of this chapter. Their emergence both reflects and fosters a substantial shift in power from labour to capital and has had a major influence on performance.

The next section briefly discusses long-term trends in the distribution of power, after which section 3 outlines a theory of power in elementary terms. Section 4 discusses the sources of labour's initial increase in power in the golden age and events during the golden age that reinforced this power shift. Sections 5 and 6 deal with the shift in power back to capital in the age of high unemployment and how legal constraints on AD have solidified capital's regained position of power. Section 7 discusses the altered international role the United States now plays in the age of high unemployment. Section 8 evaluates current trends in relation to the views of Keynes and Kalecki on unemployment, power and stability. Section 9 contains the conclusions.

2 The trend in the relative power of labour and some of its impacts

In this study we have defined power as the ability to control or command others. Two kinds of power are recognized: economic and political. They are distinguished in terms of the means that enable someone to exercise power, and not in terms of the particular purpose for which power is used.

In examining how power affects institutions and the economy, the focus is on its distribution among organized interest groups. For ease of exposition we limit the analysis to two broad categories: the large firms comprising the corporate sector of business, for which we use the terms 'business' or 'capital' interchangeably; the remaining private sector groups, referred to simply as 'labour'. The main conclusions of the chapter are not affected by this simplification.

In his description of the evolution of the distribution of power between business (or capital) and labour, Scitovsky (1978) divided the economic history of modern capitalism prior to the present episode into three phases. The first phase encompassed the development of the factory system; the second dealt with the period when the trade union movement developed; and the third covered the post-World War II period up to the early 1970s. In the first phase, because of vastly superior bargaining strength, business dominated labour markets, usually setting money wages on a 'take it or leave it' basis. The rise of trade unions greatly increased the economic power of labour in bargaining. According to Scitovsky this led to an asymmetry in money wage movements, as downward flexibility of wages was reduced and upward flexibility increased. It also led to an improvement in non-pecuniary aspects of work, for example safety conditions. What labour still lacked was 'staying power', i.e. the ability to absorb the costs of industrial warfare, such as a prolonged strike. Events of the post-World War II period changed this, with the widespread expansion of social and welfare services and payments, the accumulation of assets by workers and their unions as a result of growing affluence and the commitment of governments to full employment. Labour achieved staying power.

This shift in power had a great impact on institutions and economic performance in the golden age. As we have noted earlier, one important effect was that fairness came to the fore in wage bargaining and settlements, replacing the 'take it or leave it' wage determination of the past. The greater economic and political power of labour reduced capital's arbitrary use of power in the labour market, and settlements had to be accepted by both sides as fair, in other words, related to growing aspirations, the cost of living and to wage settlements elsewhere. As a result, changes in wages or prices could set in motion dynamic wage–price movements leading to politically unacceptable rates of wage and price inflation. In addition, this shift in power reduced capital's ability to control the workplace and increased the possibility of strike activity. Missing from Scitovsky's scenario are explanations of why unacceptable rates of inflation were avoided in some economies but not in others during the two decades of full employment following World War II, and why inflation eventually became a serious problem, issues addressed in chapters 9 to 11. Explanations are also needed for more recent events, particularly for the causes of labour's loss of power in the current episode and the advent of neoliberalism, the concern of this chapter. Scitovsky's summary of earlier trends in power is a sharp reminder of how exceptional was labour's success in challenging capital's supremacy in the golden age.

3 A rudimentary theory of power

The outline of a rudimentary theory of the distribution of power helps to organize our thinking on the effects of power on institutions and performance. Power theories such as the party control or partisan theory of economic policy focus on the exercise of power as an origin of institutional change. Two underlying premises of this theory are worth repeating: first, the economic and social divisions of a society are reflected in its institutions and political parties; and second, whereas capital prefers low inflation, labour places greater weight on full employment and therefore prefers policies that place the economy further up and to the left on a negatively sloped Phillips curve. Chapter 5 noted weaknesses in the party control theory of institutions. First, it deals only with political power, ignoring such clear examples of the use of economic power as restructuring the workplace and fairness in wage setting. Second, it assumes the distribution of political power and its impact on institutions and performance to be determined primarily by electoral success. These shortcomings are made clearer by comparison with Lindblom's analysis of the sources of capital's political and economic power, first mentioned in chapter 9. According to Lindblom (1977, chs. 13–15), in all private enterprise, market-oriented economies business has special privileges and powers stemming from its governance of economic activity, which determines economic security and living standards. These functions influence governments even if business did not engage in politics in support of pro-business representatives. But business actively participates in politics and, according to Lindblom, it has two advantages that make it more effective than other organized groups. First, it has greater financial resources at its disposal to sell its agenda, and, second, it has the organization already in place to persuade voters to accept this agenda.

This does not mean that the power of business in an economy is uncontested or that the electoral and organizational strength of labour should be given no weight. Capitalism takes many forms, and the strength and type of power that business exercises are among the causes of differences. To envisage the processes underlying the distribution of power in the post-World War II era, we assume that business holds the preferred position that Lindblom claims. However, we maintain that the power conferred on capital by its special position is variable, depending on the relative power of labour and on the performance of the economy, existing institutions and historical events. First, capital's relative power varies inversely with the strength of both the union movement and the political parties supporting its causes. Second, it varies directly with the looseness of labour markets. High rates of unemployment, especially if persistent, reduce the economic power of labour. Third, institutions that can limit capital's power include legal and social institutions that embody long-standing industrial relations practices restricting the power of business in the workplace, for example restrictions on firing workers or even 'lifetime' employment contracts. Such institutions are the foundation of the harmonious industrial relations systems in Japan and Switzerland, neither of which has strong unions to balance capital's power. In Japan, traditional social rights and obligations curb business power. In Switzerland, referenda and labour representation on advisory councils and in government perform a similar function.[2] Other institutions can increase capital's relative power by weakening the effectiveness of the democratic process; these include both national and international laws and treaties that restrict the 'fullness' of political democracy, i.e. the extent to which elected officials of a country must bear political responsibility for instituting or failing to institute regulations and laws affecting their constituents. Finally, during the post-war period, two developments unique to the episode affected capital's relative power. These were the changing state of capital's 'reputation' and the degree to which the Soviet Union was perceived by governments and business as a threat to the economic and political stability of capitalism. We should emphasize that, when referring to these possible sources of change in the distribution of power, there will be interactions between them generating self-reinforcing processes. For example, a rise in the unemployment rate may lead to the introduction of new laws further enhancing capital's power.

4 Power, social bargains and positive feedback

4.1 Power and the establishment of social bargains

With this as a background, we return briefly to some of the main institutional features described in earlier chapters that distinguish the two historical episodes making up the post-World War II era. However, here our chief concern is not with linkages between episodes; rather it is to highlight the forces accounting for differences in the distribution of power between the

---

[2] For a discussion of the industrial relations systems of these two countries, see Cornwall (1994, pp. 101–6).

two episodes and the impact of these differences on institutions and performance. We begin with the golden age and the institutional features that made it possible.

At the beginning of the 1950s, most of the OECD economies were at or near full employment. Production remained under the control of capital in a new form of capitalism; democracy was preserved in this system, which adopted social welfare measures but not socialism. Labour had achieved substantial political power and its economic power was beginning to grow. The key question addressed in chapter 9 was how this golden age episode in capitalist development arose from a past that included the rise of Soviet communism, the Great Depression and World War II. We have argued that business is unlike other interest groups; it holds a unique position in a capitalist system, a position that gives it special powers and privileges. Other things being equal, business resists efforts to reduce its economic and political power. Yet, in the golden age, capital in most of the OECD was willing to enter into cooperative arrangements with government and labour that led to a reduction in its relative power.[3] At issue are the conditions that led to this initial shift in power and the subsequent impact of further induced power shifts on economic developments of the golden age.

As described in chapter 9, by the end of World War II labour had become highly politicized and was prepared to challenge the dominating influence of business in the economy with an agenda of its own. Given the widely held belief that all groups should share in the benefits of recovery, the bad reputation its wartime activities had earned for business and the need for rapid economic reconstruction, governments (outside of the United States) were receptive to measures that would increase their own and labour's power relative to business. These included economic planning that increased governments' power, allowing them to direct the course of reconstruction, as well as the full employment policies, the expanded welfare state and nationalizations of key industries sought by labour.

However, these policies went beyond a once-over redistribution of power between labour and capital. The promised full employment would generate continued growth in labour's economic power, and this carried the danger that demands for large wage increases and strikes in support of these demands would impede recovery and lead to high inflation. Governments had prepared the way for growth in the relative power of labour, and this created a potential internal inconsistency, a conflict of domestic goals that stood in the way of a golden age. The inconsistency lay in the desire to achieve full employment and politically acceptable rates of inflation while simultaneously retaining unrestricted collective bargaining. With government

[3] The United States was a clear exception, pursuing a different domestic path.

providing leadership, social bargains were established in the early post-war years that avoided this internal inconsistency by providing an alternative to unrestricted collective bargaining, and recovery proceeded with both low unemployment and low inflation. Not all economies were able to establish a social bargain, and there was considerable variation among those that were established. Nevertheless, they had in common the objective of reconciling the goals of labour and capital, and the goals of each with national policy, both domestic and external. In terms of figure 11.2 in the last chapter, social bargains stabilized the Phillips curve LPC_0 for unemployment rates as low as U_0.

4.2 Rejection of the US model

In spite of emerging from World War II as the strongest economic and military power, the USA was unsuccessful in imposing its own preferred economic model on the countries of Western Europe. As early as the 1940s the United States had begun to promote the establishment of a multilateral system of liberalized trade, and its post-war position as economic and political hegemon ensured that American views on the post-war international order would dominate international agreements. The main event in the US domestic economy was a reassertion of power by business, supported by sympathetic governments and aided by internal strife in the US labour movement. In addition to reforming the international economic order, the USA had plans to export this fledgling neoliberal regime as the economic basis of a 'United States of Europe'.

The American view of the new international order was not without support, at least in principle. There was a broad recognition that a system of multilateral trade and payments was needed to avoid the competitive devaluations and controls that had caused so much damage in the inter-war period. Practical matters delayed the wholesale adoption of this plan, as Japan and the European countries faced large trade deficits; diminishing foreign reserves in general and a looming dollar shortage in particular added to fears that their industries were not ready to compete internationally. With the newly emerging Cold War as a catalyst, a compromise solution was found that permitted continued protection and promised American assistance for payments deficits in return for a commitment to the future liberalization of trade and payments. The basic elements of the international monetary system were fixed but adjustable exchange rates and controls on private international capital flows, features that Keynes had identified as essential to the simultaneous achievement of external balance under free trade and full employment.

Full employment was a key political issue in the UK and many European economies, and governments elected by or friendly to labour had committed themselves to this goal as part of a wider list of policies that would benefit the average citizen. This commitment ruled out acceptance of the American model of unregulated market capitalism, which accepted the dominance of business and the need to sacrifice the full employment goal, choosing inflation as the policy target instead. Interventionist policies including full employment and the welfare state were central policies of most West European governments, and were seen as essential to the political stability of many of them. Any conflict between this view and the US neoliberal preferences was avoided when the emerging Cold War made European stability the paramount concern. This caused the USA to redirect its foreign policy to strengthening and stabilizing the capitalist world, ensuring that the political and economic gains of labour in those countries would continue.

4.3 Positive feedbacks

Full employment was evidence of the success of the social bargain regimes, as well as being crucial to their continuation. But full employment is possible only when AD is strong, and continued strong AD depends upon there being no serious conflict with other macroeconomic goals. The institutions that comprised the social bargains were designed to reduce or eliminate these conflicts and to encourage modernization and economic growth. Their immediate objectives were to avoid inflation, to maintain international competitiveness, and to minimize industrial strife. Achievement of these objectives allows strong AD to persist and fosters the long-run aim of economic growth. Capital's cooperation was assured; it was unable to influence AD policy to reduce labour's power, because labour had achieved political ascendancy by the early 1950s outside the United States. Events of the two succeeding decades were to strengthen the terms of the social bargain. The ever-present threat of communism sustained the hegemon's interest in economic and political stability throughout the 'free world'. Through American aid and technology transfer, together with a strong investment effort, productivity growth accelerated everywhere. This and full employment not only provided the source of growing real wages, but also financed the expansion of a welfare state favoured by labour. Together, these benefits reinforced labour's original decision to agree to a social bargain and provided the security of employment and growing affluence that further increased its power. For capital, productivity growth and expanding markets were sources of growing profits. In addition, the social bargains brought relatively harmonious industrial relations, and the near-absence of strikes added to the growth of profits encouraged investment and further growth. These circumstances ensured the continued participation of capital in the social bargains. The interests of business, like the interests of the USA, were well served by the stability these golden age institutions provided. There was no reason not to allow them to continue. But, as long as they existed, the positive feedback – from full employment and strongly growing AD to increased productivity and affluence, and further growth in AD – would continue, and would increase labour's economic power at each step.

5 Power shifts, neoliberalism and some positive feedbacks

5.1 Establishing neoliberalism

In the previous chapter, the explosion of wages was identified as the initiating cause of the Great Inflation. The wage explosion reflected important institutional changes in the labour market. It signalled the end of the golden age and led to the introduction of AD policies whose overall stance remained restrictive long after the Great Inflation came to an end. These institutional changes and those initiated by the collapse of the Bretton Woods system set the stage for the spread of neoliberalism to economies other than the United States. Neoliberalism is a regime characterized by reduced government intervention, the deregulation of markets, cutbacks in the welfare state, and price stability as its overriding macroeconomic goal. This regime ushered in a new episode of high unemployment, of greatly reduced growth in productivity and per capita incomes, and of increases in income inequality and in the incidence of poverty.[4] These have been, and continue to be, the price of achieving low rates of inflation.

By the early 1970s most of the social bargains had collapsed. The labour unrest and wage explosions that followed led the general public to believe that labour had become too powerful and was responsible for inflation. The reputation of business rose as that of labour fell. The bad reputation capital had earned in World War II, which had caused it to restrain its use of power during the golden age, was all but forgotten. Business was now seen as the provider of affluence, and labour as preventing it from performing this task. A second motive for capital to temper its use of power was removed with the collapse of the Soviet Union in the late 1980s. This relieved both government and business of their fears of socialism. Together, these events led to a greater assertion of power by business and reduced its interest in social bargains.

---

[4] Osberg (2000) investigates five countries, and finds that between 1969/70 and 1994/95 there was a sharp increase in income disparity in both the USA and the UK, and a moderate increase in Germany. He found no increase in either Sweden or Canada.

Without social bargains, either the goal of full employment or acceptable rates of inflation had to be sacrificed. With few exceptions, throughout the OECD the decision was made to sacrifice the full employment goal and to contain inflation through restricting AD and letting unemployment rise; collective bargaining outcomes could be left to the market. The fact that little effort was made to establish a second generation of social bargains, which could have avoided a constraint on AD, suggests a growing intention of governments and business to replace interventionist domestic policies by market-determined outcomes. This lack of effort to come to terms with unions may also reflect the declining percentage of the workforce that was unionized. Except for Sweden and Denmark, this decline was evident everywhere by the late 1980s, and earlier in some countries (Chang and Sorrentino, 1991; International Labour Organization, 1998). Besides the public loss of respect for unions, changes in the structure of employment have made the industrial sector, the traditional stronghold of the labour movement, relatively less important; both have acted to reduce unions' presence as a force in the economy. The restrictive AD policies and the upward trend in unemployment rates that began in the mid-1970s reduced the power of labour further and strengthened capital's control of the work-place. This caused a major shift of economic power to business and the beginning of a new episode.

5.2 *Acceptance and reinforcement of the US model*

The changed public perceptions of business and labour paved the way for governments to follow this course, which was accompanied by claims that the only way to beat inflation was to dismantle the system that allegedly generated it. In many countries, the neoliberal agenda was expanded to include cuts to various elements of the social safety net as governments targeted deficit reduction (or even balancing the budget) as a primary goal. These trends have further weakened labour. There was also a wave of 'privatizations' as governments sold industries that had been nationalized in the wake of World War II. The symbolism was strong; not only was the 'old era' over, but governments have made an unambiguous public display of their faith in business as sole guardian of prosperity. Small, non-interventionist government had become the new norm.

Other trends have demonstrated this commitment to neoliberalism, including 'deregulation', most frequently of transportation and communications industries, where regulated monopolies were earlier established as the most efficient way to provide reasonably priced services to small and distant communities as well as to the large urban centres. These efforts to move toward a 'competitive' model have in many cases ended with an unregulated monopoly and no (or very costly) service to some communities. Finally, there has been a trend of minimizing government economic involvement by removing certain policy targets from the realm of politics. Moves to make a law or constitutional amendment requiring balanced budgets and making the central bank independent of the government are two examples. These trends tend to increase the relative economic power of business. But they also have a lasting and profound effect on labour, especially on labour that has already lost relative economic power. The ability of labour to pursue its goals via the ballot box depends on the government it elects having the legal right to use the necessary policies, and it is precisely this legal right that has been curtailed. These constraints reinforced the effects that anti-inflationary AD policies had already exerted on the distribution of economic power by moving the full employment goal beyond democratic control. Clearly, once neoliberalism is established, its small government, non-interventionist character leads to continued enhancements of the relative power of business.

6 Globalization and additional positive feedbacks

Balanced budget resolutions and greater independence for central banks were domestic manifestations of a new trend in policy, as governments introduced formal institutional constraints on their own power. In the postgolden age period this trend has reinforced the initial shift in power to capital resulting from rising unemployment rates. Most crucially, these self-imposed rules curtailed governments' power to influence unemployment rates. These are 'politically driven' constraints and are not confined to the domestic policy arena. Using slogans reminiscent of the 'no alternative' arguments for their abnegation of responsibility for domestic policy, governments have increasingly renounced responsibility for international economic relations. Citing the 'inevitability of globalization', they have signed a variety of international agreements limiting their domestic policy options. These include agreements that directly bind them to abide by regulations limiting their use of discretionary AD policies, for example Maastricht criteria; international agreements deregulating capital movements that in effect become constraints on stimulative AD policies; and trade regulations that prevent the use of import restrictions to combat sectoral rises in unemployment. These developments, whether intentional or not, have reinforced the terms of neoliberalism by removing a country's control of its international economic activities from the reach of full democracy.[5] In varying degrees, elected representatives in nation states vol-

---

[5] Universal suffrage is a key condition of 'full democracy' as the term is used here, but as the text makes clear, we impose the additional condition that elected officials must take full

untarily yielded their power to enact independent policies. They entered into agreements that would affect their constituents, but accepted no part in the governance of these agreements. Instead, international organizations staffed by unelected officials, largely under the control of the United States, were empowered to initiate agreements and to both define and interpret their terms.

Globalization refers to the integration of economies through both free trade and deregulated international capital markets. Here we provide examples of how each of these two aspects of globalization has reduced labour's power, one quite directly, the other by constraining the use of stimulative AD policy. The trend in free trade agreements has led to an increasing number of newly industrializing countries (NICs) able to compete freely with the developed economies for market shares of merchandise trade. Taking advantage of technology transfer opportunities, their rapid industrialization has been aided by the introduction of advanced (but standardized) technologies, often resulting in labour costs substantially below those of competitors in the developed economies. This in itself would contribute to the surge in exports of manufactures from the NICs to the developed economies. However, this overlooks the contribution of outsourcing – the segmentation of the production process into several components, some of which can then be contracted out to the lowest bidder. When this is technically possible, the cost advantage of the NICs will likely apply to component parts of production processes, leading to expanded outsourcing by the developed economies. In the current period, the large growth in merchandise trade relative to merchandise production in the OECD economies can be attributed both to the increased number of NICs exporting final goods to the developed economies, and also to the growth of outsourcing in the developed economies (Feenstra, 1998; Irwin, 1996). These developments act to reduce the bargaining power of labour, especially union labour (Feenstra, 1998). Producers in the developed economies, by threatening to move production abroad or to outsource links in their production chain, can exact reductions in labour compensation (wages plus benefits) or simply reduce employment, or both.[6] This reinforces the impact of higher levels of overall unemployment on capital's ability to control the workplace in the developed economies.

The deregulation of financial capital movements provides a second example of globalization's negative effect on labour's power and the

responsibility for the regulations and laws governing economic outcomes within their national boundaries.

[6] It will also lead business to demand reduced business taxation to increase competitiveness and will shift the burden of taxes from business to labour; alternatively, it leads to a general reduction of tax revenues and reduced ability to finance welfare programmes (Rodrik, 1997; Tanzi, 2000).

prospects of improved employment. It accomplishes this by creating an additional barrier to stimulative AD policies. Under an international monetary regime of deregulated financial capital and flexible exchange rates, the inflation penalty is immediate and high for any economy unilaterally attempting to pursue a full employment goal. In these circumstances, stimulative AD policies signal to managers of large stocks of mobile capital that the authorities in that economy are pursuing 'market unfriendly' policies. Since each manager will expect the others to have similar beliefs, the loss of 'credibility' of the country in question leads to capital flight, a larger than expected fall in the exchange rate and an acceleration of inflation. The stronger and more prolonged is the stimulative policy, the greater the intensity and duration of speculation against the currency, and the greater the increase in expected and actual rates of inflation. Governments are soon forced to reverse their policies in order to protect the exchange rate. Simplifying slightly, without coordinated expansionary policies, the deregulation of capital flows under a flexible exchange rate system has introduced a constraint; it rules out stimulative AD policy as an instrument for reducing unemployment rates.[7]

7 Globalization and the role of the hegemon

In this account of shifts in power, changing institutions and the advent of high unemployment, we have said little about the role of the United States in a period of increased globalization or about the unique form of American capitalism. In contrast to the majority of the OECD economies, a social bargain regime was never established in the United States. Given its weak labour movement, the acceptance of a relatively free rein for capital and a tradition of limited intervention by government on behalf of labour, this is understandable. As early as the beginning of the twentieth century, the political and economic structure of a non-interventionist regime in domestic markets was in place and remains intact. As detailed earlier, following World War II, US hopes of imposing this kind of market-dominated, non-interventionist regime on the others were shelved. Faced with the Soviet threat and strong foreign commitment to a new kind of capitalism, the United States compromised by accepting embedded liberalism, i.e. domestic interventionism embedded in a liberal international order. Following the end of social bargains and the introduction of altered international monetary institutions, there has been a strong trend toward the neoliberalism that the United States wanted to impose following World War II.

---

[7] Possible exceptions include a country whose currency serves as the international reserve currency or a country that is assessed by the financial community to have a strong payments position based on such 'fundamentals' as strong export possibilities, for example Norway.

Today, any leadership role for the United States cannot be based on overwhelming economic and military superiority, as it was following World War II; the new strength of the other OECD economies and the end of the Cold War have seen to that. However, there is one residual hegemonic role that the United States wishes to play and is best positioned to play, given its longstanding commitment to free market capitalism. This is a leadership role in a globalization process in which market forces replace interventionist policies. There is, of course, American leadership in removing controls on international capital movements, but its leadership role has another dimension. In the golden age, other governments in the advanced capitalist world committed themselves to full employment policies, and tight labour markets encouraged business loyalty to employees. In addition, these governments enacted laws that governed lay-offs and dismissals, further protecting workers. In the United States there has been no serious commitment to full employment, business has retained almost total freedom to hire and fire, and strong business loyalty to employees has been the exception. Without ties to location and employees, American business is footloose, free to move production to exploit low labour costs or to adopt a 'take it or leave it' attitude in wage settlements. Indeed, in a free trade world, facing competition from an expanding number of NICs, it has felt compelled to do so. If firms in other developed economies follow this lead and adopt the same behaviour, they draw labour into a race to the bottom.

8 Keynes and Kalecki on stability

Mainstream economics does not offer much in the way of theory or applied work on power and conflict against which to measure our analysis. The pervasive influence of the competitive model and the difficulty in incorporating power in formal models has dampened interest in these issues. Keynes' analysis (1936, ch. 24) of how persistent high unemployment affects power struggles and threatens the stability of a capitalist system and Kalecki's (1971) theory of the political business cycle are exceptions. Writing in the 1930s, when unemployment was near its historical high and totalitarian movements were growing in strength, Keynes viewed prolonged high unemployment as the cause of economic and political power struggles that could lead to the destruction of capitalism or of democracy. One danger, an economic consequence of democracy, was socialism. Militant labour, in pursuit of distributional fairness, would demand replacement of the existing capitalist system. The other danger was the political consequence of capitalism in the form of the disenfranchisement of the citizenry. Sensing an imminent attempt by labour to replace the existing economic order, capitalists would pre-empt this move by installing a fascist political order. Keynes saw full employment as necessary to avoid either outcome.

In Kalecki's theory, conflict is a natural outcome of a social order that combines capitalism with full political democracy, because of the tensions between the political demands flowing from universal suffrage and the distribution of rewards generated by the market system. Kalecki believed that extended periods of full employment capitalism and full political democracy were incompatible. To maintain control, capital had to retain some minimum amount of power, and prolonged periods of full employment denied this critical minimum. However, having the upper hand in both the market and the political arena, capital could alter the terms of the conflict and the degree of labour militancy by varying the distribution of political power (i.e. more or less democracy) and the distribution of economic power (more or less unemployment). The political business cycle was the result of capital manipulating the unemployment rate in order to ensure capitalism's economic and political 'stability'. Unfortunately, Kalecki was rather vague about the means by which capital would go about redistributing political power to achieve its goals.

Viewed from the perspective of the golden age, Keynes' analysis and remedy for capitalism appeared to be correct and Kalecki's wrong. Democracy and capitalism prevailed during an episode of prolonged full employment and historically high relative power of labour. Labour accepted welfare capitalism, and capital accepted labour's enhanced power position under booming economic conditions. Concerned with unemployment, Keynes did not consider the consequences of prolonged full employment. But this led to the wage explosions and spreading strike activity of the late 1960s, and the response of the authorities was to bring the golden age to an end. From today's perspective, after more than two decades of high unemployment, Keynes seems to have been too pessimistic. Prolonged high unemployment has not led to the instability that he feared. There is no apparent danger of socialism, and the curtailments of democratic control of economic policy have been made in an orderly fashion by democratically elected governments.

Where Keynes considered the stability of both democracy and capitalism, Kalecki's theory deals only with the stability of capitalism. A second difference lies in the time frame; by the time the *General Theory* was published, the UK had endured over 15 years of high unemployment, and this is reflected in the longer-term view of Keynes. Although Kalecki did not define a time frame precisely, his political business cycle appears to be rather short, comparable perhaps to the business cycle. A reinterpretation of Kalecki's theory to cover a longer period allows us to assess its conclusions and applicability to post-World War II events, especially to the advent and course of the current episode.[8] Although high unemployment has not resulted in either right-wing totalitarianism or socialism, there has been considerable scaling back of the welfare state (partly owing to depressed AD conditions) and this has been accompanied by a proliferation of political constraints on AD. Both of these have reinforced the effects of the original restrictive AD policies that ended the golden age. Their effect on the distribution of power has been to guarantee capital more than the minimum amount of power Kalecki argued was needed for capitalism's survival. Both by increasing unemployment and by denying full democracy, stability in the form of low inflation, low strike volume and capital's control of the workplace has been achieved.

This long-run reinterpretation of Kalecki's political business cycle seems to fit the post-World War II facts quite well. The golden age episode of low unemployment together with the current period of high unemployment amount to a sequence very similar to a Kalecki political business cycle. In both cases the downturn in economic activity was a policy response to increased labour militancy, taking the form of measures to reduce labour's economic and political power. However, there are significant divergences between the historical record and Kalecki's theory. We have already noted that our post-war sequence of two episodes lasts half a century, whereas Kalecki's cyclical theory has a shorter time horizon. There is an additional difference of note. In the initial phase of the sequence (i.e. the golden age), a distribution of economic and political power between capital and labour arose from a process of consultation, compromise and cooperation. In Kalecki's scheme, changes in the distribution of power are initiated and carried out by capital; whatever the phase of the political cycle, capital never relinquishes its dominating power position.

9 Conclusions

In the conclusion to chapter 11, we were left with the possibility that stimulative AD policies might be used to restore full employment if a new generation of social bargains could be put in place to counter a likely instability of the Phillips curve at unemployment below current rates. In this chapter, we have explored additional constraints on the use of AD policies; some put expansionary AD policies beyond the reach of democratic control, so that governments can no longer promise the full employment essential to any social bargain. These constraints are characteristic of the neoliberal economic regime adopted in response to the shift of relative power from

---

[8] Phelps Brown (1971, 1975) and Salvati (1984) have explained post-war movements in unemployment as a long-run sequence along Kaleckian lines.

labour to capital. Also symptomatic of the power shift is a lack of interest in social bargains, both because of capital's enhanced control of the workplace and because such institutions are not part of a neoliberal system; there are both practical and ideological barriers against social bargains. The apparent lack of concern with continued high unemployment can be explained in terms of the acceptance of the neoliberal model.

Viewed from the perspective of the entire post-war era, the relationship between unemployment and economic and political stability remains unclear. The golden age supports the Keynesian view that full employment ensures economic and political stability, but the entire post-war period seems to point toward a sequence resembling Kalecki's political business cycle, although over a much extended time period. However, Kalecki's theory assumed recurring cycles: following a bout of unemployment, labour would scale down its aspirations and its militancy and capital would then initiate another boom. This leads to some questions. First, are we on the verge of a revival of capitalism in the OECD, with unemployment about to fall to low or full employment rates? And, if we are not, will continuing high unemployment lead to a critical point at which we again face the dangers foreseen by Keynes in the 1930s? Or, third, will neoliberalism collapse as new institutions form, bringing a new golden age? In the final chapter we consider these questions in the light of history, with special attention to the likelihood of unemployment falling to golden age rates within any reasonable time frame.

13　A neoliberal future?

1 Introduction

In chapter 12 it was suggested that the historical sequence in unemployment rates over the past half-century might be interpreted as a longer-run
version of Kalecki's political business cycle. Those who see a pattern of
recurring long cycles in the historical record go further and interpret the
post-war era as two phases of the most recent long cycle in macroeconomic
activity. In this view the recovery of the American economy in the late 1990s
marks the early stages of the boom phase of a new long cycle. Although not
necessarily based on long cycle notions, similarly optimistic views are
shared by those who welcome the spread of neoliberalism as the wave of the
future. This regime of reduced government intervention, deregulation and
reduction of the welfare state derives its appeal in part from a longstanding
belief in capitalism's ability to renew itself, provided that the private sector
is relieved of 'political interference'. Its recent growing appeal and support
can also be traced to the greater international economic integration and the
argument that increased globalization requires the developed capitalist
economies to strengthen existing neoliberal tendencies if they are to
survive. The role of government is to assist capital by removing obstacles to
the spread of unregulated international markets in a future of increasing
globalization.

In this concluding chapter we identify what we believe to be the central
lessons uncovered by our study of capitalist development, and then attempt
to answer the questions posed at the end of chapter 12: will growing acceptance and implementation of the basic tenets of neoliberalism usher in an
era of sustained full employment; if neoliberalism fails to deliver full
employment, will this set in motion a series of radical institutional changes;
and will neoliberalism come to a non-violent end, and capitalism re-make
itself yet again and produce a new golden age? The historical record of the
OECD economies over the past half-century provides some clues about the
likely effect of continued neoliberalism on macroeconomic performance.

The answers to the second and third questions depend on political trends, and are addressed in the light of past political events.

2 What can we learn from history?

A defining feature of the golden age was full employment. This was not true of all the OECD economies, but it was true of enough to allow us to characterize the golden age episode in these terms. In contrast, the episode of advancing neoliberalism has been one of high unemployment, as shown in table I.1. Contrary to the neoclassical competitive market model, the economies that achieved full employment in the golden age were those with institutions that most severely restrained the free play of market forces. These institutions provided incentives for labour and capital to behave in ways consistent with national goals such as full employment and acceptable inflation rates; Austria, Norway, Sweden and Japan are among the countries that have benefited from these non-market solutions. Further, the historical record does not support the neoclassical view that full employment is the normal condition of market capitalism, but shows high unemployment to have been a common feature of capitalist economies in the twentieth century (see table 2.1). This has been particularly true of economies whose institutions most closely resemble neoliberalism, for example Canada, the United Kingdom and the United States.

The post-war record strongly supports the view that full employment required the joint action of government, capital and labour to create and sustain an institutional environment that made social bargains possible. No invisible hand could be counted on to perform this task. More specifically, institutions were required that would relieve the economy of constraints on aggregate demand and its growth. There were three kinds of institutions.

First, there were institutions embodying cooperation and trust in industrial relations and a widely shared determination to ensure the distributional fairness of the economic system. These allowed a bargain to be struck between government, capital and labour that would keep inflation down to politically acceptable rates at full employment. This required labour's willingness to abandon unrestricted collective bargaining, i.e. market-determined wages, and accept moderate money wage increases in exchange for benefits such as full employment and rising real wages, an expanded welfare state and 'fair' treatment at the workplace. What we have emphasized on several occasions is that the social bargains and the industrial relations systems that supported them represented a significant departure of labour markets from the competitive institutional forms so heavily favoured in economic textbooks and professional journals.

The second group of institutions relieving economies of constraints on aggregate demand embodied an interventionist role for governments to ensure the success of the social bargains. This required government to guarantee the benefits that were offered to induce wage restraint and cooperation in industrial relations, such as full employment and social safety nets. This clearly distanced the economy very substantially from a neoliberal *laissez-faire* model.

Finally, full employment necessarily required an institutional framework that promoted the achievement of external balance, i.e. an acceptable payments position at full employment. Chapter 9 discussed how most OECD economies were able to maintain external balance during the golden age. The international monetary regime was based on an adjustable pegged exchange rate and regulated international capital movements. These reduced uncertainty and prevented widespread speculation in foreign currency and financial capital markets, removing a potential constraint on aggregate demand. Aided by interventionist governments, social bargains delivered acceptable rates of inflation at full employment, and the international monetary regime reconciled external balance with full employment. These institutions, not the invisible hand, fostered the golden age, a lesson of history now largely forgotten.

Following the chain of causation back one step more, we found that the traumatic events of the inter-war period were in large part responsible for creating institutions favourable to full employment in the golden age. These included the Great Depression, the radical disruptions of World War II and the massive reconstruction programmes that followed it, and the emergence from the war of a victorious Soviet Union believed to have imperialist plans. The depression and the war had led to broad acceptance of the demand that all should share the benefits of the recovery; they had also restrained the power of corporate business because of the bad reputation it had acquired during the 1930s and World War II; and post-war reconstruction created the need for cooperation between capital, labour and government. Perhaps of greatest urgency was the determination of governments to convince their citizens that capitalism offered a superior alternative to Soviet communism. These developments reinforced the political power of labour at the end of World War II. The way this power was exercised differed among countries. In many it included strong representation in government, allowing labour to pursue its own interests directly. In Japan traditional social norms rather than direct representation gave labour its political voice, while in Switzerland labour was represented in coalition governments as well as on powerful advisory councils. A second lesson of history is that labour must have political power and broad public support for its cause before the institutions can be established that will achieve full employment and create social safety nets that guarantee a fair income distribution.

Since the end of the golden age, the relative power of capital has risen. Following Lindblom (1977), we have argued that business holds a special place in a capitalist economic system because of the crucial functions it performs. The decisions of business determine the standard of living, the organization of work, what is to be produced, and how and where it is to be produced. In short, business governs the economy and elected governments cannot ignore this. This is the source of business power and privilege, which have continued uninterrupted, even during the golden age. The difference in the golden age was that labour's relative power was greater than usual in capitalist systems. The current episode is therefore a restoration of capital's customary position, and the high unemployment and a less interventionist form of governance follow from the restoration of old policy priorities. These reflect the preferences of corporate business. Institutions have been established to give a high priority to price stability and to ensure a reduced role for government in both domestic and international economic affairs. Market-determined outcomes in the labour market have replaced social bargains; flexible exchange rates and deregulation of international capital markets have replaced pegged exchange rates and capital controls. The possibility that prolonged high unemployment is related to the institutions of neoliberalism has been overlooked by those in power. Following the end of the golden age, the market has been given another chance to show its ability to produce a full employment, growing economy. It has recorded yet another failure to do so. At the time of writing (August 2000), it is over a quarter of a century since the golden age ended, a period too long for any future recovery to be claimed as evidence of success! The third lesson of history is that the market cannot be relied upon to guarantee full employment.

This change in political preferences and institutions was largely due to the poor reputation labour obtained following the Great Inflation. Rightly or wrongly, the general public and governments held labour responsible for the inflation. In contrast, the reputation of business had steadily improved with the growing affluence of the golden age. The break-up of the USSR was taken as further proof of the failure of leftist and pro-labour policies; capitalism was declared to have won the day. This was a view easy to accept for a large segment of the population which was too young to have experienced life prior to the full employment and rising living standards of the golden age. From their viewpoint, it seemed that overly powerful labour had brought prosperity to an end. Political views to the right, favourable to business interests, were readily accepted.

A comparison of the linkages that initiated the two most recent episodes reveals an asymmetry in the weight of events required for radical shifts in both relative power and institutions. The current episode of high unemployment in the OECD was initiated by a period of accelerating inflation, and high inflation rates persisted until the 1990s in spite of restrictive AD policies and high unemployment. These relatively undramatic events are to be compared with the great upheavals that led to the institutions of the golden age: world-wide economic collapse, a devastating world war and a clear threat to capitalism in the shape of an existing credible alternative system of economic organization. This asymmetry reflects the inherent power of business and the difficulty for labour in countering this power. The fourth lesson of history is that the conditions needed for labour to have its voice heard are far-reaching and difficult to achieve, because it must gather sufficient strength to balance the well-established and very great power that business wields under capitalism.

Based on the historical records of a sizeable number of developed capitalist economies, the lessons of history are easily summarized. There is no evidence that the market can guarantee full employment, but ample evidence that institutions can be devised that will do so. The problem is that these institutions depend upon labour's relative power being strong enough to convince capital to participate in their formation and operation. Lastly, labour seldom reaches this level of relative power under capitalism, which gives the advantage to capital.

3 What of the future?

A conclusion of chapter 12 was that, following the golden age, governments relinquished much of their power to implement independent expansionary policies. This has deprived them of the ability to promise full employment to induce labour to re-establish social bargains. Given that neoliberal institutions rule out the use of policies to guarantee full employment, can neoliberal capitalism produce an episode of full employment in the near future, for example sometime during the first decade of the new millennium? Our view is that there is no reason to believe that the continuation of the neoliberal policies discussed in chapter 12 will lead to a sustained period of full employment. Whether intended or not, the institutional changes that have implemented the basic elements of neoliberalism introduce an AD policy asymmetry. Expansionary fiscal policies are limited by the fear of violating the terms of balanced budget laws or international treaties, and restrictive policies must be used to ensure such violations are avoided. Expansionary monetary policies are also restricted because policy-induced payments deficits are considered 'market unfriendly' by dealers in foreign exchange and international capital markets. Adverse capital flows or currency depreciations are likely to be met with restrictive policy, reversing or at least halting employment gains. Unregulated capital flows mean that this barrier to full employment is triggered rapidly, almost certainly before any inflationary bias reappears. At the same time, the widespread fear of igniting latent inflationary tendencies will remain.

The ability to restore and sustain full employment conditions requires the establishment of institutions that solve both problems of inflation and the aversion of business to any reduction of its powers, as did the institutions of the golden age. Unfortunately, until now there has been no sustained effort to reintroduce the institutions necessary to restrain inflationary pressures at full employment. We anticipate that, in the absence of social bargains, a sustained period of low unemployment comparable to golden age rates will lead to unacceptable rates of inflation in most developed capitalist economies. The response will be restrictive AD policies and a rise in unemployment rates. The induced shifts in power to labour brought by sustained low unemployment would reinforce the desire for restrictive policies in these economies. How soon such policies are initiated depends on the speed of recovery of workers' aspirations. The spread of involuntary, part-time employment and the threats of forced early retirement, of 'footloose' capital to relocate to areas of lower wages or higher unemployment and of continued immigration (legal and illegal) of foreign workers will act to restrain demands for rising real incomes. But rising strike levels and wage demands in the economies with falling unemployment rates suggest unacceptable inflationary pressures will occur long before full employment has been attained.

However, it is claimed that this argument is refuted by what has already happened in the USA; the official unemployment rate in mid-2000 stands at 4 per cent. Our first response is to refer to the finding in chapter 2 that the official unemployment figure significantly underestimates the amount of slack in the American labour market. When allowance is made for involuntary part-time employment, discouraged workers and the impact of current high rates of incarceration on the underemployment measure, the American unemployment rate remains significantly above its golden age average of 4.8 per cent.

Whether or not the official unemployment figures reflect an absence of involuntary unemployment, our second response is that the real issue is whether or not the American economy can generate the sustained level of AD needed to maintain officially measured unemployment at 4 per cent over the near future. We would argue that it cannot. The boom of the 1990s in the United States was driven by rapid growth in expenditures (and indebtedness) of the household sector, financed by foreign lenders and the 'irrational exuberance' of the stock market. The steady rise in the ratio of household debt to income has made this sector an unlikely source of continued strong growth of AD. More generally, as long as full employment depends on private sector spending, especially by households, with no government standing ready to rectify spending shortfalls, fluctuations in private expenditure will dominate fluctuations in GDP. All of this is highly speculative to be sure, but the point is that under neoliberalism the present boom conditions in the USA are likely be short lived.[1]

This raises a second question. If a sustained expansion does not materialize, either because restrictive policies are introduced early in the recovery owing to fears of inflation and increased labour power, or because private sector spending is not strong enough to generate a sustained boom, could continued high unemployment lead to the kinds of radical institutional changes seen by Keynes and others in the 1920s and 1930s when contemplating a continuation of the unemployment of that period? The fascism or communism that seemed likely then no longer does so, if for no other reason than unemployment is unlikely to become so serious over the near term. Although there have been increases in the membership of fascistic political groups in many OECD countries, these are still regarded as fringe parties. In the minds of the great majority of the population, fascism is still closely linked to the horrors of World War II; in some countries, such as Spain and Portugal, the bulk of the population has first-hand experience of life under fascism and the limits to free expression it entails. Currently, the adoption of socialism seems even less likely. Prior to World War II, the Soviet Union appeared to be a viable example of socialism; it provided employment at a time when elsewhere high unemployment was creating misery for millions. The collapse of Soviet and East European socialism was taken as proof of its failure. But, even if it had survived, it would not have been an attractive alternative. The years since World War II have seen the growth of huge disparities as OECD per capita incomes rose dramatically faster than USSR incomes. Even allowing for recent cutbacks, the current OECD welfare measures are a vast improvement over the 1930s, considerably reducing the hardships of unemployment. Few in the West, few even of the unemployed, would exchange their standard of living for life in the Soviet Union. At present there seems to be no reasonable alternative to capitalism, and so no reason for governments to fear socialism or fascism as Keynes did.

The final question concerns whether, in failing to achieve the target of sustained full employment, neoliberalism, rather than being overturned and replaced by a different economic system, merely collapses under the weight of prolonged high unemployment and demands for a political solution. An obvious possibility is that neoliberalism's characteristic trend of increasing income disparities, already very evident in the USA and the UK,

---

[1] A similar scenario is likely in the United Kingdom.

and its threat of increased job insecurities and a loss of social safety nets, will provide a common cause among those adversely affected and strengthen arguments and sentiment against neoliberalism. The unfair outcomes of these trends might be expected to bring the broad public support that proved to be a valuable boost to labour's political power and influence in the late 1940s. If labour is seen to be enduring hardships, political parties may re-evaluate left-wing policies. If the will exists, a political brake can be applied to neoliberalism. Would such a development be sufficient to initiate a move towards the kind of reformed capitalism that emerged at the end of World War II?

To answer this question we believe it is sufficient to consider what was necessary to bring into existence the reformed capitalism that arose following World War II. This type of peaceful near-revolutionary change is unlikely because of the weakness of political demand for the institutions it requires. Until recently, the labour movement was losing ground, representing a declining fraction of the workforce – the combined effect of the falling share of employment in manufacturing, with its high rate of membership, and slow progress in unionizing workers in the service sector, which now has the largest share of total employment in most OECD economies. In addition, labour has not yet lived down its reputation of causing inflation, and so would not gain the broad-based support that it had in the late 1940s. The same breadth of support is no longer there for left-wing political parties. To increase their chances of election, these parties have taken steps to distance themselves from this perception of labour, which has meant moving toward the right and formulating policies that appease business. The result has been the loss of consistent representation of labour's interests. Events in the period leading up to the golden age tell us that, for labour's voice to be heard, it must have a well-articulated programme and confidence that its claims are fair, it needs broad public support and agreement with its claims, and it must use its political power effectively to elect governments that represent its interests. None of these elements is in place today, and there is no sign that they will be assembled in the near future.

4 A final statement

Our analysis of the likely paths of neoliberalism draws a rather bleak picture of the near future. Over two decades of neoliberalism have revealed its similarities to the *laissez-faire* regimes of earlier times – prosperity for the few and insecurity for many. This insecurity becomes actual hardship when fluctuations in performance bring extended periods of high unemployment. In direct contrast, the experience of the golden age shows that extended episodes of poor performance are not caused by 'acts of God' or some natural law, and that malfunction can be avoided. Prolonged episodes of high unemployment and low growth result from there being constraints on aggregate demand. The golden age followed the establishment of institutions that removed these constraints. This is evidence that these constraints are never binding; they are 'man-made' and can be unmade if the political will exists.

We maintain that the business of government is to intervene in the economy to remove impediments to its proper functioning through policy-induced changes in institutions. Capitalism itself is a human construct and requires direction in order to serve human ends. It has demonstrated its capacity to generate income and wealth, the means to achieve social goals. It is up to society to define those goals and to develop the institutions that will ensure they are achieved. This is quite clear in Jospin's translation of Fernand Braudel's *La dynamique du capitalisme*, which provides us with a succinct description of the nature of capitalism:

[Its] suppleness and adaptability make capitalism a dynamic force. But it is a force that of itself has no sense of direction, no ideals or meaning – none of the elements vital to a society. Capitalism is a force that moves, but it does not know where it is going. (Jospin, 1999, p. 8)

Bibliography

Abramovitz, M., 1986, 'Catching up, Forging ahead, and Falling behind', *Journal of Economic History,* 46, 386–406.

Aglietta, M., 1979, *A Theory of Capitalist Regulation*, London: New Left Books.

Akerlof, G., Dickens, W. and Perry, G., 1996, 'The Macroeconomics of Low Inflation', *Brookings Papers on Economic Activity*, No. 1.

Alchian, A., 1950, 'Uncertainty, Evolution, and Economic Theory', *Journal of Political Economy*, 58: 211–21.

Alesina, A. and Roubini, N. with G. Cohen, 1997, *Political Cycles and the Macroeconomy*, Cambridge, MA: MIT Press.

Allen, K. and Stevenson, A., 1974, *An Introduction to the Italian Economy*, London: Martin Robertson.

Alogoskoufis, G. and Manning, A., 1988, 'Unemployment Persistence', *Economic Policy*, 3(2): 427–69.

Armstrong, P., Glyn, A. and Harrison, J., 1984, *Capitalism since World War II*, London: Fontana Paperbacks.

Arrow, K., 1962, 'The Economic Implications of Learning by Doing', *Review of Economic Studies*, 19 (June).

Ayres, C., 1962, *The Theory of Economic Progress*, New York: Schocken Books.

Barro, R., 1997, *Determinants of Economic Growth: A Cross-country Study*, Cambridge, MA: MIT Press.

Baumol, W., 1968, 'Entrepreneurship in Economic Theory', *American Economic Review*, 58, (May).

Baumol, W., Blackman, S. and Wolff, E., 1989, *Productivity and American Leadership: The Long View*, Cambridge, MA: MIT Press.

Bernanke, B., 1983, 'Non-monetary Effects of the Financial Crisis in the Propagation of the Great Depression', *American Economic Review*, 73, (June).

Beveridge, W. H., 1944, *Full Employment in a Free Society. A Report*, London: George Allen & Unwin.

Blanchard, O. and Summers, L., 1987, 'Hysteresis in Unemployment', *European Economic Review*, 31 (1–2): 288–95.

Borenstein, I., 1954, 'Capital and Output Trends in Mining Industries, 1870–1948', Occasional Paper 41, National Bureau of Economic Research, New York.

Bowles, S. and Edwards, R., 1985, *Understanding Capitalism: Competition, Command, and Change in the US Economy*, New York: Harper & Row.

Bowles, S., Gordon, D. and Weisskopf, T., 1990, *After the Wasteland: A Democratic Economics for the Year 2000*, Armonk, NJ: M. E. Sharpe.

Boyer, R., 1988a, 'Technical change and the Theory of "Regulation"', in G. Dosi, C. Freeman, R. Nelson, G. Silverberg and L. Soete (eds.), *Technical Change and Economic Theory*, London and New York: Pinter Publishers, 67–94.

1988b, 'Formalizing Growth Regimes', in G. Dosi, C. Freeman, R. Nelson, G. Silverberg and L. Soete (eds.), *Technical Change and Economic Theory*, London and New York: Pinter Publishers, 608–30.

Boyer, R. and Petit, P., 1990, 'Kaldor's Growth Theories: Past, Present and Prospects for the Future', in W. Semmler and E. Nell (eds.), *Nicholas Kaldor and Mainstream Economics*, London: Macmillan.

Brett, E. A., 1985, *The World Economy since the War: the Politics of Uneven Development*, London: Macmillan.

Brittan, S., 1975, 'The Economic Contradictions of Democracy', *British Journal of Political Science*, 5 (April): 130–59.

Bromley, D., 1989, *Economic Interests and Institutions*, Oxford: Basil Blackwell.

Calmfors, L. and Drifill, J., 1988, 'Bargaining Structure, Corporatism and Macroeconomic Performance', *Economic Policy*, 3 (April): 13–62.

Calomiris, C., 1993, 'Financial Factors in the Great Depression', *Journal of Economic Perspectives*, 7 (Spring).

Cameron, D., 1984, 'Social Democracy, Corporatism, Labour Quiescence and the Representation of Interest in Advanced Capitalist Society', in J. Goldthorpe (ed.), *Order and Conflict in Contemporary Capitalism*, Oxford: Clarendon Press.

1986, 'The Growth of Government Spending: the Canadian Experience in Comparative Perspective', in K. Banting (ed.), *State and Society: Canada in Comparative Perspective*, Toronto: University of Toronto Press.

Carlin, W. and Soskice, D., 1990, *Macroeconomics and the Wage Bargain*, Oxford: Oxford University Press.

CEPR, 1995, *Unemployment: Choices for Europe*, London: Centre for Economic Policy Research.

Chang, C. and Sorrentino, C., 1991, 'Union Membership Statistics in 12 Countries', *Monthly Labor Review*, December (US Bureau of Labor Statistics).

Cheng, L. and Dinopoulos, E., 1992, 'Schumpeterian Growth and International Business Cycles', *American Economic Review*, May.

Chiappori, P., 1989, 'The Growth Effects of 1992: Discussion', *Economic Policy*, 4 (October).

Clark, C., 1957, *The Conditions of Economic Progress*, 3rd edn, London: Macmillan.

Clark, K. and Summers, L., 1979, 'Labor Market Dynamics and Unemployment: a Reconsideration', *Brookings Papers on Economic Activity*, No. 1.

Coase, R., 1937, 'The Nature of the Firm', *Economica*, 4.

Colander, D., 1996, 'The Macrofoundations of Micro', in D. Colander (ed.), *Beyond*

Microfoundations: Post Walrasian Macroeconomics, Cambridge: Cambridge University Press.

1999, 'A Post-Walrasian Explanation of Wage and Price Inflexibility and a Keynesian Unemployment System', in Mark Setterfield (ed.), *Growth, Employment and Inflation*, London: Macmillan, 211–25.

Commons, J. R., 1950, *The Economics of Collective Action*, Madison: University of Wisconsin Press.

Cornwall, J., 1972, *Growth and Stability in a Mature Economy*, London: Martin Robertson.

1977, *Modern Capitalism: Its Growth and Transformation*, London: Martin Robertson.

1992, 'Stability and Stabilization of Mature Economies', in K. Velupillai (ed.), *Non-Linearities, Disequilibrium and Simulation*, London: Macmillan.

1994, *Economic Breakdown & Recovery: Theory and Policy*, Armonk, NY: M.E. Sharpe.

Cornwall, J. and Cornwall, W., 1992, 'Export-led Growth: a New Interpretation', in W. Millberg (ed.), *The Megacorp and Macrodynamics: Essays in Memory of Alfred Eichner*, Armonk, NY: M.E. Sharpe, 209–23.

1997, 'The Unemployment Problem and the Legacy of Keynes', *Journal of Post Keynesian Economics*, 19 (Summer).

Cornwall, J. and Maclean, W., 1984, *Economic Recovery for Canada: a Policy Framework*, Toronto: James Lorimer & Company, in association with the Canadian Institute for Economic Policy.

Cornwall, W., 1991, 'The Rise and Fall of Productivity Growth', in J. Cornwall (ed.), *The Capitalist Economies: Prospects for the 1990s*, Cheltenham, UK: Edward Elgar, 40–62.

1999, 'The Institutional Determinants of Unemployment', in Mark Setterfield (ed.), *The Political Economy of Growth, Employment and Inflation*, London: Macmillan, ch. 5.

Crafts, N., 1995a, 'You've Never Had It So Good? British Economic Policy and Performance, 1945–60', in Barry Eichengreen (ed.), *Europe's Post-War Recovery*, Cambridge: Cambridge University Press, 246–70.

1995b, 'The Golden Age of Economic Growth in Western Europe, 1950–1973', *Economic History Review*, 48 (3): 429–47.

Crafts, N. and Toniolo, G., 1996, 'Post-War Growth: an Overview', in N. Crafts and G. Toniolo (eds.), *Economic Growth in Europe since 1945*, Cambridge: Cambridge University Press, 1–37.

Crouch, C., 1985, 'The Conditions for Trade Union Wage Restraint', in L. Lindberg and C. Maier (eds.), *The Politics of Wage Inflation and Economic Stagnation*, Washington DC: Brookings Institution.

Cukierman, A., 1992, *Central Bank Strategy, Credibility, and Independence: Theory and Evidence*, Cambridge, MA: MIT Press.

Cukierman, A., Webb, S.B. and Neyapti, B., 1992, 'Measuring the Independence of Central Banks and Its Effect on Policy Outcomes', *World Bank Economic Review*, 6: 353–98.

Curtis, D.C.A. and Murthy, K.S.R., 1999, 'Restructuring and Economic Growth in OECD Countries: 1964–1992', *Eastern Economic Journal*, 25(1): 17–30.

Debelle, G. and Fischer, S., 1994, 'How Independent Should a Central Bank Be?', *Goals, Guidelines, and Constraints Facing Monetary Policymakers*, Federal Reserve Bank of Boston Conference Series No. 38.

Dosi, G., Freeman, C., Nelson, R., Silverberg, G. and Soete, L. (eds.), 1988, *Technical Change and Economic Theory*, London: Pinter.

Dow, J.C.R., 1990, 'How Can Real Wages Ever Get Excessive?', National Institute of Economic and Social Research, Discussion Paper No. 196.

Duesenberry, J., 1958, *Business Cycles and Economic Growth*, New York: McGraw-Hill.

1991, 'A New American Inflation?' in J. Cornwall (ed.), *The Capitalist Economies: Prospects for the 1990s*, Aldershot, UK: Edward Elgar.

Duijn, J. van, 1983, *The Long Wave in Economic Life*, London: Allen & Unwin.

Eichengreen, B., 1992, *Golden Fetters: The Gold Standard and the Great Depression, 1919–1939*, New York: Oxford University Press.

1995a, 'Mainsprings of Economic Recovery in Post-war Europe', in B. Eichengreen (ed.), *Europe's Post-War Recovery*, Cambridge: Cambridge University Press, 3–35.

1995b, 'The European Payments Union: an Efficient Mechanism for Rebuilding Europe's Trade?', in B. Eichengreen (ed.), *Europe's Post-War Recovery*, Cambridge: Cambridge University Press, 169–95.

Elster, J., 1989, 'Social Norms and Economic Theory', *Journal of Economic Perspectives*, 3.

Fagerberg, J., 1994, 'Technology and International Differences in Growth Rates', *Journal of Economic Literature*, 32: 1147–75.

1996, 'Heading for Divergence? Regional Growth in Europe Reconsidered', *Journal of Common Market Studies*, 34: 431–48.

Feenstra, R., 1998, 'Integration of Trade and Disintegration of Production in the Global Economy', *Journal of Economic Perspectives*, 12 (Fall).

Fisher, I., 1933, 'The Debt–Deflation Theory of Great Depressions', *Econometrica*, 1 (October).

Flanagan, R., Soskice, D. and Ulman, L., 1983, *Unionism, Economic Stabilization and Incomes Policies: European Experience*, Washington DC: Brookings Institution.

Flora, P., 1983, *State, Economy, and Society in Western Europe, 1815–1975*, vol. 1, *The Growth of Mass Democracies and Welfare States*, London: Macmillan.

Fortin, P., 1996, 'The Great Canadian Slump', *Canadian Journal of Economics*, 29 (4).

Frankel, M., 1962, 'The Production Function in Allocation and Growth: a Synthesis', *American Economic Review*, 52: 995–1022.

Freeman, C. (ed.), 1983, *Long Waves in the World Economy*, London: Butterworth.

Freeman, R., 1988, 'Institutions and Economic Performance, *Economic Policy*, No. 6.

1995, 'The Limits of Wage Flexibility to Curing Unemployment', *Oxford Review of Economic Policy*, 11 (Spring).

Friedman, M., 1953, 'The Methodology of Positive Economics', *Essays in Positive Economics*, Chicago: Chicago University Press.

1968, 'The Role of Monetary Policy', *American Economic Review*, 58 (March).

1977, 'Nobel Lecture: Inflation and Unemployment', *Journal of Political Economy*, 85 (June).

Friedman, M. and Schwartz, A., 1963a, *The Great Contraction 1929–1933*, New York: National Bureau of Economic Research.

1963b, *A Monetary History of the United States, 1867–1960*, Princeton, NJ: Princeton University Press.

Galbraith, J., 1997, 'Time to Ditch the NAIRU', *Journal of Economic Perspectives*, 11(1).

Gambetta, D., 1988, 'Can We Trust Trust?' in D. Gambetta (ed.), *Trust: Making and Breaking Cooperative Relations*, Oxford: Basil Blackwell.

Gelderen, J. van, [Fedder, J.], 1913, 'Springvloed', in *De Nieuwe Tijd*, 18 (April–June): 253–77, 369–84, 445–64.

Glyn, A., Hughes, A., Lipietz, A. and Singh, A., 1990, 'The Rise and Fall of the Golden Age', in S. Marglin and J. Schor (eds.), *The Golden Age of Capitalism*, Oxford: Clarendon Press, 39–125.

Goldthorpe, J., 1978, 'The Current Inflation: Towards a Sociological Account', in F. Hirsch and J. Goldthorpe (eds.), *The Political Economy of Inflation*, Cambridge, MA: Harvard University Press.

Goodwin, R., 1990, *Chaotic Economic Dynamics*, Oxford: Oxford University Press.

1991, 'Schumpeter, Keynes and the Theory of Economic Evolution', *Journal of Evolutionary Economics*, 1(1): 29–48.

Gordon, D., 1978, 'Up and down the Long Roller Coaster', in *U.S. Capitalism in Crisis*, New York: Economics Education Project of the URPE.

1980, 'Stages of Accumulation and Long Economic Cycles', in T. K. Hopkins and I. Wallerstein (eds.), *Processes of the World System*, vol. 3 of *Political Economy of the World System Annuals*, Beverly Hills, CA: Sage Publications.

1991, 'Inside and outside the Long Swing', *Review*, 14(2): 263–312.

Gordon, R., 1989, 'Hysteresis in History: Was There Ever a Phillips Curve?' *American Economic Review*, 79 (May).

1997, 'The Time-varying NAIRU and Its Implications for Economic Policy', *Journal of Economic Perspectives*, 11(1).

Gordon, R. and Wilcox, J., 1981, 'Monetarist Interpretations of the Great Depression: An Evaluation and Critique', in K. Brunner (ed.), *The Great Depression Revisited*, Boston: Martinus Nijhoff.

Gourevitch, P., Martin, A., Ross, G., Allen, C., Bornstein, S. and Markovits, A., 1984, *Unions and Economic Crisis: Britain, West Germany and Sweden*, London: Allen & Unwin.

Grubel, H. and Lloyd, P., 1975, *Intra-Industry Trade: The Theory and Measurement of International Trade in Differentiated Products*, New York: John Wiley.

Hansen, A., 1939, 'Economic Progress and Declining Population Growth', *American Economic Review*, 29 (March).

Hargreaves Heap, S., 1994, 'Institutions and (Short-run) Macroeconomic Performance', *Journal of Economic Surveys*, 8(1): 35–56.

Hasan, H. and de Broucker, P., 1982, 'Duration and Concentration of Unemployment', *Canadian Journal of Economics*, 15 (November).

Hausman, J., 1978, 'Specification Tests in Econometrics', *Econometrica*, 46: 1251–7.

Heilbroner, R., 1986, *The Nature and Logic of Capitalism*, New York: W.W. Norton.

Hibbs, D., 1987, 'Political Parties and Macroeconomic Policy', in *The Political Economy of Industrial Democracies*, Cambridge, MA: Harvard University Press.

Hicks, J., 1974, *The Crisis in Keynesian Economics*, New York: Basic Books.

Hobsbawm, E., 1994, *Age of Extremes: The Short Twentieth Century, 1914–1991*, London: Michael Joseph.

Hocking, R., 1976, 'The Analysis and Selection of Variables in Multiple Regression', *Biometrics*, March: 1–49.

Hodgson, G., 1988, *Economics and Institutions: A Manifesto for a Modern Institutional Economics*, Cambridge: Polity Press.

1993, 'The Economics of Institutions', *European Association for Evolutionary Political Economy Newsletter*, June: 7–11.

International Labour Organization, 1998, *Yearbook of Labour Statistics*, 57th issue, Geneva: International Labour Office.

Irwin, D., 1996, 'The United States in New World Economy? A Century's Perspective', *American Economic Review*, 86 (May).

Jenkins, M., 1996, 'Central Bank Independence and Inflation Performance: Panacea or Placebo?', *Banca Nazionale del Lavoro Quarterly Review*, 49 (June): 241–70.

Jospin, L., 1999, *Modern Socialism*, London: Fabian Society.

Kaldor, N., 1957, 'A Model of Economic Growth', *Economic Journal*, 67 (December).

1963, 'Capital Accumulation and Economic Growth', in F. Lutz (ed.), *The Theory of Capital*, London: Macmillan.

1981, 'The Role of Increasing Returns, Technical Progress and Cumulative Causation in the Theory of International Trade and Economic Growth', *Further Essays on Economic Theory and Policy*, New York: Holmes & Meier.

1985, *Economics without Equilibrium*, New York: M.E. Sharpe.

Kalecki, M., 1971, 'Political Aspects of Full Employment', in *Selected Essays on the Dynamics of the Capitalist Economy*, Cambridge: Cambridge University Press, ch. 12.

Katz, L. and Krueger, A., 1999, 'The High-Pressure US Labour Market of the 1990s', *Brookings Papers on Economic Activity*, No. 1: 1–87.

Kendrick, J., 1961, *Productivity Trends in the United States*, Princeton, NJ: Princeton University Press.

Kennedy, K. and Dowling, B., 1975, *Economic Growth in Ireland: the Experience since 1947*, Dublin: Gill and Macmillan.

Keohane, R., 1984, 'The World Political Economy and the Crisis of Embedded Liberalism', in J. Goldthorpe (ed.), *Order and Conflict in Contemporary Capitalism*, Oxford: Oxford University Press.

Kerr, C., 1960, *Industrialism and Industrial Man*, New York: Oxford University Press.

Keynes, J. M., 1936, *The General Theory of Employment, Interest and Money*, London: Macmillan.

Kondratiev, N., 1925, Translation in 'The Long Wave in Economic Life', *Review of Economic Statistics*, 17 (November 1935): 105–15.

Korpi, W., 1983, *The Democratic Class Struggle*, London: Routledge & Kegan Paul.

Kotz, D., 1987, 'Long Waves and Social Structures of Accumulation: a Critique and Reconstruction', *Review of Radical Political Economics*, 19(4).

1990, 'A Comparative Analysis of the Theory of Regulation and the Social Structure of Accumulation Theory', *Science & Society*, 54(1).

Kuznets, S., 1961, *Capital in the American Economy*, Princeton, NJ: Princeton University Press.

Lachman, L., 1947, 'Complementarity and Substitution in the Theory of Capital', *Economica*, 14 (May).

1948, 'Investment Repercussions', *Quarterly Journal of Economics*, 63 (November).

Lamfalussy, A., 1961, *Investment and Growth in Mature Economies*, New York: Macmillan.

1963, *The United Kingdom and the Six: an Essay on Economic Growth in Western Europe*, Homewood, IL: Richard Irwin.

Layard, R., et al., 1991, *Unemployment: Macroeconomic Performance and the Labour Market*, Oxford: Oxford University Press.

Lebergott, S., 1964, *Manpower in Economic Growth: the American Record since 1800*, Toronto: McGraw-Hill.

Lewis, W.A., 1949, *Economic Survey 1919–1939*, London: George Allen & Unwin.

Lindbeck, A., 1983, 'The Recent Slowdown of Productivity Growth', *Economic Journal*, 93: 13–34.

Lindbeck, A. and Snower, D., 1987, 'Union Activity, Unemployment Persistence and Wage–Employment Ratchets', *European Economic Review*, 31 (February–March).

Lindblom, C., 1977, *Politics and Markets*, New York: Basic Books.

Lipsey, R., 1965, 'Structural and Demand Deficient Unemployment Reconsidered', in A.M. Ross (ed.), *Employment Policy and the Labor Market*, Berkeley: University of California Press.

Lorant, J., 1966, 'The Role of Capital-Improving Innovations in American Manufacturing during the 1920s', unpublished PhD dissertation, Columbia University.

Lown, C. and Rich, R., 1997, 'Is There an Inflation Puzzle?' *Federal Reserve Bank of New York Economic Policy Review*, December.

Lucas, R., 1988, 'On the Mechanics of Economic Development', *Journal of Monetary Economics*, 22 (July).

McCallum, J., 1983, 'Inflation and Social Consensus in the Seventies', *Economic Journal*, 93.

1986, 'Unemployment in the OECD Countries in the 1980s', *Economic Journal*, 96: 942–60.

McCombie, J., 1991, 'The Productivity Growth Slowdown of the Advanced Countries and Intersectoral Reallocation of Labour', *Australian Economic Papers*, 30: 70–85.

McCombie, J. and Thirlwall, A., 1994, *Economic Growth and the Balance-of-Payments Constraint*, London: Macmillan.

Mackie, T. and Rose, R., 1991, *The International Almanac of Electoral History*, London: Macmillan.

Maddison, A., 1991, *Dynamic Forces in Capitalist Development*, Oxford: Oxford University Press.

Maier, C., 1987, 'The Politics of Productivity: Foundations of American International Economic Policy after the War', in *In Search of Stability: Explorations in Historical Political Economy*, Cambridge: Cambridge University Press, 121–52.

Main, B., 1981, 'The Length of Employment and Unemployment in Great Britain', *Journal of Political Economy*, 89 (June).

Malinvaud, E., 1977, *The Theory of Unemployment Reconsidered*, Oxford: Basil Blackwell.

Mandel, E., 1964, 'The Economics of Neo-capitalism', *Socialist Register*, 56–67.

1980, *Long Waves of Capitalist Development*, New York: Cambridge University Press.

Mankiw, N., 1994, *Macroeconomics,* 2nd edn, New York: Worth Publishers.

Marglin, S., 1990, 'Lessons of the Golden Age: an Overview', in S. Marglin and J. Schor (eds.), *The Golden Age of Capitalism*, Oxford: Clarendon Press, 1–38.

Mensch, G., 1979, *Stalemate in Technology: Innovations Overcome the Depression*, Cambridge, MA: Harvard University Press.

Minsky, H., 1975, *John Maynard Keynes*, New York: Columbia University Press.

Mishel, I., Bernstein, J. and Schmitt, J., 1997, *The State of Working America 1996–97*, Armonk, NY: M.E. Sharpe.

Mishkin, F., 1978, 'The Household Balance Sheet and the Great Depression', *Journal of Economic History*, 38 (December).

Mokyr, J., 1990, 'Punctuated Equilibria and Technological Progress', *American Economic Review, Papers & Proceedings,* May.

Moore, G. (ed.), 1961, *Business Cycle Indicators,* vol. II, National Bureau of Economic Research, Princeton, NJ: Princeton University Press.

Nelson, R., 1995, 'Recent Evolutionary Theorizing about Economic Change', *Journal of Economic Literature*, 33(1): 48–90.

Nelson, R. and Winter, S., 1982, *An Evolutionary Theory of Economic Change*, Cambridge, MA: Harvard University Press.

North, D., 1981, *Structure and Change in Economic History*, New York: W.W. Norton.

1987, 'Institutions, Transaction Costs and Economic Growth', *Economic Inquiry*, 25.

1990, *Institutions, Institutional Change and Economic Performance*, Cambridge and New York: Cambridge University Press.

1991, 'Institutions', *Journal of Economic Perspectives*, 5: 92–112.

1994, 'Economic Performance Through Time', *American Economic Review*, 84(3): 359–68.

Norton, B., 1988, 'Epochs and Essences: a Review of Marxist Long-Wave and Stagnation Theories', *Cambridge Journal of Economics*, 12: 203–24.

OECD, 1995, *Economic Outlook*, 58, Paris: OECD, December.

1999, *Economic Outlook*, 65, Paris: OECD, June.

1999, *Economic Outlook*, 66, Paris: OECD, December.

1995, *Employment Outlook*, Paris: OECD.

1997, *Employment Outlook*, Paris: OECD.

1999, *Employment Outlook*, Paris: OECD.

1991, *Historical Statistics 1960–1990*. Paris: OECD.

1995, *Historical Statistics 1960–1993*. Paris: OECD.

1997, *Historical Statistics 1960–1995*, Paris: OECD.

1999, *Historical Statistics 1960–1997*, Paris: OECD.

Labour Force Statistics, various issues.

1978, *Towards Full Employment and Price Stability*, Paris: OECD.

O'Hara, P., 1994, 'An Institutionalist Review of Long Wave Theories: Schumpeterian Innovation, Modes of Regulation, and Social Structures of Accumulation', *Journal of Economic Issues*, 28: 489–500.

Okun, A., 1973, 'Upward Mobility in a High Pressure Economy', *Brookings Papers on Economic Activity*, No. 1.

Osberg, L., 2000, 'Long run Trends in Economic Inequality in Five Countries: a Birth Cohort View', Dalhousie University, Department of Economics, Working Paper No. 2000–1.

Paldam, M., 1980, 'Industrial Conflict and the Phillips Curve – an International Perspective', Memo 80–4/5, Institute of Economics, Aarhus University.

Perez, C., 1983, 'Structural Change and Assimilation of New Technologies in the Economic Social Systems', *Futures*, October: 357–75.

Perry, G., 1975, 'Determinants of Wage Inflation around the World', *Brookings Papers on Economic Activity*, No. 2: 403–47.

Phelps, E., 1962, 'The New View of Investment: a Neoclassical Analysis', *Quarterly Journal of Economics*, 77 (November).

Phelps, E., et al., 1970, *Microfoundations of Employment and Inflation Theory*, New York: Norton.

Phelps Brown, E.H., 1971, 'The Analysis of Wage Movements under Full Employment', *Scottish Journal of Political Economy*, 18 (November).

1975, 'A Non-monetarist View of the Pay Explosion', *Three Banks Review*, No. 105, March

Pissarides, C., 1988, 'Unemployment and Macroeconomics: an Inaugural Address', *Centre for Labour Economics Discussion Paper*, No. 3–4, London School of Economics, March.

Porter, P., 1990, *The Competitive Advantage of Nations*, London: Macmillan.

Posen, A., 1995, 'Declarations Are Not Enough: Financial Sector Sources of Central Bank Independence', in B. Bernanke and J. Rotemberg (eds.), *NBER Macroeconomics Annual 1995*, Cambridge, MA: MIT Press.

Reichlin, L., 1995, 'The Marshall Plan Reconsidered', in B. Eichengreen (ed.), *Europe's Post-War Recovery*, Cambridge: Cambridge University Press, 39–67.

Richardson, G., 1959, 'Equilibrium, Expectations and Information', *Economic Journal*, 69: 223–37.

Rodrik, D., 1997, 'Has Globalization Gone Too Far?' Institute for International Economics, Washington, DC.

Romer, C., 1993, 'The Nation in Depression', *Journal of Economic Perspectives*, 7 (Spring).

Romer, P., 1986, 'Increasing Returns and Long-Run Growth', *Journal of Political Economy*, 94 (October).

1990, 'Endogenous Technological Change', *Journal of Political Economy*, 98 (October).

Rosser, B., 1995, 'On the Complexities of Complex Economic Dynamics', *Journal of Economic Perspectives*, 9 (Fall).

Rostow, W., 1978, *The World Economy: History and Prospect*, London: Macmillan.

Rostow, W. and Kennedy, M., 1979, 'A Simple Model of the Kondratieff Cycle', in P. Uselding (ed.), *Research in Economic History*, 4: 1–36.

Rothschild, K., 1971, *Power in Economics: Selected Readings*, Harmondsworth, UK: Penguin Books.

Rowthorn, R. and Wells, J., 1987, *De-Industrialization and Foreign Trade*, Cambridge: Cambridge University Press.

Rutherford, M., 1983, 'J.R. Common's Institutional Economics', *Journal of Economic Issues*, 17: 721–44.

1989, 'What Is Wrong with the New Institutional Economics and What Is Still Wrong with the Old?', *Review of Political Economy*, 1.

Salop, S., 1979, 'A Model of the Natural Rate of Unemployment', *American Economic Review*, 69.

Salvati, M., 1984, 'Political Business Cycles and Long Waves in Industrial Relations', in C. Freeman (ed.), *Long Waves in the World Economy*, London and Dover, NH: Frances Pinter (Publishers), ch. 15.

Schotter, A., 1981, *The Economic Theory of Social Institutions*, Cambridge: Cambridge University Press.

Schumpeter, J., 1934, *The Theory of Economic Development*, Cambridge, MA: Harvard University Press (translation of German publication of 1912).

1935, 'The Analysis of Economic Change', *Review of Economics and Statistics*, 17(4): 2–10.

1939, *Business Cycles: a Theoretical, Historical and Statistical Analysis of the Capitalist Process*, 2 vols., New York: McGraw-Hill.

1942, *Capitalism, Socialism and Democracy*, New York: Harper & Brothers.

1944, *Readings in Business Cycle Theory*, Philadelphia: Blakiston Company.

Scitovsky, T., 1978, 'Market Power and Inflation', *Economica*, 45 (August).

Scott, M., 1989, *A New View of Economic Growth*, Oxford: Clarendon Press.

Setterfield, M., 1995, 'Historical Time and Economic Theory', *Review of Political Economy*, 1.

Setterfield, M., Osberg, L. and Gordon, D., 1992, 'Searching for a Will o' the Wisp: an Empirical Study of the NAIRU', *European Economic Review*, 36.

Shapiro, C. and Stiglitz, J., 1984, 'Equilibrium Unemployment as a Worker Discipline Device', *American Economic Review*, 74.

Shonfield, A., 1965, *Modern Capitalism: the Changing Balance of Public and Private Power*, Oxford: Oxford University Press.

Silberman, J. and Weiss, C., 1992, 'Restructuring for Productivity', World Bank Industry and Energy Department, Working Paper No. 64.

Skott, P., 1999, 'Wage Formation and the (Non-)Existence of the NAIRU', *Economic Issues*, March.

Solomou, S., 1987, *Phases of Economic Growth, 1850–73: Kondratieff Waves and Kuznets Swings*, Cambridge: Cambridge University Press.

Solow, R., 1994, 'Perspectives on Growth Theory', *Journal of Economic Perspectives*, 8(1): 45–54.

Soskice, D., 1978, 'Strike Waves and Wage Explosions, 1968–70: an Economic Interpretation', in C. Crouch and A. Pizzarno (eds.), *The Resurgence of Class Conflict in Western Europe since 1969*, vol. 2, New York: Holmes & Meir, 221–46.

1990, 'Wage Determination: the Changing Role of Institutions in Advanced Industrialized Countries', *Oxford Review of Economic Policy*, 6(4): 36–61.

Summers, R., 1985, 'Services in the International Economy', in R. Inman (ed.), *Managing the Service Economy: Prospects and Problems*, Cambridge: Cambridge University Press, 27–48.

Sundrum, R., 1990, *Economic Growth in Theory and Practice*, London: Macmillan.

Svennilson, I., 1954, *Growth and Stagnation in the European Economy*, Geneva: Economic Commission for Europe.

Tanzi, V., 2000, 'Globalization and the Future of Social Protection', International Monetary Fund, W/P/00/12, Washington, DC.

Temin, P., 1993, 'Transmission of the Great Depression', *Journal of Economic Perspectives*, 7 (Spring).

Tobin, J., 1993, 'Price Flexibility and Output Stability: an Old Keynesian View', *Journal of Economic Perspectives*, 7 (Winter).

Trevithick, J., 1976, 'Inflation, the Natural Unemployment Rate and the Theory of Economic Policy', *Scottish Journal of Political Economy*, 23: 37–53.

Tylecote, A., 1992, *The Long Wave in the World Economy*, London: Routledge.

Ulmer, M., 1960, *Capital in Transportation, Communications, and Public Utilities: Its Formation and Financing*, New York: National Bureau of Economic Research.

United Nations, 1972, *Economic Survey of Europe in 1971*, New York: United Nations.

US Bureau of Labor Statistics, 1995, *Monthly Labor Review*, August.

1995, *Monthly Labor Review*, October.

US Department of Commerce, 1976, *Survey of Current Business*, Washington DC, January.

1976, *Survey of Current Business*, Washington DC, September.

1989, *Survey of Current Business*, Washington DC, September.

Veblen, T., 1899, *The Theory of the Leisure Class*, New York: Macmillan.

1919, *The Place of Science in Modern Civilisation and Other Essays*, New York: Hubsch.

Wartenberg, T., 1990, *The Forms of Power: from Domination to Transformation*, Philadelphia: Temple University Press.

Weisskopf, T., Bowles, S. and Gordon, D., 1985, 'Views of Capitalist Stagnation: Underconsumption and Challenges to Capitalist Control', *Science & Society*, 69(3): 259–86.

Western, B. and Beckett, K., 1999, 'How Unregulated is the US Labor Market? The Penal System as a Labor Market Institution', *American Journal of Sociology*, 104(4): 46–76.

White, H., 1980, 'A Heteroskedasticity-consistent Covariance Matrix and a Direct Test for Heteroskedasticity', *Econometrica*, 48: 817–38.

Witt, U., 1992, 'Evolutionary Concepts in Economics', *Eastern Economic Journal*, 18 (Fall).

1993, 'Emergence and Dissemination of Innovations: Some Principles of Evolutionary Economics', in R. Day and P. Chen (eds.), *Non Linear Dynamics and Evolutionary Economics*, Oxford: Oxford University Press.

Wyplosz, C., 1987, 'Comments', in R. Layard and L. Calmfors (eds.), *The Fight against Unemployment*, Cambridge, MA: MIT Press.

1994, 'Demand and Structural Views of Europe's High Unemployment Trap', *Swedish Economic Policy Review*, No. 1.

Index